Dr. Jack's

LEADERSHIP LESSONS
LEARNED FROM A LIFETIME IN
BASKETBALL

Dr. Jack's

LEADERSHIP LESSONS LEARNED FROM A LIFETIME IN BASKETBALL

DR. JACK RAMSAY

WILEY

JOHN WILEY & SONS, INC.

Published by John Wiley & Sons, Inc., Hoboken, New Jersey.
Published simultaneously in Canada.

For general information on our other products and services please contact our Customer Care Department within the United States at (800) 762-2974, outside the United States at (317) 572-3993 or fax (317) 572-4002.

Wiley also publishes its books in a variety of electronic formats. Some content that appears in print may not be available in electronic books. For more information about Wiley products, visit our web site at www.wiley.com.

Library of Congress Cataloging-in-Publication Data:

Ramsay, Jack, 1925-
  Dr. Jack's leadership lessons learned from a lifetime in basketball /
Jack Ramsay.
   p.   cm.
  Includes index.
  ISBN 0-471-46929-7 (cloth : alk. paper)
   1. Ramsay, Jack, 1925-   2. Basketball coaches—United
States—Biography.   3. Leadership—United States—Case studies. I.
Title: Doctor Jack's leadership lessons learned from a lifetime in
basketball. II. Title.
  GV884.R33 A34 2004
  796.323'092—dc22

2003057095

Printed in the United States of America.

10 9 8 7 6 5 4 3 2 1

To the present-day Ramsay Clan and its heritage—those relations who came to this great country to establish a foothold, so that we who followed had the opportunity to choose our individual ways of life.

I begin with my wife, Jean, and include our respective families: my father, John, and my mother, Anne Foster; and Jean's parents, Joseph Duffey, and his wife, Anne Callahan, and the families that preceded each of them. Then there are the spousal relationships of our children: daughters—Susan (husband, Vincent Dailey; parents: Vincent and Honora McGrath), Sharon (husband, James O'Brien; parents: William and Bernice Cecelia Kavanagh), and Carolyn (husband, Andrew Goodman; parents: Edwin Lawrence and Anita Siegal); sons—John (wife Michele Twomey; parents: John and Irene MacDermott) and Christopher (wife Cristina Martinez-Fonts, parents: Alberto and Florinda Sanchez). All have contributed to the makeup of the current Ramsay family.

My father had no brothers, nor did I. So the continuance of this branch of Ramsays is left to Nicholas, Jacob, and Luke Ramsay, the offspring of our son, John. The Ramsay Clan is in good hands.

If

If you can keep your head when all about you
Are losing theirs and blaming it on you;
If you can trust yourself when all men doubt you,
But make allowance for their doubting too;
If you can wait and not be tired by waiting,
Or, being lied about, don't deal in lies,
Or, being hated, don't give way to hating,
And yet don't look too good, nor talk too wise;

If you can dream—and not make dreams your master;
If you can think—and not make thoughts your aim;
If you can meet with triumph and disaster
And treat those two imposters just the same;
If you can bear to hear the truth you've spoken
Twisted by knaves to make a trap for fools,
Or watch the things you gave your life to broken,
And stoop and build 'em up with wornout tools;

If you can make one heap of all your winnings
And risk it on one turn of pitch-and-toss,
And lose, and start again at your beginnings
And never breathe a word about your loss;
If you can force your heart and nerve and sinew
To serve your turn long after they are gone,
And so hold on when there is nothing in you
Except the Will which says to them: "Hold on";

If you can talk with crowds and keep your virtue,
Or walk with kings—nor lose the common touch;
If neither foes nor loving friends can hurt you;
If all men count with you, but none too much;
If you can fill the unforgiving minute
With sixty seconds' worth of distance run
Yours is the Earth and everything that's in it,
And—which is more—you'll be a Man my son!

—Rudyard Kipling

Contents

Foreword

THE FIRST TIME I saw Jack Ramsay was in 1968 when he was coaching for the Philadelphia 76ers. I was at the Garden, back from six years overseas as a *New York Times* foreign correspondent, and I was just embarking on a new incarnation as a serious Knicks fan. I don't remember much about the game, who won or lost, but what I do remember was Jack, his intensity and the fierce, passionate way he worked the refs. Every call seemed to be life or death to him—and maybe for a nanosecond it actually was. To those of us assembled there to cheer for the Knicks he seemed to be right out of central casting, playing perfectly the role of the enemy incarnate. There he was, face flushed, arguing what seemed like an endless series of calls. So I did what any well-brought-up New York boy would do in a situation like that: I booed him.

Then in a few years we became friends and I stopped booing. He was, it turned out, also a passionate reader and had read one of my books on Vietnam. We met one night when mutual friends arranged a dinner after a game, and we had a wonderful time together. Now, nearly 35 years later, we're still friends. (One of the first things I asked him about that night at the Garden was the feverish pitch with which he coached: Wasn't he in danger of a heart attack? I asked. No, he assured me, he was quite healthy; the emotion was just a way of blowing off some of the tension.)

Back when he coached for Philly, and then for Buffalo, we had a certain routine: I'd go to the game and then meet him for dinner afterward, and we would talk late into the night. He was thoughtful, curious, and always open. We would talk first about basketball, and then about politics. (The protest against the Vietnam War was reaching a crescendo in those days, and I think he wanted answers for himself, but also so he could understand how his players felt, many of whom were black and significantly more alienated from the political process.) I thought he did some of his best coaching in Buffalo—taking a team without a big man, a team that had a lot of disparate parts that did not readily fit, and talking any number of players into giving an additional dimension to their game. All in all he created a team that was a great deal of fun to watch.

And I came to admire him. Jack has no con to him, no artifice. He's an old-fashioned man, direct, sometimes a bit blunt, with a highly developed ethical sense, one in which there is still a clear and well-drawn line between right and wrong. In a sports world where one finds, with increasing frequency, altogether too many big-name coaches with a dual value system—a benign one created specifically for export to the larger public and projected through calculated media appearances, and then a real value system, albeit a covert one, where the line between right and wrong is crossed all the time (the value system many coaches use when they think no one is around)—Jack remains a throwback. There are not two of him—there is only the one. What you see is what you get.

I was thrilled back in 1976 when he got the Portland job. I had been fascinated by Bill Walton's college play, but had been surprised by his difficult adjustment to the pro game in his first two years, so I wondered what would happen when he got together with Jack. If ever there were a case, I thought, of a coach and a player who were made for each other, this was it. I still think of the 1976–1977 Blazers, and the 1977–1978 team (until Walton's foot gave way in the playoffs against Seattle), as an aficionado's team. If you love the game, you loved that team. The ball moved from player to player as if in a clinic. The shot selection was always good. Everyone was in position for a rebound. No one was out of position on defense. The fast break started in almost perfect connection to the rebounding. You were always a bit surprised when a player on that team took a bad shot or made a careless pass. What was special about that team was that the whole was infinitely greater than the sum of its parts. The players were young, and a dynasty seemed in the offing.

And then very quickly it all went sour. All the modern viruses of contemporary big-time sports entered the picture. Soon after Walton's foot went out, he was gone; and other players became dissatisfied with their status and with the pay scale. Somewhere in there I had the idea of doing a book on what happened, not in the championship season, which is what most writers generally try to do, but instead what happens when the forces that created a championship are torn asunder, and the pressures of modern-day materialism with its accompanying subsidiary pressures attack a no-longer-immune smaller world. That is what big-time sports in this era are really like.

I took the idea to Jack, and asked what he thought. He knew it was going to be a difficult year and that his team was not talented, and that expectations because of the earlier triumphs were still too high. I told him that there was a real chance, given the degree of difficulty for the season ahead, that he might not like the book and that our friendship might become a casualty of a, painful year. What is good for a writer, conflict among the principals, is not necessarily what is good for the coach. And he, confident that he was not going to be any different as a man in a difficult season than in a triumphant one, said not to worry. The idea, he thought, was a good one, and he was interested in what his world looked like from the outside.

It was a very tough season indeed, but it never dented our friendship. Almost everything that could go wrong did go wrong: serious injuries to key players, player disaffection over salaries, myriad tensions between the ownership and the coaches and the players. Jack might be the most passionate of coaches, and defeat might still be unbearably painful—you did not want to go out to dinner with him after a losing game that season—but he never changed as a man, and he never blamed others for what was going on. He was as passionate, ethical, and honorable when everything was collapsing on him as he had been when everything was going right just a few years earlier and he was obviously on his way to becoming coach of the year. We all know how easy it is to be graceful in the best of times, but watching so driven a man in the worst of times, when exterior forces were working so hard against him was, in itself, an education.

He has mellowed a bit over time of our friendship. I'm amused that he has ended up as a member of the media, primarily as a broadcaster. Not surprisingly, he's a good one, too, as in coaching, always well prepared, always straight. I tease him a bit that he has gotten a little soft on the refs, because he'll say several times during a broadcast that the ref had made a good call, which was not the way it went in the old days. I'm glad that he has written this book—it's wonderful and surprisingly candid; but it is also a book that will find a wide readership among not just basketball fans but people from all walks of life. It is vintage Ramsay, part memoir and part clinic—all in all, a wonderful distillation of what the game he loves so much is all about. I think you'll like the book just as you would like the man who wrote it.

DAVID HALBERSTAM

David Halberstam has written 19 books of which the last 14 have been national best-sellers. They include: The Best and the Brightest, Breaks of the Game, War in a Time of Peace, *and* The Teammates. *Also, he has won a Pulitzer prize for his work on Vietnam.*

Acknowledgments

A GREAT MANY PEOPLE helped to make this book a reality. John Monteleone first contacted me about this project in behalf of editor Michael Hamilton, of John Wiley & Sons. I had been considering doing a book about the NBA for some time. John made the connection with Wiley, Mike suggested a leadership theme, and the book became more than just a story of NBA basketball.

Wiley assigned Janice Borzendowski to organize my meandering prose and give it continuity. Janice did a marvelous job making the pieces fit, suggested changes in the existing text, and gets special thanks for her assistance and encouragement.

Next, I want to acknowledge the contributions of those involved with the National Basketball Association in the past and present, who willingly gave their time to provide information that was important to the research for this book. NBA Commissioner David Stern, Dallas team owner Mark Cuban, and NHL Commissioner Gary Bettman were especially gracious fitting me into schedules already jammed to capacity. The same was true of many of these former NBA players: Bob Pettit, Bill Russell, Jerry West, Dave Bing, Billy Cunningham, Bill Bradley, Bill Walton, Johnny Davis, Earvin (Magic) Johnson, Michael Jordan, Sam Bowie, Larry Bird, Kevin McHale, and Joe Dumars. Present-day players Kevin Garnett, Tim Duncan, Shaquille O'Neal, Kobe Bryant, Steve

Nash, and Avery Johnson were equally cooperative, as were coaches Phil Jackson, Pat Riley, Gregg Popovich, Maurice Cheeks, Rick Adelman, Flip Saunders, Jim O'Brien, Paul Silas, and Jim Lynam.

Former NBA coaches Bill Fitch, Chuck Daly, Jerry Reynolds, Paul Westhead, Don Casey, and longtime University of North Carolina basketball coach, Bill Guthridge, also contributed valuable information. Special mention goes to the players from the 11 teams that I coached at St. Joseph's College, and that institution's present-day director of athletics, Don DiJulia; players from the 1977 champion Portland Trail Blazers; and longtime basketball associate and friend, Jack McKinney, for their many recollections of events shared. I also recalled past conversations with basketball pundits Pete Newell, Arnold (Red) Auerbach, Stu Inman, Donnie Walsh, and the late Wilt Chamberlain.

NBA representatives Tim Frank, Zelda Spoelstra, Tom Carelli, Todd Harris, and Dana Jones provided excellent perspectives on time sequences and league personalities; and while I received excellent cooperation from NBA media relations personnel in general, Tom James (San Antonio Spurs), John Black (Los Angeles Lakers), Bill Bonsiewicz (Boston Celtics), Tim Donovan (Miami Heat), and Gregg Elkin (Dallas Mavericks) made special efforts in my behalf.

Collegiate sports publicists Larry Dougherty (then at St. Joseph's and now serving in the same capacity at Temple University), Bob Lyons, formerly at La Salle College, and Craig Sachson (Princeton University) helped me dig out facts and figures from the past to accurately fill in blanks in my memory bank. I also appreciated the cooperation from many executive assistants of those mentioned earlier, but especially Sue Ray, of the Bing Group; and George Kohler, Michael Jordan's all-purpose assistant. There were many outside the NBA circle—particularly Sue Lindsay, Steve Spinner, Sydney Tiller, and Steve Kauffman—who provided facts or personal insights that widened my knowledge about some of the individuals or incidents included in this book.

I want also to thank members of the print media who provided needed resource information—especially Phil Jasner and Bob Vetrone Jr., *Philadelphia Daily News*; Celeste Whittaker, *Camden Courier-Post*; Tim Brown and Mark Heisler, *Los Angeles Times*.

I want to express my deep appreciation to David Halberstam, who—when I told him that I was putting this book together—said immediately, "I'll do the Foreword for it, if you'd like." I have been a great Halberstam admirer since I read *The Best and the Brightest* (New York: Random House, 1973) in the early 1970s and am pleased to have him as a friend. I am honored to have his name and mine on the same publication.

Final thanks go to Charlotte Saikia of Publications Development Company of Texas, for her deft touch in preparing this manuscript for print.

J. R.

INTRODUCTION

Hoop Journey

From Barn Door to the NBA

THE HOOP BUG BIT me when I was 12 years old, after my dad hung a rim on the barn door near our house in Milford, Connecticut. I shot baskets there for hours on end. When it got too dark outside, I went into the house and shot rolled-up socks through an open-ended Quaker Oats box hanging above the kitchen door—much to the amusement of my three older sisters.

I went on to play basketball on the grade school team, then on Milford High School's junior varsity team as a freshman. I liked everything about school—my classes, some special teachers, and my friends—but I loved basketball. The level of competition couldn't have been very good, but it didn't matter.

Milford was a small school; we played basketball games in the grade school auditorium. Backboards were suspended from the walls at either end of the floor; canvas padding covered radiators on the baselines; and the court's width was limited by a stage on one side and, on the other, by a balcony that extended about 3 feet over the court. The jayvee coach,

Mr. Jensen, was also the high school mechanical drawing teacher and had never played the game. Game scores were sometimes in the teens, and I felt good about myself when I scored six points. On game nights, when the teams came on the floor to warm up, the public address system played recorded music by the "big bands." Artie Shaw's "Begin the Beguine" was very popular and was always among the pieces played. (To this day, whenever I hear that music, I recall shooting layups for the MHS jayvee basketball team.)

When I was in 10th grade, my parents separated, and my mother and I moved to the Philadelphia area, where I entered Upper Darby High School, which was much larger than Milford. Leaving a friendly, small-town community and the friends that I had grown up with was an emotional ordeal. I also had to make many adjustments in our changed family structure, which added to the stress for a teenager who was entering a different school in the month of November. I struggled at first with the academic demands, which were significantly greater at Upper Darby (UD), but I made the jayvee basketball team and gradually began to feel at home in my new environment. By the end of the school year, I realized that moving to Upper Darby, where I could receive a higher-quality education and participate in a more competitive level of athletics, was going to be a positive experience for me.

Gradually, my family life also improved. One of my sisters, Mary, got a job in Philadelphia and came to live with my mother and me. My other sisters lived away from home. Anne, the oldest, was married and lived with her husband in Orange, New Jersey; and Virginia (called Gig) was a nurse at a New Haven, Connecticut, hospital. So there were just the three of us—my mom, Mary, and I—living comfortably in a rented house in Bywood, a quiet section of Upper Darby Township. My father, who had retained his mortgage business in New Haven, came to visit on some weekends, mostly during the basketball season, and often attended my games. But his visits frequently ended in bitter arguments with my mother, and it was more peaceful when he left, or didn't come at all.

My academic work improved to the point where my grades made me eligible to attend quality colleges. I became a starter on the basketball and baseball teams in 11th and 12th grade, and tended goal for the soccer team in my senior year. Upper Darby played in the Suburban I conference, generally considered the strongest outside Philadelphia. We had good teams, but finished second to rival Lower Merion each year. In the structure of Pennsylvania interscholastic athletics at the time, only league champions went to the state basketball playoffs, so I never got to the playoffs in any of the years I played.

During that high school period, my basketball skills improved. The higher level of competition helped considerably, and even though I played on the school's baseball and soccer teams, I always found time to work on some facet of my basketball game. Although Upper Darby didn't qualify for the state playoffs, it entered a county Kiwanis tournament in my two varsity years. We never won it, but I made the All-Tournament team and received the outstanding player award in my senior year. I was also voted the school's outstanding senior athlete. The next step was to get a scholarship to college.

Neither of my parents had schooling beyond eighth grade, but my mother made going to college a must for my future. My high school coach, Carson Thompson, who had pitched for the 1936 United States Olympic

The Coaching Bug Bites

The competition with Lower Merion, which not only won the Suburban I title but also the state championship in basketball in both of my varsity seasons at Upper Darby, gave me my first opportunity to see the impact that a coach could have on his team. Bill Anderson, who coached Lower Merion, stressed tight man-to-man defense and give-and-go offense. His teams looked the same year after year, even though different players performed. Few of his players became prominent at the college level, but they all played well within Anderson's system. His teams were fundamentally sound and totally unselfish. They were frustrating teams to play against because they were hard to score on and never beat themselves. My interest in coaching probably began when I observed how Anderson achieved such excellent team play and consistent success.

baseball team, was dedicated to his student athletes. At the end of our senior season, he took several of his players to small area colleges to work out in an effort to get them athletic scholarships. This was common practice at the time, permitted by the loosely regulated policies of collegiate athletics. Those workouts went well for me—Ursinus College offered me a scholarship—but I was looking for a school with a stronger basketball tradition. Through a chance connection my mother made with a St. Joseph's College alumnus, I had the opportunity to work out for Bill Ferguson, the St. Joe's coach. On the designated day, about 40 players from Pennsylvania and New Jersey came to the St. Joseph's Prep gym (the college didn't have one), and we scrimmaged for about three hours under Ferguson's watchful eye. I felt that I had done pretty well and this belief was confirmed when, at the end of the workout, Ferguson told me to apply for admission. I did so, and in a couple of weeks I received a letter offering me a scholarship. I was thrilled, and my mother was very proud.

College Basketball

St. Joseph's was a wonderful experience. It had a small enrollment of about 250 students that year (1942) because of the military draft and enlistments that followed the United States' entrance into World War II. The Jesuit priests were excellent teachers, and the basketball team played a national schedule. I made the varsity as a freshman and was a bit awestruck to play on the same team with George Senesky, who would lead the nation in scoring that season, make All-America First Team, and be selected as the Helms Foundation College Player of the Year.

Coach Ferguson—called "Ferg" by his players—was an austere man in his mid-40s when I first met him, a high school math teacher and part-time banker by profession. He wore his business attire to practice and games: black suit, white shirt, and conservative tie. He was a devout Catholic and a man of high morals who was vehemently opposed to the use of alcohol or tobacco. He expected the same abstinence from his players.

Ferg was not an X-and-O guy. His highest priority was constant, all-out effort—which he termed "the old ginegar"—and his teams were known for their never-say-die attitude. On offense, he wanted the ball passed, instead of dribbled, but there were no set plays, no plan of attack other than the fast break, and scrimmaging dominated his practices. Ferg had a network of high school coaches throughout Pennsylvania who sent him good players, and he produced some outstanding teams during his 25-year tenure.

A Chance to Play

As one of two freshman on the varsity, I was happy just to be there, and although I wasn't getting much playing time, I learned a lot by scrimmaging against Senesky at practice each day. At last I got my chance to play when St. Joe's was routed by St. John's in New York's Madison Square Garden. It had been billed as a big game—matching the scoring of Senesky with that of Harry Boykoff, St. John's big center. As it turned out, Boykoff did most of the scoring (45 points), and Ferguson, unhappy with his team's effort, sent me in the game early in the second half with instructions to get things going. I let it all hang out: I fouled, dove for loose balls, got a couple of steals, and even scored. After the game, Ferguson delayed his entrance into the locker room for several minutes, then walked in, said "Nice game, Jack," and turned and walked out. Even Senesky, whom I idolized, later said, "Nice game, Rammy." It was a big moment in my young basketball life.

Before the next practice, Ferg took me aside to ask if I could handle moving into the starting lineup. I said that I could and asked what he wanted me to do. He gave me a couple of general thoughts about hustle and hard play, then added, "When George flashes up from the baseline, pass him the ball and cut off him." But when I did that in the scrimmage, my defender left me as I cut by, and tied up George with the ball. George looked around and said, "Whose man is this?" I said, "Mine." He said, "Get him the hell out of here."

I looked at Ferg. Ferg looked at the floor and said nothing. After that, I was unsure what to do, mostly stayed out of George's way, and lost

> ### Early Leadership Lesson
>
> Ferguson never explained his decision for not playing me, and I wasn't bold enough to question it. In retrospect, he may have used me to build a fire under some of the team's regulars. For whatever reason, I remained a bench player as a freshman, though I did get in the game earlier and played longer after that. I held no malice toward Ferg for the incident, but I tucked it in the back of my mind as an inappropriate way for a coach to deal with a player. I finished the season wanting more than ever to be a starter on future St. Joe's teams.

my aggressiveness along with my confidence. I knew I was being too tentative, and could sense my opportunity slipping away, but I couldn't regain my intensity. Although I practiced with the first team the next day, and was listed to start on game day, I never got off the bench.

The Big Timeout: World War II

Much more serious matters than basketball were going on in the world at that time. The war was not going well for the United States in either Europe or the Pacific, and like most young men at the time, I felt a sense of duty to do my part. In 1943, when I turned 18, I joined the Navy and was sent to Villanova University in the Navy's V-12 program to complete academic requirements for officer training school. After attending Columbia University Midshipman's School, I was commissioned an ensign in December 1944. I spent most of my active duty as a platoon leader in an Underwater Demolition Team (later known as Navy SEALS), and then as captain of a refrigerated cargo ship.

Underwater Demolition Team 30

Underwater Demolition Team 30 (UDT 30), a unit composed of 100 officers and enlisted men, was the last of the Navy's underwater demolition teams to be commissioned during the World War II era. We did our basic training at Fort Pierce, Florida, and joined the other 29 teams at Coronado, California, to prepare for the invasion of Japan. We embarked from San Diego on a troop-carrying destroyer to rendezvous with a large segment of the Navy fleet for the big event. Our team was in top physical shape, could swim forever and, like the other UDTs, specialized in blowing

Ties That Bind

I developed a lifelong friendship with fellow officer Wade Haggard, who became an outstanding educator in the public school system in Seattle, Washington. Wade and I had mini-reunions every time my NBA team played in his city. I saw only a couple of the other members of the platoon after the team broke up, and both meetings were basketball-related.

The first reunion was with Bob McKay, who had become the recreation officer at Attica, New York, State Penitentiary. Through his efforts, I took the Buffalo Braves to Attica to conduct a practice for the inmates just before Christmas in 1975. Bob and I had a chance to talk about our days as frogmen before the practice began.

When the team came on the floor, there was a generous round of applause, but special cheers resounded for Kenny Charles, one of my players who had grown up in a tough section of New York City. Kenny waved to the group, then went over, shook hands, and exchanged warm greetings with about a dozen of the prisoners. He later explained to me, "Coach, there are a lot of my old friends from the 'hood up here. I was one of the few who stayed straight."

About four years later, before a game I was coaching in the Forum against the Lakers, I felt a tap on my shoulder. Someone thrust a picture of my UDT 30 platoon in front of me and asked, "Do you remember any of those guys?" I looked around and immediately recognized one of the platoon members, standing there with a big grin on his face. Alvin Jacobson had changed very little. "I remember you, Jacobson," I responded and we exchanged hugs and a hearty handshake.

up obstacles in the water and on beaches so that landing craft could freely discharge troops on D-Day. We had a great team, led by Lt. Commander Murray Fowler—a Harvard professor in civilian life—and looked forward to the invasion with great anticipation.

Of course, the invasion never happened. Shortly after we left San Diego, the United States dropped the atomic bomb on Hiroshima, then Nagasaki. The invasion was put on hold, and our ship returned to San Diego. Not long after that, Japan surrendered. While the combat veterans on other teams looked on the surrender as a blessing, it was a tremendous letdown for our young group. Team 30 stayed together for another couple of months in Oceanside, California, while the Navy sought new assignments for its members. I left the team with reluctance and a twinge of sadness. It was a close-knit group, based on mutual trust and respect in a risky environment.

Putting the Squeeze On: Learning to Lead under Pressure

When the group disbanded, my orders were to join USS YP643, an inter-island refrigerated cargo ship at Kwajalein, one of the Marshall Islands in the southwest Pacific Ocean. The ship's complement called for two officers and 25 enlisted personnel. When I arrived, the captain put in for his discharge from the Navy, soon got it, and went back to the United States. That made the executive officer the captain, and made me the new exec. After about two weeks, another officer arrived, so the current captain put in for his discharge, and got it—making me the new captain of USS YP643. There I was, 20 years old, with little shipboard experience, suddenly in command of a U.S. Navy vessel. I was about to have some interesting experiences.

About two months after I assumed command, we were anchored in the lagoon at Kwajalein, when the ship was directed to return to Pearl Harbor, Hawaii, then to San Francisco for decommissioning. The Navy was sending most of its wartime vessels back to the States, and convoys of ships were returning daily. The procedure was to group vessels of like speed in the convoys. My ship, a converted tuna fishing boat, had a top speed of 9 knots, but the slowest speed of any convoy was 10 knots.

There were no convoys listed for ships as slow as YP643, and I was well aware that the members of my crew, many of whom had been in the far Pacific for more than two years, were ready to gnaw on hawsers in their anxiety to get home. It looked as if they would have a long wait.

I explained our plight to the ship's chief boatswain's mate, a career Navy man named Wright, who knew the ship's capabilities well. He listened carefully, then said that if we jettisoned all excess ballast and got the ship as light in weight as possible (it wouldn't be a very comfortable voyage) we could make 10 knots. I agreed to try it—and the crew was ecstatic. I waited for the harbormaster to announce the next convoy with a 10-knot speed, and asked to be included. The other vessels were mostly LCIs (Landing Craft, Infantry), which had a maximum speed of 12 knots, but could handle 10 knots easily. At a meeting with the other ship captains, there were questions about the speed of YP643, the only wooden-hulled ship in the group. I assured them that we could make the required 10 knots. The harbormaster gave me a long, searching look, then gave us permission to join the convoy—then added that if we didn't keep up, we would be sent back to Eniwetok, the barest and most forlorn of all the Marshall Islands.

We made feverish preparations. The ship was floating like a cork it was so high in the water, but we made 10 knots on a trial run. On the designated departure date, we started out on the 3,200-mile trip, pulling up the rear of the convoy. The ship, unaccustomed to the demands placed on it, vibrated and groaned, pitched and rolled, but after three days, we were still keeping speed with the others.

At dawn of the fourth day, I was awakened by a sharp knock on my cabin door. "Cap'n, you'd better come to the bridge." I recognized Wright's voice, and scrambled quickly to the deck. There wasn't another ship in sight! Apparently, there had been a change in course during the night and our man at the wheel didn't alter his original course and, worse, didn't notice that the running lights of the other ships were disappearing from sight. From the bridge level, the horizon is 15 miles away, so I knew we were beyond that distance from the rest of the convoy. I was angry, but didn't have time to waste reprimanding the people on duty.

I got on the radio and called the convoy commander by his ship's code name—Spindle-shanks 52—identifying my ship—Squeezebox 43. He was not pleased to hear from me. "Where the hell are you, Captain?" he bellowed. I gave him our approximate position and awaited his reply. He didn't respond for what seemed like an eternity . . . then agreed to slow the group's speed so that we could catch up. We were able to do that in another four hours and stayed with them the rest of the way to Pearl Harbor. They left Pearl two days later without us . . . and I couldn't blame them.

After needed repair work, YP643 hooked on with another convoy bound for San Francisco. We had one more critical incident when our fuel lines became clogged with dirty diesel oil and we had run out of filters. Hanson, my head man in the engine room, had no emergency plan. I knew nothing about diesel engines, but suggested that we clean the filters by hand so we could get going. It somehow worked and we got underway after being dead in the water for about two hours. Once again, a reluctant convoy commander took pity on us and waited. We finally limped into San Francisco Bay and started the decommissioning process, which took about a month. The ship had to be bone-dry and drained of fuel oil; and every bit of metal—engine parts, guns and mounts, other machinery, every nut and bolt—had to be cleaned, greased, and rendered waterproof. It was a demanding task, but most of the ship's complement was ready for discharge when the job was completed, so they all gave it their full effort. That done, I was ordered to a separation center at the Philadelphia Navy Yard. On July 4, 1946, I said my farewell to the military service. It had been a great experience, but I was ready to get on with the rest of my life.

Back on Campus

I returned to St. Joseph's in the fall of 1946, eager to complete my degree work and to play more basketball. I took a curriculum that qualified me to teach English and social studies in secondary schools, and I played three more years of basketball for Ferguson. I was in the starting lineup all three of those years and captained the team as a senior. Those teams were good, but not great. We achieved our best record in my sophomore year when many servicemen returned to finish their college education. We had a 15-and-8 record, with memorable wins over Nevada, Oklahoma A&M, and St. John's. My junior season was cut short when I was undercut while in the air going for a rebound, in a game against Western Kentucky. I fell hard, head first to the floor, and sustained a concussion that kept me out of action the rest of the season.

In my senior year, when I was team captain, we struggled to a mediocre .500 season. I was disappointed with my play and the team's record. It was an unhappy ending to my college basketball days, although many positives came from playing at St. Joe's. We faced some of the nation's best teams and pulled off a few upset wins, and I thoroughly enjoyed the comradeship with my teammates. And maybe most impressionable of all, I learned I didn't like losing one bit.

The Die Is Cast

During my time at St. Joe's, we played doubleheaders with Temple and LaSalle at Philadelphia's Convention Hall in a program organized by Ned Irish, the president of New York's Madison Square Garden. Irish arranged for some of the best college teams from the West to make trips eastward with stops at Buffalo, Philadelphia, and New York. St. Joseph's played teams coached by some of the legends of the game—men like Hank Iba (Oklahoma A&M), Joe Lapchick (St. John's), Forest Twogood (UCLA), Jack Gardner (Kansas), and Nat Holman (CCNY). The influence these men had on their teams fascinated me. Each team had its unique style that those outstanding coaches put in place. The high level of team play that I saw as I played against them maximized the skills of the best players. Those teams were among the nation's best every year, and it was obvious that their coaches played a leading role in that success. I wanted to have that experience with a team of my own. It was then that I decided on coaching as a profession.

Cutting a Career Path

Just before college graduation, I married my fiancée, Jean Duffey, and we honeymooned in Maine where I worked as the waterfront director at a boy's camp. I began teaching and coaching at St. James High School, in Chester, Pennsylvania, in the fall of 1949—a position that Ferguson helped me obtain—and then took the same kind of job at Mount Pleasant High in Wilmington, Delaware. I taught and coached at each school for three years and learned a lot about both tasks.

My first year of coaching was the most difficult. St. James was a member of the strong Philadelphia Catholic League and had graduated most of the players from a good team the previous year, leaving me only one reserve player returning. We were outclassed and outcoached—always a bad combination. But we made progress over the next two seasons and made the playoffs in my third year there. Jack McKinney, who later played for me at St. Joseph's and became my assistant there and with the Portland Trail Blazers, was one of the players who went through my early growing pains as a coach.

Mount Pleasant was a suburban school in an upper-income setting. Most of the students came from professional families, and academic achievement was a top priority. Participation in sports was acceptable but ranked a distant second to classroom success and social events. That was fine with me. I enjoyed teaching students who wanted to learn and excel in their studies—but I also wanted them to make the same commitment on the basketball court. Most of the athletes played three sports, and the basketball program had been loosely run without much success. Delaware had no organized leagues or state playoff competition at that time, so success was measured by the season record. My teams there weren't great, but they had winning records that improved each year, and I left feeling better about my ability to coach.

During those six years, I also played in the Eastern Pro League, for Harrisburg and then Sunbury, and started graduate studies toward a master's degree at the University of Pennsylvania. Jean and I began to raise a family, which would eventually total five: three girls (Susan, Sharon, and Carolyn) and two boys (John and Christopher). Those five married when they grew up and have blessed Jean and me with 13 wonderful grandchildren.

My teaching/coaching salary at St. James was $2,400 a year, and although that sum doubled at Mt. Pleasant, the need for additional income for a growing family was imperative. Playing in the Eastern League helped during the winter months. I was paid $40 to $50 a game, and we played 30 to 40 games a season, depending on playoff participation. But summer employment was always a necessity, and I worked a variety of jobs: sandwich maker, cabdriver, wholesale milkman, laborer at an oil refinery, swim club manager—whatever I could find to provide extra income. It was a busy life.

College Coaching

I left Mount Pleasant to return to St. Joseph's as its head coach. It was an incredible career break. I inherited a team of juniors and seniors who were ready to win after playing .500 ball for two seasons. We had a 23–6 record that first season (1955–1956), were Philadelphia Big Five champions, and finished third in the National Invitation Tournament. That was the beginning of an 11-year coaching stint for me at St. Joe's, during which the Hawks participated in 10 postseason tournaments and made it to the Final Four once. I also taught in the Education Department, became director of athletics, continued my graduate studies, and received a doctorate in education from Penn in 1963.

Although there were mostly great times at St. Joseph's, there was also one almost devastating season (more about that later). I coached some outstanding college players. Four of them played in the NBA (Bob McNeill, Matt Guokas, Cliff Anderson, and Steve Courtin), four became NBA head coaches (McKinney, Guokas, Jim Lynam, and Paul Westhead), and many others coached at the high school and college levels. For the most part, I was privileged to work with students of the highest quality. They were great, tough-minded competitors who played their hearts out for team success. My experiences at St. Joseph's as a student, athlete, coach, and administrator were immensely fulfilling and helped form me as a Christian person.

The NBA

In 1966, I left St. Joe's to become general manager of the Philadelphia 76ers. The Sixers (the former Syracuse Nationals) had been purchased by two pro basketball fans, Ike Richman and Irv Kosloff in 1963, who moved the franchise to Philadelphia. Richman was an attorney who ran the team's activities from his law office; Kosloff, occupied with running his own business (Roosevelt Paper Company), was an interested, but silent partner. When Richman suddenly died of a heart attack at a Sixers-Celtics game in the winter of 1966, Kosloff needed someone to run the day-to-day operation of the team, and he contacted me.

In the spring of the same year, I had developed an edema on the retina of my right eye, which deprived that eye of vision except for a halo fringe. The condition was attributed to the stress of coaching, and my doctors recommended that I step away from that activity at least for a while. Around then, the National Basketball Association was starting to develop into a more viable professional sport, and the opportunity to enter it at such a prestigious level intrigued me. So I met with Kosloff in his home in suburban Philadelphia to talk about the job. Kosloff, who was a very gracious man, immediately made me feel comfortable. He told me what the job entailed, asked me questions about myself, and answered those I had for him. The meeting went well: Each of us was satisfied with the other's responses, and I accepted his offer of a three-year contract starting at $25,000, plus bonuses based on team success. I was excited about this new challenge.

The job kept me busy. Like many NBA teams of that era, the Sixers had only a skeleton force of full-time people. Other than me, there was only a coach (Alex Hannum), a trainer (Al Domenico), 10 players, and two other staff members—secretary Marcia Schmidt and ticket manager Mike Iannarella. Harvey Pollock, the team's statistical guru, worked full-time for the Philadelphia Recreation Department; but he had also prepared publicity releases and tallied game stats on a part-time basis for the Philadelphia Warriors before they moved to San Francisco. He continued in that capacity for the Sixers. We shared a small office in the lobby of the downtown Sheraton Hotel with Eddie Gottlieb (former owner of the Warriors, then serving as a league consultant) and we did all the Sixers' office work there.

I was responsible for scheduling preseason games, selecting regular-season home dates, and making the team's travel arrangements; signing players to contracts; scouting prospective talents; negotiating contracts for playing sites and for radio and television deals; and hiring home-game personnel (ticket sellers, ticket takers, and police security). I also watched practice, attended all home games, traveled to nearby away games—like New York, Baltimore, and Boston—and made one or two road trips with the team. It was fascinating work but not stressful, and in three months the edema on my eye had disappeared.

The Sixers of 1966–1967 were a marvelous team. They posted a 68–13 record and won the NBA Championship. They were superbly coached by Alex Hannum, and the player roster included three future Hall of Famers—Wilt Chamberlain, Hal Greer, and Billy Cunningham. The team excelled in all facets of the game. The defense was strong and the rebounding powerful. The players ran the floor quickly on the fast break, executed the half-court offense with precision, and shot the ball with accuracy. Chamberlain was a dominating force. He scored seemingly at will from the basket area and was the team leader in assists. The Sixers beat Boston 4–1 in the Eastern Finals—ending the Celtics' string of eight consecutive NBA titles—and then defeated San Francisco, 4–2, in the NBA Finals. (In a media poll taken in 1980 to commemorate the 35th anniversary of the NBA, that Sixers team was named the NBA's Greatest Team. Red Auerbach was named the Greatest Coach and Bill Russell the Greatest Player in the same poll.)

The following season, however, the Celtics, down three games to one, won the next three to upset Philadelphia in the Eastern Finals, and a disappointed Hannum left the Sixers to coach the Oakland ABA team in his home state of California. Hannum's departure left a coaching vacancy, which I somewhat reluctantly filled, at Kosloff's request. I intended to coach for just that season, but we had a successful year, and that one season somehow stretched into a 20-year NBA coaching career—with stops at Buffalo, Portland, and Indiana. Each franchise was different and each left vivid images etched in my memory.

I had the honor of association with two truly great teams: the Sixers of 1967 and the Portland Trail Blazers of 1977. Those Blazers, molded around Bill Walton's pinpoint passing and the intimidating presence of Maurice Lucas, represent my closest brush with basketball Nirvana. That group remains one of the great joys of my life.

After I left NBA coaching in the 1989 season, NBA Commissioner David Stern asked me, along with some other NBA coaches, to give instructional clinics in countries around the world. For the next five years, Hubie Brown and I were on tour in the summer months giving clinics for coaches and players all over the globe. Dick Motta, Rick Adelman, Paul Westhead, Jim Lynam, George Karl, Dave Cowens, and Del Harris were among the coaches who joined us on some of those trips; Calvin Murphy and Bill Walton headed up a list of former players who also participated. Not only were the clinics a success in teaching the game, but they helped the NBA establish an intercontinental beachhead for marketing and television purposes. It was a gratifying experience. During that same period I also helped coach the Belgian national team in international tournament competition—another memorable association with basketball.

From Coach to Commentator

Like many things in life, my move into television and radio came unexpectedly. I had become friends with journalist Jim Barniak when he covered the Portland-Philadelphia NBA Finals in 1977 for the *Philadelphia Bulletin*. When the *Bulletin* went out of business, Jim became sports director for Prism, a cable television network in Philadelphia that aired Sixers games. Barniak had asked me previously to join him in television work when I finished active coaching, and I took him up on his offer in 1989. Jim did the play-by-play, and I did the color commentary for Sixers games for three years, until Jim died suddenly in 1992. Billy Cunningham, then a managing partner for the Miami Heat, asked me to come to Miami to help telecast Heat games, which I did for the next eight seasons.

During the NBA Finals in 1991, ESPN invited me to provide studio commentary for the Lakers-Bulls series. That began a 12-year association with ESPN as their NBA analyst. In 1995, ESPN received the radio contract to broadcast the NBA Game of the Week, and I joined with superb play-by-play man Jim Durham to air those games, and have continued in that capacity through the 2003 season. For the past three years, I have also contributed to the NBA section of ESPN.com. The combined duties became a full-time job at ESPN and has been a wonderful association for me.

How lucky can a guy get? For all but the earliest years of my life, I have played, coached, and been associated with a game that I have loved since my father bolted that basketball hoop to the barn door in Milford. I feel like I've never really worked a day in my professional life.

It has been a great tour, and I've learned a lot of lessons over those years. I'd like to tell you about them.

Lace 'em Up

The Foundations of Success

THE OLD LOCKER ROOM expression *lace 'em up* means "get ready to play!" For me during my playing days, that literally meant to pull my sneaker laces up tight and get ready to do battle. Tightly laced sneakers gave me the feeling of having a strong, solid base from which I could run faster, jump higher, and make quicker changes of direction.

In life, we all have to lace 'em up every day of our lives. Every day is "game day." There are no off-days or travel days, and there is no end of the season. No matter what we do in life—whether man or woman; homemaker or breadwinner; white- or blue-collar worker; craftsperson, tradesperson, or politician; artist or athlete; student or new graduate—we each have a job to do and we must be ready to give every day our best effort. To do that well, we must have a passion for what we do and strive to do it to the best of our ability. Lace 'em up tight!

Master coach, John Wooden, thought lacing one's shoes was so important that he always taught a session on the manner in which players should lace their sneakers. Coach Wooden felt that unless a player's feet were sound and secure, he couldn't be expected to perform the game's basic functions. When I coached the Trail Blazers, I noticed that Bill Walton, one of Wooden's prize pupils, always pulled his laces tighter just before practice began. He still adhered to Wooden's message: Lace 'em up tight!

Be Yourself

A foundational principle of success—in any endeavor—is to be yourself. Every person has his or her own personality, and though shaped by genetics, by environment, and by experience, essentially we are who we are. That is not to say we can't improve certain aspects of our personalities—such as making an effort to be more outgoing, less critical, or more cooperative. Self-improvement is certainly beneficial, and we should all strive to be the best person we can be—but by being ourselves. Trying to be someone else, no matter how admirable we may think that person is, just doesn't work. Others will easily see through that facade, and the result can be disastrous.

Bruce Ogilvie, one of the pioneers in sports psychology, who worked with the Trail Blazers all the years I was with that organization, called it having a *transparent personality*. He listed it as one of the primary traits for success for those in authority. "Be who you are," Bruce said. "You may be Mr. Nice Guy or you may be an SOB, but you must be that person all of the time."

Develop Self-Confidence; Set Goals

Self-confidence goes hand in glove with being yourself. Confidence is tangible and must be sincere. It is the product of knowing what the task is and that you can accomplish it. It comes from successfully completing the task over and over again. False confidence will ultimately reveal itself, whereas true self-confidence is constant and won't evaporate under pressure.

One-of-a-Kind Leader: Mark Cuban

I coached for four owners during my career in the NBA. All were eminently successful in their chosen fields: Irv Kosloff (Philadelphia 76ers) started his own paper business (Roosevelt Paper Company); Paul Snyder (Buffalo Braves) founded Freezer Queen, which specialized in the preparation of frozen foods; Larry Weinberg (Portland Trail Blazers) began a real estate development business in the Los Angeles, California, area, taking advantage of the great demand for housing following World War II; and Herb and Mel Simon (Indiana Pacers) ran an international land development business that specialized in the construction of shopping malls.

Mark Cuban is not like any of them. Simply put, he is the most unique owner in the history of the NBA. On January 4, 2000, he paid the most money ever ($280 million) for an NBA franchise and set about revitalizing the struggling Dallas team—which, in its four most recent seasons, had a combined 89–207 record and was currently 9–23. His upbeat attitude and total personal involvement immediately breathed life into the moribund organization, and without changing any players or coaching personnel, the Mavericks became a winning team. They went 31 and 19 the rest of that season to finish with a 40–42 record. Seemingly overnight, the Mavericks had become a hot-ticket item in Big D.

As it turns out, engineering dramatic successes is something of a specialty for Cuban. Mark was born and raised in Mt. Lebanon, Pennsylvania (near Pittsburgh), the oldest of three sons. His father upholstered car interiors for a living, while Mark grew up loving basketball and developing a fascination with ways to make money. (He once sold garbage bags—$6 per hundred—door-to-door to earn money to buy basketball shoes.) When he finished high school, he enrolled at Indiana University after his research of the top 10 business schools showed that it was the least costly to attend. Mark finished his senior year at the University of Pittsburgh, then moved to Dallas to join some of his college friends. He started working for a computer software company (Your Business Software), but quickly

(continued)

grew tired of the menial details of the job (opening the store and sweeping up), so he opened his own computer consulting firm, MicroSolutions, Inc. It didn't seem to matter that Cuban wasn't especially knowledgeable about computers; he took on any jobs that came his way, then studied texts to find out how to do them. A basic rule for him was "Make the effort to learn as much as you can. Real success comes from giving more than you thought you could, and preparing yourself for every opportunity. In a lot of things, I taught myself. I wanted to make sure that I knew how to do everything myself." In seven years, the company's gross earnings reached $30 million a year and he sold out to CompuServe.

His next venture developed as a result of helping out one of his friends (Todd Wegner) from Indiana who wanted to listen to the university's basketball games. Cuban figured out a way to receive those broadcasts over the Internet, then formed a company called Broadcast.com. That company went public and was eventually purchased by Yahoo.com; 300 of the company's employees became millionaires. Cuban is estimated to have come away with $3 billion.

With that background in mind, it should not be surprising that after buying the Dallas Mavericks, Cuban quickly jumped into every phase of its operation. He personally took part in a telephone ticket-selling campaign that required each caller to make 100 calls a day. "I told them that anyone mentioning the team's [won-lost] record would be fired on the spot."

He also came up with a mantra: "Every minute of every day is selling time." To make good on that, Cuban tripled the size of the sales force and brought in a new sales director and marketing manager. He instructed them that they weren't selling basketball, they were selling fun at the games. He found new ways to entertain the fans with dance teams, up-tempo music, and video presentations.

It didn't take long to see the wisdom of his approach. The team soon began to play better and fans began flocking to the team's new arena, the American Airlines Center.

He prioritized personnel. When he met with Coach Don Nelson, the first question Cuban asked was, "Are you having any fun?" When Nelson told him no, Cuban responded, "We'll have to change that." That same day, Cuban held a meeting with the players before practice. A self-described "5–10, 200-pound basketball junkie," he broke the ice by challenging star player Dirk Nowitzki to a one-on-one contest. Needless to say, he came away a loser, but it served his greater purpose: to open the doors of communication.

Accentuating the positive, Cuban told the players that the franchise was going forward from that day. Then he asked them what he could do to help change things for the better. Gary Trent (now with Minnesota) was the first to speak, essentially saying that the players felt that nobody cared. Other players expressed similar thoughts. A laundry list of complaints followed, from the quality of team travel to parking availability at the arena. Cuban noted all their gripes and assured the players that they would be taken care of. He said, "Let me prove to you that I'm going to do everything possible to make this the best franchise in the NBA. In return, I expect your best effort."

This was in stark contrast to the previous owner, Ross Perot, Jr., who was primarily concerned with the bottom line and had cut expenditures to the bone. Cuban went in the other direction: He provided luxury air travel, five-star hotel accommodations, and numerous other amenities. He had each player's locker equipped with a flat-screen, 13-inch television monitor, a stereo, DVD player, CD player, and a PlayStation. He catered a fine-dining buffet for players of *both* teams after home games in Dallas. Returning from road trips, players found their cars washed and waiting for them. Cuban also added nine coaches to Don Nelson's staff, to provide specialized instruction and more one-on-one teaching opportunities.

Not only did these changes dramatically affect the morale and performance of Cuban's team, but he regards the additional costs as having been a good business investment as well. "We had a payroll of over $40 million at the time. It made sense for me to spend a little more money to get 150 percent return in production."

Cuban spares no expense when it comes to improving the player roster. Since taking over in 2000, he has signed off on a number of significant player deals after conferring with Nelson. By the

(continued)

2002–2003 season, only four players remained from that team: Nowitzki, Steve Nash, Michael Finley, and Shawn Bradley. Roster additions, which include Nick Van Exel, Raef LaFrentz, Tariq-Abdul Wahad, Eduardo Najera, Adrian Griffin, and Walt Williams, plus the contract extensions to Finley and Nowitzki, have pushed the Mavs' payroll (about $80 million) over the league salary cap and into luxury tax territory. Cuban is willing to spend that to improve the team and plans to work hard in other areas to make up the difference in dollars.

Cuban has a hand in everything that happens with the Mavs. He confers with Nelson about player personnel, oversees contract negotiations, organizes game promotions and ticket sales, creates new souvenir clothing items, and even sees that the arena restrooms are spotless. He is on hand for almost every game that the team plays, home or away. He travels with the team, sits near its bench at games, and sometimes sticks his head into Coach Don Nelson's timeout huddles ("I don't meddle in the coaching. I just want to know what's going on").

Cuban is, without doubt, the Mavericks' biggest and most visible fan, highly elated in victory, a subdued sufferer in defeat. A now-favorite focus of television camera operators, he's often caught leaping up, pumping his fists in the air on key scoring plays, or shouting out his dismay and/or disdain at an official's call that went against his team.

The team has responded positively to Cuban's approach. In 2001, the Mavs' record jumped to 53–29, and they finished second in the Mid-West Division. In 2002, the record improved to 57–25, again finishing second in the division. In 2003, Dallas won 60 and lost 22, and tied for first place in the division with San Antonio.

Mark Cuban's goal is to win an NBA championship, something that Dallas has never done; but he says, "I have no timetable for that. I just want us to keep moving forward." The Mavs are doing just that. In the 2003 playoffs, Dallas reached the Conference Finals with a gutsy effort before losing to the eventual champion, San Antonio, in seven hard-fought games.

Cuban's leadership concepts are serving him well. "If you want to get the most from the people working with you, it's important to acknowledge their efforts, make them feel appreciated. I like to surprise people with nice things. Having the players' cars washed when they get back from a trip is one of those. These are little things, but they show people that we care about them. I also try to put people in a position to succeed. It gives them responsibility and challenges them to make their best effort. It shows that I have confidence in them."

"Having fun is important, too," he emphasizes. "We have a nice environment for our players and a beautiful, new arena. Our locker room is first-rate. Our players like playing here. I want our fans to enjoy the total experience of Mavericks basketball. We work hard to make that happen. When they have fun, we have fun."

As to his renowned visibility, he says, "I think it's important to be out front where people can see you. Most NBA owners are removed from the scene. Their [teams'] fans don't even know who some of them are. I want our players and fans to see that I'm totally involved with this team and that I really care about it and them."

He's adamant, too, about the value of knowledge: "Have all the information possible before reaching a decision. You've got to know everything that's going on if you're going to make smart judgments." Likewise, he says, "Preparation is very important. Everybody has the will to win, but only those who prepare are going to get there."

In life, confidence comes from feeling secure about your relationships with family, friends, and associates; your job; your leisure-time activities; and your religious faith. Those characteristics are not innate; they are the products of good nurturing, careful guidance, and the will to achieve. There is a resultant satisfaction with the present and a sound basis for continuing that lifestyle or improving on it in the future. You can meet head-on the inevitable problems that arise, with a strong expectation of solution. You can approach each day with interest and energy. Faced with dissatisfaction with their station in life, confident people analyze the situation, make logical plans to improve it, then go to work to achieve their goals.

The legendary Larry Bird was well known for his thorough and regular practice regimen. I recall bringing my team into the Boston Garden two hours before a Celtics game and hearing the swish of the net and an occasional bounce of the ball as we walked down the corridor to the visitors' locker room. One of my rookie players asked what was going on. Without looking, I told him that it was Larry Bird getting ready for the game. We stopped and could see the dimly lit court through a tunnel in the evenly spaced sections of seats. There was one player shooting and a ball boy retrieving. It was Bird—the best shooter in the game at the time—honing his skills for yet another test. He always followed the same routine—starting inside the free-throw line, concentrating on his form, then moving out, eventually to three-point range, working from one side of the floor to the other. He rarely missed from any distance. He performed that ritual before just about every game he played and acquired the utmost confidence in his shooting ability.

The Boston Celtics took Larry Joe Bird as the sixth pick in the first round of the 1978 NBA Draft when he was a junior at Indiana State, knowing that he was returning to play his senior year and wouldn't play for them until the 1979–1980 season—or possibly not at all. NBA rules governing the signing of underclassmen stipulated that the Celtics had until the date of the following draft to sign Bird to a contract. If they didn't sign him, they lost their rights to him and Bird went into the pool of players eligible for that draft. The Celts signed Bird—a decision, like the one to acquire Bill Russell from St. Louis in 1956—that turned out to be among the wisest in the storied history of the Boston franchise.

In the year they waited for Bird to finish his college career (1978–1979), the Celtics finished 29 and 53—dead last in the Atlantic division. The following year, Bird's first season with the team, the Celtics won a league-best 61 games, finished first in their division, and reached the Conference Finals before losing to Philadelphia. The personnel was essentially the same—except for the addition of Bird and Coach Bill Fitch. Bird averaged 21 points and 10 rebounds that season, was selected Rookie of the Year, and was named to the All-NBA First Team. In the next season, Boston added Robert Parish and Kevin McHale to the roster and won the NBA championship. The front line of Bird, McHale, and Parish became the best in the NBA. Later additions of Dennis Johnson and Danny Ainge to the backcourt gave the Celtics one of the greatest starting lineups of all time. Bill Walton, the former Trail Blazer center, although hampered by injuries, also joined the Celtics roster in 1985 and helped Boston to one of its finest seasons.

Making the transition from college ball to the NBA is difficult for most players (some highly touted prospects never make it). But Bird made the adjustment easily. I asked him when he knew that he could play in the league. He said, "It was before training camp. Some of the veterans were having workouts—Dave Cowens, Tiny Archibald, Rick Robey, and some others. They were good players, but the first time I played with those guys, I made the plays I wanted to make. I knew right then that I belonged."

Bird had a great career with the Celts. During his 13-year tenure in Boston, the team won three championships and made it to the Finals two other times, but lost. He made the All-NBA First Team nine consecutive times and was the league's Most Valuable Player three times. He's known as Larry Legend in Boston for good reason.

Bird always demonstrated enormous self-confidence and made a habit of winning close games with last-second shots. He did it several times to my Portland team. In one such game at Boston, the lead changed constantly in the last period. It came down to which team would make the last field goal. Clyde Drexler put the Blazers up by one, with about four seconds left in the game. Boston took a timeout. I assigned two defenders, Jerome Kersey and Steve Colter, to play Bird, with the purpose of denying him the ball. On the inbounds pass attempt, Kersey deflected the ball out of bounds. It was still Boston's ball, but with only two seconds remaining. This time Bird positioned himself, leaning over the sideline to take the pass from Dennis Johnson (Bird knew no defender was permitted to touch the pass from Johnson). Once he had the ball in his hands, he turned toward the baseline and lofted an arching shot from the deep corner. The shot hit nothing but net. I stood watching with awe and amazement while the Celtics celebrated their win.

I asked him recently if he remembered that game. "Oh yeah. I remember it well. I knew that I'd get the shot off. Two seconds is plenty of time, and when I turned I got a good look at the basket. And it wasn't from behind the board like some people said. I kind of fell to the baseline after I shot it. But I had a good look." He smiled as he recalled the moment. I'm still in awe. Where did that confidence come from?

"When I was in high school (Springs Valley High School, Indiana) I could do everything but shoot. In my sophomore year, we were playing in a Christmas tournament and were winning the game by a few points at halftime. I thought I was playing all right, but my coach, Jim Jones, said to me, 'If you don't start scoring, you're not going to play for me.' I wanted to play, so I started shooting more. I felt that if my coach had that much confidence in me, I should have confidence in myself. I think that's where that started." He carried that confidence through high school, college, and into the NBA.

Bird remembers an incident prior to the three-point shoot-out contest in 1986, when he asked the other contestants, "Which one of you guys is coming in second?" He admits, "There was a little gamesmanship in that, but they [the other contestants] weren't full-time players; they didn't take big shots with the game on the line in front of 20,000 people. I was used to taking those shots. I knew if I could get by the first round, I'd win it." And that's what he did.

Another of countless demonstrations that show how confidence paid off for Bird came in a last-second game situation when K. C. Jones was the Celtics coach. "Case" drew up a play on his clipboard that involved several screens for the game-winning shot. Bird, standing on the edge of the huddle, looked at the Xs and Os that K. C. had just finished drawing, took his towel, erased the play, and said, "Just give me the ball." According to Bird, at least part of that tale is apocryphal: He denies erasing K. C. Jones's play from the coach's playboard at the end of the game timeout. "I did say, 'Just get me the ball.' But I didn't erase the board. You know how it is: When you draw up a play with one or two options, and you end up not getting the ball to the player who's supposed to shoot it? Well, I wanted to be sure the ball got in my hands."

And once the ball was in his hands, things almost always turned out right for the Celtics.

In sports, confidence comes from successful repetition in practice under simulated game conditions. That base enables the performer to feel comfortable participating in live games. Competence there leads to success in critical game situations. Practice should provide individual and team competition in all the drillwork, with time taken to focus on end-of-game situations. Real game conditions cannot be truly duplicated, but simulations help players to get ready, and then each successful game performance fortifies the confidence base.

Hundreds of big, game-turning plays linger in your mind when you've coached over 35 years, but some stick out more than others. I recall one such play that occurred when St. Joseph's played in the Queen City Tournament (Buffalo, New York) during the Christmas holidays in 1961. We met the tournament host, Canisius, after we had both lost to first-round opponents. The game was close throughout, and in the final seconds, my point guard, Jim Lynam (later an NBA coach), was fouled driving to the basket. We trailed by a point at the time, so the free throws were critical. Bob MacKinnon, the Canisius coach, took a timeout to put more pressure on Jim. During that period, I talked to my team about what to do if we were ahead or behind after the free throws, but didn't say anything to Lynam directly. He was well aware of the importance of his upcoming shots. As the horn sounded to resume play, he looked me in the eye and said, "Don't worry coach, I'll make them both." And, against the din created by the partisan home fans, he calmly netted both shots that enabled his team to win. Jim knew he could make those shots. He had done it in practice countless times; and he had done it in other games.

When I coached Philadelphia, Billy Cunningham had developed into an unstoppable scorer with excellent poise, and I had come to rely on him to score down the stretch of close games. He seldom failed to deliver. Billy always saw the big picture. I recall a game in Seattle when the Sonics had rookie Gar Heard defending Cunningham. At a timeout in the first half, Billy said, "Coach, we're going good right now, but if we need a hoop later on, I can take that kid [Heard] every time." Later in the game, he did what he said he'd do.

Bob McAdoo was another extremely confident player. Mac was a scoring machine when we were both with the Buffalo Braves (now the LA Clippers). He had great range, a lightning-quick first step when driving to the hoop or back-cutting his man, and an accurate turn-around jumper from the low post. He was too fast for centers and big forwards, and jumped over smaller defenders. He led the NBA in scoring three straight years and was the league's MVP in 1975.

In Buffalo's opening round of the 1976 NBA playoffs against Philadelphia, the series was tied at a game each, and the deciding game was in Philly. We trailed by 2 points in the closing seconds when McAdoo was fouled taking a short jumper in the basket area. As he took the ball at the free-throw line from referee Jake O'Donnell, he noticed the backboard was swaying side to side. A Sixers' fan was pulling on one of the support cables attached to the backboard and was causing the board—and basket—to move laterally.

Jake spotted the overzealous rooter, ordered him to stop—which he did—then gave the ball back to McAdoo with orders to shoot. But even though the fan had ceased pulling on the cable, the board was still swaying. Mac looked at Jake, who again signaled for him to shoot. So McAdoo eyed the moving target, hit it twice to send the game into overtime, where the Braves won to advance to the next round.

What was there about Jim Lynam, Billy Cunningham, Bob McAdoo, and Larry Bird that made them such successful clutch performers? They were all fierce competitors who relished game-deciding situations. They all had an intense desire to win, and each exuded self-confidence.

Inspire Confidence in Others

Once you have confidence, it behooves you to inspire it in others. When my Portland team fell behind Philadelphia 0–2 in the 1977 NBA Finals, I talked over several approaches to our plight with my assistant coach, Jack McKinney, on the red-eye flight back to Portland. Jack suggested returning point guard Dave Twardzik to the starting lineup in place of rookie John Davis. Twardzik had sprained his ankle badly in the Denver series, and Davis had stepped in to do a nice job in his absence. But Dave's ankle was now healed, and since he had started most of the games in the regular season, McKinney's thought was a sound consideration.

We also talked about using our zone press more often to up-tempo our offense, as it had done frequently in the regular season. We considered other changes before Jack returned to his seat, and I sat by myself in the darkened plane, trying to decide on the best course of action for the Blazers in the upcoming, critical Game 3.

I knew that we had not played well in either of the first two games. We were a bit out of sync from a nine-day interval between the Western Conference Finals and the start of the Championship Series in Philadelphia. I also detected a bit of nervousness among our players—most of whom were experiencing their first taste of NBA playoff competition. The Sixers, on the other hand, were a veteran team led by the superb Julius Erving, and they were playing at the top of their game. Before we landed, I decided that changing the lineup would send the wrong message to my team. It would say, in effect, that we weren't good enough to beat the Sixers. I didn't want to send a negative signal, so I decided not to change anything *except* the way we played. I was convinced that what we needed was to get back to playing our best game. We had blown out the Sixers in a regular season game in Portland. I wanted my players to feel confident that we could duplicate that kind of performance.

So in the team meeting we had prior to practice later that day, I said as much to the players. I stressed that we had to defend and rebound at our best level; fast-break, push the ball at every opportunity—even after the Sixers scored—and if we didn't have the break, then to execute our half-court sets with sharpness and precision. My parting statement to the team: "Let's play *our* game!"

The message seemed to be what the players wanted and needed to hear. We had a great practice, then won the next two games in Portland by 22- and 32-point margins. With our confidence restored, we won Game 5 comfortably in Philadelphia and returned to Portland to hold on and win Game 6 by a 2-point margin—as well as the NBA Championship.

The players win games on the court, of course. I am not about to imply that my locker room talk was the reason we came back to win. But it may have helped Walton (the Series MVP), Lucas, Gross, Davis, Hollins, Neal, Twardzik, Gilliam, and Calhoun regroup with the confidence they needed to get that job done.

Confidence to Spare: Air Jordan

Michael Jordan, arguably the greatest clutch player of all time, traces his championship-making confidence to a single moment early in his career: "The thing that made me realize—and made everyone realize—that I was capable of playing on the highest level was when I hit that [game-winning] shot in 1982," he said, referring to the jumper he made to win the NCAA championship against Georgetown. "I think that gave me the confidence [to believe] that I belonged on the highest level in basketball at that particular time—which was college, Division I, at the University of North Carolina. From that point, the confidence just continued to build."

Indeed, as MJ continued to grow as a player, he developed so much confidence that he didn't hesitate to spread it around to his teammates. Jordan had a history of making decisive, last-second shots and relished the opportunity to hit gamewinners. However, he also appreciated and showed great trust in his less-talented (by NBA standards) teammates who played big in the clutch—players like Bobby Hansen, John Paxson, and Steve Kerr, all of whom made game-winning plays orchestrated by MJ.

One of those occasions was in Game 6 of the Bulls-Jazz NBA Finals in 1997. Chicago needed a hoop in the closing seconds of the game to end the series, and Phil Jackson took a timeout to set up the last-shot play. Everyone knew Jordan would get the ball, and that was the play that Phil drew up. I was doing the broadcast for ESPN Radio and watched closely from our courtside position near the Bulls bench as the Bulls broke their huddle with the score tied and scant seconds on the clock. Michael stood still as the others moved out onto the court, then pulled Steve Kerr back and said something to him. Steve said something back, and then both went to their assigned spots on the floor to put the ball in play from out of bounds.

Jordan ended up with the ball on the left side of the floor, top of the circle extended, drove toward the middle, and was double-teamed hard by two Jazz players. He passed the ball to Steve, who was standing alone inside the top of the circle, and Steve nailed the game-winner to give the Bulls their fifth NBA Championship. Michael wrapped him in a bear hug as the game ended.

In our postgame interview, I asked Steve what Michael had said to him after the timeout. He answered that Michael told him to be ready, because he thought he'd be doubled. "And what did you say," I asked. "I told him that I'd make the shot." Two confident guys: one (Kerr) feeding off the good vibes coming from the other (Jordan).

Tap the Power of Positive

Add self-confidence to a positive attitude and you've got a winning game plan. If you think you can, you can. If you think you will, your chances of success increase even more. You can gain much by taking the negative out of your thought processes altogether. Think in terms of dos instead of don'ts. Every golfer has watched players miss a 4-foot putt, then listened to them say, "I just can't make those short ones." Of course they can't: They don't think that they can.

In coaching and leading, a positive approach makes all the difference. A positive outlook on the team's ability permeates the atmosphere for everything that happens with that team in meetings, practices, and games. I recall stopping a training camp scrimmage following an especially brilliant segment of play in my first season with Portland (1976) to say to the players, "We can win if we play like that! I mean win the whole thing . . . the NBA championship." I saw belief in their eyes. Players know when they're playing well, but I wanted to reinforce their positive feelings with my sense of where we were and where we could go.

Positive thinking applies not only to the big picture, but to detail work as well. It is much more productive to stress dos than don'ts. In drillwork with point guards, "Head up—see the floor," is a positive statement when you want them to keep their eyes off the ball while dribbling. And a short "Head up" call during scrimmages or games gets the message across quickly and positively. "Block out!" tells your rebounders to find an opponent and use the proper footwork to make solid, balanced, butt-to-front contact; and to hold that position before jumping in the

Rebound from Rejection: Dave Bing

At the 1966 NCAA Eastern Regional semifinals I sat with my assistant, Jack McKinney, at the scorer's table near midcourt in the Raleigh Arena watching Syracuse play Davidson. Our St. Joseph's team was scheduled to play the winner of the game and we wanted to get one last look at our future opponent. Syracuse, under Coach Fred Lewis, used a half-court trapping defense in which Dave Bing played a wing position. Bing's first responsibility was to double-team the opposing player in possession of the ball after he crossed the half-court line.

In one sequence, the Davidson point guard brought the ball into the front court, hoping to draw Bing to him, then pass to a teammate in the corner. As the ball crossed half-court, Bing juked back and forth a couple of times, then came hard at the Davidson player. When the Davidson player was a step away from Bing, he went in the air to pass. Bing also went up . . . and up . . . and up. It happened right in front of McKinney and me. From my seat at courtside, I was looking at Bing's sneakers—he had to have been four feet off the floor! Bing caught the ball a split second after it was passed, landed on the floor, took one dribble, and fired a scoring pass to a teammate going to the basket. I looked in amazement at McKinney, who was slack-jawed. Neither of us had ever seen another play like that. Syracuse beat Davidson that night, and later lost to Duke in the finals, but that play by Dave Bing stands out in my memory yet.

Bing graduated from Springarn High School (Washington, D.C.) in 1962 (where a few years earlier the great Elgin Baylor had starred), and was among the most sought-after players of his year. He had his sights set on Princeton, and although he was a very good student, admissions officials thought he was not well enough prepared by his inner-city school to succeed at Princeton, and so they turned down his application. Dave was crushed by the rejection—it had never happened to him before. But in what would become typical of Bing's winning approach to all challenges, he quickly moved on.

Bing's second choice was Syracuse, anything but a basketball power at the time; indeed, it had just experienced a 29-game losing streak. However, Coach Lewis told Dave that he was going to rebuild the Syracuse program around him and that he had other outstanding recruits entering in the same year. Dave was further impressed by the two student-athletes who showed him around the campus: football greats Ernie Davis, the 1962 Heisman trophy winner, and John Mackey, who later starred for the Baltimore Colts as a tight end. Neither emphasized athletics; instead, they talked mostly about the educational opportunities that Syracuse afforded. Bing bought in.

Syracuse was a wonderful experience for Bing. He was confident he could make it as a basketball player, but he wanted to be sure he would make it as a student, too. He learned a lot about how to study from his roommate, Frank Nicoletti, also a freshman basketball player. Frank had come to Syracuse from St. Peter's Prep—an excellent academic school—where he had learned good study habits, and Dave followed his example. Dave didn't want to fail—the rejection from Princeton was still in his mind, and he wasn't about to let it happen again.

Dave recalled, "I went to every class—which some of the athletes didn't do," he said. "Then when I got back to the dorm, I studied what had just been covered in class. That allowed me to keep up with the rest of the class."

In his first year, when freshmen were ineligible for varsity competition, the frosh beat the varsity decisively in practice games before enthusiastic throngs at the new Manley Fieldhouse. (Jim Boeheim, coach of the 2003 NCAA championship Syracuse team, was one of Bing's teammates.) Bing led the Orangemen to postseason tournaments in three highly successful seasons. He was captain all three years and was the team's leading scorer. He was an All-American selection in his junior and senior years, and in 1966 graduated from Syracuse with a major in economics.

Bing was the number-one draft choice of the Detroit Pistons in 1966—the second player chosen. He was named the NBA Rookie

(continued)

of the Year for that season and led the NBA in scoring the next year with a 27.4 average. Dave was an All-NBA first team selection twice (1968 and 1971) and second team once (1974). He played in seven All-Star games and was the game's MVP in 1976. He was the recipient of the J. Walter Kennedy Citizenship Award for 1977.

Bing played nine years at Detroit and was the first Piston to have his number (21) retired. He played two more seasons at Washington, then one at Boston before retiring with a 20-point career scoring average. He was elected to the Naismith Basketball Hall of Fame in 1990 and was included among the Top 50 players in NBA History in 1996. That is quite a resume for any athlete—but it was only the beginning for Dave Bing (more on Bing in Chapter 10).

direction of a missed shot. "Block out" and "Head up" are cryptic and positive. They carry a "do this" message, rather than a "don't do that."

It is also important to be aware of implicit negativity, a lesson I learned early in my NBA career from something I overhead the great Celtics coach Red Auerbach say: "Ramsay may be a good coach, but he doesn't talk to anybody when his team loses." I had long admired the rapport that Red had with his players; and his record for winning was unmatched. After hearing his comment, I made it a point to say something constructive to my team immediately after every game—win or lose.

Cultivate a Winning Attitude

It's one small step from developing a positive attitude to cultivating a winning attitude. The will to win is in all of us, but it burns more fiercely in some than in others. There have been innumerable NBA players with a powerful will to win (they wouldn't have made it to that level of competition without it), but the most determined that I observed in the NBA over the years were—in chronological order—George Mikan, Bill Russell, Jerry West, Dave Cowens, Larry Bird, Magic Johnson, Michael Jordan, Hakeem Olajuwon, Shaquille O'Neal, and Kobe Bryant. These players demonstrated not only a tremendous will to win, but an absolute refusal to lose—special character traits limited to a relative few.

An important aspect of a winning attitude is the recognition that there are different definitions of winning, depending on the situation. The will to win is no less meaningful when it garners only a very personal sense of achievement, as opposed to public acclaim. I recall when Wayne Cooper (Coop), a veteran Blazer center, came to the LA Summer League to work on his game. It was an ideal setting for coaches to give individual instruction and to get to know players more personally. I really enjoyed that time; it was pure coaching. The rookies and free agents worked hard to learn the Portland style of play, and veterans came voluntarily to sharpen their games. It also was a more relaxed atmosphere in which coaches could improve their own physical conditioning. In the early morning hours, I joined hundreds of runners, swimmers, and cyclists out in the warm southern California clime, getting ready for upcoming competitions.

Coop learned from trainer Ron Culp that I was at the beach before practice each day, running in the sand and swimming in the ocean, conditioning for triathlons later in the summer, but specifically training for an upcoming annual pier-to-pier two-mile swim race held at Manhattan Beach. The night before the race, I bumped into Coop coming out of the hotel dining room. "Are you going to win it?" he asked. When I told him that I didn't expect to, that there would be about 300 contestants—some at the world-class level—and that I'd be satisfied to finish the race within the two-hour time limit, he looked shocked. "I can't believe I'd ever hear you say that you didn't think you could win!" But for me and many others in that event, the definition of winning was finishing the swim in less than two hours. I tried to explain that to Cooper, but he had watched me go all-out as a coach to win too many basketball games and couldn't imagine that I'd be any different in other competitions.

Another important aspect of the will to win is to stay focused on what you're trying to win, even if others misinterpret your objective. When the Blazers championship team started to break up after the 1978 season, the author David Halberstam (whose book *The Best and the Brightest* I had truly admired) asked if I thought Portland management would permit him to follow the team closely so that he could do a book on that franchise and the NBA in general. I had become friends with David Halberstam through another noted writer, Gay Talese, a friend from Ocean City, New Jersey, with whom I played tennis when I was coaching Buffalo, so I felt comfortable taking the matter to team president, Harry Glickman, who gave the project his blessing.

For several weeks, beginning with training camp, Halberstam attended practices, sat in on team meetings, and traveled to games with the team. He interviewed all the players and management personnel extensively. He took copious notes and spent long hours holed up in his hotel room transcribing and filing his material. He also kept saying that he wanted to sit down with me and talk about my role with the team, but we never got around to it.

When the book was nearly ready for print, Halberstam called to tell me that he had finished the part in the book about me, and would send me those galley proofs. I reminded him that we had never really sat down to talk about it, but he felt he had gotten a good insight into my function by observing me and talking to others.

I am not an especially introspective person, so I was interested to see what David had written; and I admit I awaited the galley proofs with a mixed feeling of curiosity and trepidation. After reading the proofs, I had no serious objections except for one small part that I felt needed clarification. At the time, I was second in total NBA wins to Red Auerbach, and David had written that I was so obsessed with gaining more career wins than Red that, when the Blazers played Boston, it wasn't the Celtics that I thought about, ". . . it was Auerbach, Auerbach, Auerbach."

When I called Halberstam with my feedback, I told him that when we played Boston, I never thought about Red (who was not the Celtics coach at the time and often didn't attend games between the two teams) and that I was totally focused on what my team had to do to beat Boston, not what I had to do to beat Auerbach's record. I added that I didn't think a lot about career wins, and certainly not during the season, because if the Blazers didn't win enough games, my career could be over quickly.

David listened without comment, and when I was finished, he said, "You have to allow me a little poetic license. But I'll see what I can do to

Man to Watch: Bill Russell

One good reason I had to keep my focus on beating Boston—as opposed to Auerbach's record—was named Bill Russell. When I was coaching Philadelphia in 1968–1969, he was still player/coach of the Celts. In a game at the Boston Garden that season, the Sixers managed to get a 2-point lead going down the stretch of a closely played game. The Celts had possession with about 20 seconds left to play and worked the ball to Sam Jones, who missed a corner jumper. Darrell Imhoff got the rebound and outlet the ball to Archie Clark near half-court, with no Celtic between him and the hoop. In retrospect, Clark should have dribbled out the clock and taken the win. But since no one was in front of him, he continued in for the layup.

From nowhere came Russell, the only Celt to pursue Clark. Archie never saw him coming, and when he released his shot at the basket, Russ smacked the ball off the backboard, grabbed the rebound, and fired a length-of-the-court pass to Jones. Sam, not one to miss two big shots in a row, nailed the jumper to tie the game as the horn sounded.

We were stunned. I tried to rally my players' spirits during the ensuing timeout, but Russell's incredible play had sucked the life out of us and resuscitated his own team. The Celts went on to win the game in overtime. That extraordinary play was typical of the fierce intensity Russell brought to every game he played.

fix it." When *The Breaks of the Game* was published, Halberstam gave me an autographed copy. I scanned through the book to find the section about me coaching against the Celtics. Halberstam's "fix" was to drop two Auerbachs, so it now read that I was focused on "Auerbach." (We're still good friends.)

The vast majority of people that I've met want to do well in what they consider to be essential tasks. That in itself demonstrates a will to win. When we apply that principle to our daily lives, then we're striving to be the best that we can be. How much better would the world be if everyone accepted that as their personal goal?

Home Court Advantage

Teaching and Learning

WHEN I BEGAN COACHING at St. James High School, I had just finished a decent college career against some of the best coaches, teams, and players in the country. I continued playing in the Eastern Pro League—a good, eight-team league at the time—and played well enough to make either the first or second All-League team four times. I thought I was a pretty good player who knew the game and how to teach it. I got a rude awakening.

I found that my knowledge of the game was limited and my teaching skills were inadequate. I showed my young players how I played without teaching them how they should play. I failed to break down the game into its basic elements and taught whole concepts instead of part to whole. I had always played man-to-man defense—so my team played it—but many of the teams we faced played zone defense, and I didn't prepare my team properly for that. I played a fast-break game, but my players lacked the skills to play it well, and I made no adjustments.

That first season in the Philadelphia Catholic League, we had our heads handed to us by teams with skilled coaches. I didn't like the experience one bit. From that point on, for each of the more than 36 years I coached basketball, I learned something that I could apply to my craft. What I discovered along the way is that there's really no limit to the potential knowledge one can gain in any endeavor; no one knows all there is to know about anything. Those who achieve the greatest success are those who have what Bruce Ogilvie, a pioneer in sports psychology, described as an "insatiable curiosity" about their craft, and they never stop trying to learn more.

Learn from Others

Determined never again to experience that kind of failure, I concentrated on learning how to coach. I traveled to coaching clinics and attended games at every level—high school, college, and professional. While watching good teams, I tried to pick out facets of their games that I could apply to the kind of game I wanted my teams to play. I sent for films of NCAA Final Four Tournament games and pored over them, running them back and forth, picking out fundamentals that I had been neglecting to teach my teams.

Jack McCloskey and Stan Novak, two teammates with the Sunbury team in the Eastern League, were also high school coaches. We all lived in the Philadelphia area and carpooled to our weekend games in upstate Pennsylvania. Each week, we would rehash the games our high school teams played and go over the tactics and strategies we had used. It was, essentially, a weekly clinic on wheels that benefited me greatly as a coach. (McCloskey went on to coach at the University of Pennsylvania and Wake Forest University, and at Portland in the NBA; and was general manager of the Pistons championship teams before going to Minnesota as its general manager. Novak coached a record 30 years in the Eastern League, then joined McCloskey as the Pistons' chief scout, and later accompanied him to Minnesota.)

Detail Man: Pete Newell

Pete Newell, one of the all-time great coaches, theorists, and teachers of the game, has positively influenced an extraordinary number of coaches and players. Because of his highly developed sense of the game and how to teach it, Newell was connected with one NBA team or another for all of the 22 years that I was involved with the league. I had studied the game films of his teams at the University of California—especially the National Championship team of 1960—and gleaned a lot of helpful information from them. Then, in my early coaching days with the Sixers, I had the chance to meet Pete when he was general manager of the San Diego franchise.

In the summer, Newell held voluntary workouts (for which he accepted no pay) at Loyola-Marymount University for NBA players who lived in the Los Angeles area. My Portland team was among other NBA teams that played their summer league games there. I often came over early to Blazer practices to watch Pete drill his players. He had 6 to 10 players of all positions there. They met every other day throughout the summer and spent a lot of time on footwork drills for defense and one-on-one offense. The workouts were low-key. Pete gave his instructions quietly, and the players worked hard at following them. It was fascinating to watch his attention to detail. Some of the top players in the league—such as Kermit Washington, Kiki Vandeweghe, and Gail Goodrich—were there to get in shape for the NBA season, working on the fundamentals of the game.

Newell later held enormously popular sessions for big men only—aptly named Pete Newell's Big Man Camp. Players came from all over the world to learn from one of the game's master coaches. Newell brought in some of his former students—including Washington—to serve on the staff. He charged a fee to attend these sessions, explaining, "I wanted to give some of my older players a chance to make some money out of this."

I talked with Newell about the game frequently during those summers and still remember the day he asked me, "When your

(continued)

player comes to the wing to receive a pass, which of his feet is up?" I hadn't paid attention to that detail and admitted as much. Pete had obviously noticed that my players weren't consistent in the way they received the ball at that position, and this was his way of offering a suggestion. He then explained why he thought it was better to always receive the ball with the inside foot (the foot nearer the foul lane) as the extended foot. First, it allowed that foot to become the player's pivot foot. From that position, the player was able to face his defender and could assume the "triple-threat" position (whereby he could pass, dribble, or shoot) closer to the basket and with the defender at a disadvantage.

It made immediate sense to me, and thereafter was always part of my teaching technique. Breaking down skills like that is an important part of good teaching. Pete Newell is one of the very best at doing just that.

I learned about the zone press—a defense I was often given credit for originating—from Woody Ludwig, the coach at Pennsylvania Military College (now Widener College). Like St. James High School, PMC was located in Chester, Pennsylvania. In my senior year at St. Joseph's, we scrimmaged PMC. They played a small college schedule and weren't considered a very strong team. The scrimmage went easily for St. Joe's—until Ludwig applied full-court, zone pressure late in the workout. We had never seen anything like it before and proceeded to turn over the ball frequently. The tactic took us completely out of our game. I tucked away that experience in my memory bank, and when I was at St. James, I learned all the adjustments Ludwig used in that defense. By the time I was coaching at St. Joseph's, the zone press was part of my defensive game plan—thanks to Woody Ludwig.

Other coaches taught me a lot without knowing it—coaches like Frank Keaney, Henry Iba, Ken Loeffler, Pete Newell, Eddie Donovan, and Red Auerbach. Playing against Keaney's team at Rhode Island State was an early lesson in fast-break basketball; and Iba's Oklahoma teams, known for their rock-ribbed defense and ball-control offense, left me physically bruised, but in admiration of their teamwork. Loeffler's La Salle teams won both the National Invitation Tournament (NIT) and the National Collegiate Athletic Association (NCAA) Tournament with Tom Gola as their star by using a five-man, pass-and-screen offense. Donovan's St. Bonaventure teams had a similar game with a flash post mixed in; and Auerbach's early Celtics played pressure defense, with Bill Russell guarding the hoop, and Bob Cousy, Bill Sharman, and Tom Heinsohn running the break. All those coaches were outstanding mentors for me or any other young coaches with inquiring minds.

No one attains success in coaching by himself. For whatever accomplishments I achieved, there were countless coaches and players who contributed to my success. Most coaches feel the same way. Pat Riley, Phil Jackson, and Gregg Popovich, all highly successful NBA coaches, are quick to acknowledge a debt to their mentors.

Pat Riley

In November 1981 when Lakers' owner Jerry Buss wanted to replace Paul Westhead as coach, his original plan was to bring back Jerry West—who had coached the Lakers from 1976 to 1979. But West had no desire to return to coaching, so at the press conference held to announce the coaching change, West took the microphone first and said that Pat Riley (one of West's teammates on the 1972 championship Lakers team) would leave the television booth (he was then doing color commentary on Lakers' telecasts) and take over as head coach. Riley, who at that time had no coaching experience at any level, stepped up and said, "Well, if no one else wants this job, I'll take it."

Initially, Riley leaned heavily on the counsel of assistant Bill Bertka. But Riley, who didn't take the job to fail, became obsessed with learning as much as he could about how to succeed at his new profession. As a launch point, he recalled principles implemented by his former coaches: in high school, Walt Przbylo, and in college, the legendary Adolph Rupp. Both were strong disciplinarians.

Riley, who admits he was a "street kid who knew all the answers" at Linton High School (Schenectady, New York), says that Przbylo "kicked my ass into a discipline mode. He thought I had talent and didn't want to see me blow it. He started me off by sending me to a second gym to practice with the freshman. He straightened me out pretty quickly." Riley also remembers the meetings Coach Przbylo had with his players before every practice. "He called it 'Backs to the Bleachers' because that's where his squad sat while he talked to them about the status of their game and what they would work on that day on the court." Riley has incorporated that same tactic with every NBA team he has coached, starting with that first Lakers team.

Rupp, Riley says, was like a military general. He had a rigorous practice schedule from which he never deviated. He used the same drills and practiced the same plays on offense over and over. Everyone worked hard, and in complete silence, for no one dared to question the "Baron."

Riley says that those two men, Przbylo and Rupp, influenced his coaching more than any others. But he credits his knowledge of good player communication techniques to Bill Sharman, who coached the Lakers when Riley played there. Sharman was an accomplished detail man who had come to the Lakers at a time when they needed a change of direction. (Butch Van Breda Kolff and Joe Mullaney had preceded him, and although both took their teams to the NBA Finals, neither was able to lead their talented squads to the championship.)

Sharman was an innovative coach. He had his team run in place in the locker room before taking the floor for pregame warm-ups, and he was the first coach to make day-of-game shootarounds a mandatory practice. Wilt Chamberlain, a member of that team, resisted the idea, preferring to go to the beach and play volleyball on mornings of a home game. Eventually, however, Sharman cajoled Wilt into trying out the shootaround routine, which he came to enjoy. Coincidentally, the Lakers began a winning streak that reached a yet-unbroken record of 33 straight games.

Sharman made it a practice to talk with each of the reserve players at least once a week. He was up front with them, telling those who weren't going to see any playing time to keep working at their games. At the time, Riley was in the rotation, but was not getting consistent minutes and was unhappy about it. He remembers that Sharman came to him, draped an arm around his shoulders, and said, "Let's talk." Then he led

Riley to the side-court and encouraged him—telling him that he liked how "Riles" was playing and to keep working, that his minutes would increase. And so they did. Riley became a part of a tight player rotation on that Lakers team, which won the NBA Championship in 1972. "I still have a picture of Bill talking to me at a Lakers practice, taken while we stood at courtside."

Riley worked all those techniques into his coaching persona. He has a rigid, well-thought-out game plan; he works his players very hard on the practice floor; he sits and talks to them—backs-to-the-bleachers style—before each practice; and he makes time to speak to individuals to bolster confidence and inspire their continued efforts. In Los Angeles, the proof of Riley's memorable "Showtime" game plan could be counted on four fingers, each with a championship ring on it.

But some Lakers players complained that Riley's workouts were overly intense and fatiguing, and Riley was reportedly eased out as coach in 1990. He spent a year as a television analyst; then in 1991, he became coach of the New York Knicks, who were coming off a 39–43 season. Riley immediately jump-started the Knicks to a 51-win season. The Knicks won or shared the Atlantic Division title three of the four years that Riley coached them. New York also reached the NBA finals in 1999, losing to Houston in seven games.

In 1995–1996, Pat agreed to take over at Miami, whose team, the Heat, had a 32–50 record the previous year. When I asked him how he'd react to coaching a team that might finish under .500, he said simply, "I'm going to work very hard to turn this franchise around. My goal is to be part of a championship parade on Biscayne Boulevard. But however it turns out, I'll deal with it."

It didn't take long for Riley to heat things up for the struggling franchise. In his first season there, the team's record improved to 42–40, earning them a spot in the playoffs. The next season, Miami won 61 games, only to be dispatched from the playoffs by the champion Chicago Bulls. Riley's Heat reached the playoffs four more times, but he has yet to see the championship parade march.

Another measure of Riley's success is that players like to play for him. Near the close of his career, Rod Strickland, an extremely talented point guard with a history of missed practices and erratic game appearances, came to Miami during Riley's tenure. General managers, coaches, and players around the league wondered—sometimes aloud—how this apparent conflict of personalities would work out. Strickland told me a year after leaving the Heat, "It [playing under Riley] was great. I wish I had had the chance to play for him earlier in my career."

Likewise, P. J. Brown and Jamal Mashburn, both of whom Riley traded after the Heat had been upset by New York in the playoffs of 2000, had high praise for Riley. They said that they still applied practices they learned from Riley about preparing mentally for games.

In 2001–2002 and 2002–2003, however, Riley's coaching success, once unparalleled in NBA history, took a hard hit. His teams finished under .500 missing the playoffs for the first time in his career, and Riley has taken some harsh criticism from the media and fans that usually accompany losing seasons. But his enthusiasm and confidence remain intact. He is applying the same dedication to resurrecting the current team that he did to bring championship seasons to Los Angeles. He works very hard, uses the same coaching principles, and is "dealing" with the results. He doesn't like the current status of his team by any means, but predictably, won't walk away from the job until he sees his team back as a playoff competitor and championship contender.

Gregg Popovich

Unlike Pat Riley and Phil Jackson, Gregg Popovich did not first run the hardwood as an NBA player before he began running plays from the sidelines as a coach. But his deep knowledge and understanding of the game and his outstanding leadership skills have earned Popovich a spot alongside them as a top-ranking NBA coach. And he, too, is quick to acknowledge his coaching mentors, including Dean Smith, Larry Brown, and Don Nelson, for laying the foundation on which he has built a successful career.

Popovich ("Pop") grew up in East Chicago, Indiana, where his father, like most of the other men of Serbian-Croatian heritage in the community, worked in a steel mill. Gregg attended Merrillville High School, where he was cut from the basketball team as a sophomore. Honing his skills against tough playground opponents in neighboring Gary, Pop came back to make the team as a junior. "I had a different game—I was a 6–2 postplayer—but did okay with it and was the team's leading scorer in my senior year," he remembers. However, he failed to be recruited by any college for his basketball talent and so made plans to go to Wabash (Indiana) College. But when some of his football-playing buddies were recruited by the Air Force Academy, Pop sought out a local congressman who obtained an appointment for him. At the Academy, Pop majored in Soviet Studies, played two years of varsity basketball for Coach Bob Spear and, as a senior, was captain and leading scorer of the team.

After graduation in 1970, he was commissioned as a second lieutenant and initially was assigned to Intelligence School in Washington, D.C. When a general in charge of the U.S. Armed Forces basketball team preparing to tour Eastern Europe and the Soviet Union, learned of Pop's availability, he had him transferred to that "duty." Pop played on that team in 1971 and represented the U.S. military on the 1972 national AAU championship team, which also toured the Soviet Union. He was also a candidate for the 1972 U.S. Olympic basketball team, but was not selected, and so he returned to the Air Force Academy as an assistant to Hank Egan, who had replaced Spear. Pop stayed in that capacity for six years, and during that time, he earned a master's degree in physical education at the University of Denver.

By 1979, Pop had tired of the demands of Division I recruiting and left the Academy to take over a then-losing basketball program at Pomona-Pitzer, a prestigious academic institution in California. It took him a while to turn things around, but in 1985–1986, Pomona-Pitzer won the Southern California IAC championship—its first in 68 years—and a berth in the NCAA Division III tournament. Pop's winning ways had begun.

On a mandatory sabbatical leave from Pomona-Pitzer in 1987, Pop used the time well, spending part of it with Coach Dean Smith at North Carolina and part with Larry Brown at Kansas. The latter connection led to Pop's next position, for in 1988, when Brown left Kansas to take the head coaching job at San Antonio, Pop joined him as an assistant, a position he kept for four years. When Brown left the Spurs to take a job with the Los Angeles Clippers in 1992, Popovich went to Golden State as an assistant to Don Nelson for two years. He returned to the Spurs as general manager in May 1994 and has been with the organization ever since.

In December 1996, after the Spurs got off to a 3–15 start under Bob Hill, Pop took over as interim coach. His goals at the time, he says, were to get the team straightened out, finish the season, then hire a new coach for the next year. He met the first two goals, but not the third. During that season, the Spurs suffered a stretch of bad luck (David Robinson played in only six games and Sean Elliott in 39, and the team finished with a 20–62 record), but Pop's handling of it had gained the players' attention and respect, and so he stayed on as head coach. And his—and the team's—luck was about to change.

In June of the same year, the Spurs won the lottery and drafted Tim Duncan. The rest, as they say, is history. Duncan led the Spurs to a 56-win turnaround season in 1998, as the team finished second to Utah in the Mid-West Division. In the following, lockout-shortened season, San Antonio won the NBA championship.

Taking Duncan as a lottery pick was a no-brainer, but no one disputes that it was the highly astute personnel maneuvers by Pop, in partnership with R. C. Buford (the team's general manager, who also came to the Spurs as an assistant to Larry Brown in 1988), that crafted the San Antonio Spurs into a championship-caliber team. With the sole purpose of fleshing out an effective unit around Duncan, Pop and Buford alternately acquired, retained, or dealt players to other teams. In fact, of the 12 players on the championship roster in 2003, only 2, other than Duncan, were acquired through the draft: Tony Parker, the 28th pick in the first round in 2001, and Manu Ginobili, the 57th selection in the second round in 1999. It was interesting to watch the 2002–2003 Spurs develop. They had become younger, more athletic, and shot the ball better from the edges. Stephen Jackson, Speedy Claxton, and Manu Ginobili had the young legs, and veterans Kevin Willis and Steve Kerr added maturity. Before the season was over, all had made huge contributions, and Pop used them well.

Dynamic Duo: Tim Duncan and Gregg Popovich

Tim Duncan was the San Antonio Spurs' first pick in the 1997 NBA College Draft, and from the beginning, he more than held his own. He showed that he could score, defend, rebound, and block shots. At the end of his rookie season, he had averaged 21 points, just under 12 rebounds, and tallied more than 200 blocks. The Spurs won 56 games to finish second to Utah in the Mid-West Division, and Duncan was named Rookie of the Year and selected as a member of the All-Rookie and All-NBA first teams that season—an auspicious beginning in the NBA.

But though his actions spoke volumes—no one questioned who was the key player on the team—the more vocal leadership roles were already filled by the Spurs' charismatic point guard Avery Johnson (known as the "Little General") and David Robinson ("the Admiral"), one of the top centers in NBA history, who was the team's patriarch. Duncan was content to be the quiet force behind the team's progress, and throughout the following season (1998–1999), he continued to improve his game, leading the Spurs to the NBA championship that season (he was named the Finals Most Valuable Player).

But when Avery Johnson left the team following the 2001 season, Duncan, encouraged by Coach Gregg Popovich, began to add his voice to his leadership arsenal. "After Avery left, I felt that I needed to step up and become more vocal. The team needed it." Simple as that. Like his coach, Duncan doesn't hesitate to take responsibility for how the team plays, frequently announcing to his teammates in the locker room after a tough defeat that the loss was on his shoulders. And despite his dominance as a player, he is completely unselfish, following Pop's game plan fully and productively and never losing sight of the role his teammates play in his own success. He will bear-hug a teammate who has just made a big play; look directly into the eyes of another to impart some last words after a timeout; or offer words of encouragement or an invitation to lunch to one who has had a difficult practice.

(continued)

Duncan has become arguably the best power forward of all time. By the end of the 2003 season, Duncan had been named to the All-NBA first team in each of the six seasons he played in the league, and he was again selected as the Finals MVP for the 2003 playoffs—which the Spurs won against New Jersey in six games. And he just keeps getting better. He now has great versatility in his game, good footwork at the low post, and can score from there with turnaround jumpers, jump hooks, and quick drop-step moves. He makes strong drives to the basket away from the post; and if defenders back off him, he knocks down jumpers—which he likes to bank from the left side from 15 to 17 feet. He is very quick off the floor, getting to the offensive glass, and has strong hands for quick finishes on put-back scores. (Sacramento's coach, Rick Adelman, calls Duncan the best rebounder he's ever seen.) He has also become a sound passer—especially when double-teamed at the post. Duncan defends big players well in the basket area and is an outstanding help defender and shot blocker. He runs the floor both ways and demonstrates good judgment when handling the ball on the Spurs fast break.

Just as notable is that back-to-back regular-season MVPs and a second NBA Finals MVP haven't changed Duncan. He remains somewhat quiet, but is a vocal, forceful leader when the occasion demands.

Throughout that season, the Spurs maximized their strengths and minimized their weaknesses. They did the reverse to their opponents, forcing them to play a game that was less than their best. Spurs players knew their roles and contributed their skills accordingly to develop a complete team. They grew in poise and skill during the season and through the playoffs. They made appropriate adjustments within the game as demanded.

Like all championship teams, the 2003 Spurs merit a "well-coached" label. The players carried out the prescribed game plan and played within its structure. Their leading player, Duncan, played the ultimate team game. On offense, he attacked single defenders or found open teammates with passes when double-teamed. He was also the team's stopper and re-bounder at the defensive basket.

Pop, a fierce competitor, remained understated and self-effacing throughout, typically deflecting the credit for team success to his players. (He shrugged off a compliment I paid him for his part in a big win with a mumbled "Thanks, Coach" and quickly switched to describing how well his players had performed. He even looked uncomfortable and somewhat embarrassed on receiving the NBA's 2003 Coach of the Year Award.) Shrug it off though he might, Gregg Popovich has become an outstand-ing coach. He has a workable game plan, uses his personnel extremely well, and makes in-game adjustments effectively. The NBA Finals against New Jersey provide a perfect example: Pop utilized a 3–2 zone defense to great advantage, a tactic that I regard as the decisive factor in the Spurs 4 games to 2 series victory. The Spurs hadn't used a zone very often during the regular season, but they practiced it once every week or 10 days so that, if the time came when they needed it, they would have it ready. That time came in the Finals.

Pop said after the series was over, "We knew the Nets depended so much on the fast break and the timing of their cuts and screens in their half-court offense and that if we could stop their break and then get them out of their half-court game, it might be enough for us to win." The Spurs did both. They kept the Nets' break under control with strong of-fensive board work of their own and a relentless focus on transition de-fense by every player. Then they put the zone to work for segments of every game to keep the Nets from acquiring a consistent rhythm of half-court offense. The Nets never came up with a satisfactory zone attack.

Pop applied the zone and took it off with just the right timing and fre-quency. In Game 4 of the Finals, the Nets held a 2-point lead with about a minute to play and had the ball. The Spurs had been playing man-to-man defense, but for that one occasion, Pop called for the zone, and Ginobili came up with a steal of a casual Jason Kidd pass. With a chance to tie or take the lead, Manu pushed the ball into the front court, then pulled up and fired a three-pointer that missed. The Nets got the rebound, then held on to win that game and tie the series. But Pop's decision to use the zone caught the Nets off guard and gave his team a chance to win. (Nets assistant coach, Mike O'Koren, gave the move a two-thumbs-up rating. "That was a gutsy call by Pop—and a good one," was how he described the stratagem to me before Game 5.) The seed of that tactic may have been sown during the time Pop spent as an assistant to Don Nelson. "I learned a lot from Nellie about the NBA game and how to play it: how to assess opponents and utilize the rules to best advantage."

Like all successful leaders, Pop is true to himself and is unique. He is extremely well organized in handling myriad coaching duties; he knows the NBA game thoroughly, works hard at developing an effective team game, and is very demanding of his players. (He is known for his direct, and often profane, approach in his dealings with them. "I tell our players from the beginning that I won't play any mind or motivational games with them, that I'm going to be honest and open with them. I try not to ever embarrass them, but I never want them to wonder where they stand with me.") And he doesn't play favorites—he'll even jump all over Duncan. All the players accept his approach and respond positively because they respect him and know what they need to do on the floor to satisfy him.

Even Tony Parker, who came to the team in 2001 and perhaps more than any Spurs player has borne the brunt of Pop's critical wrath, has said, "I know that Pop is only trying to get me to do what's best for the team. He's kind of like a father to me. I can take that." For his part, Pop also knows the value of maintaining a balance, explaining, "If I've been a little tough on Tony, I'll take him to a restaurant for dinner [when we're] on the road and order a bottle of French wine, then explain why I went after him hard and give him a chance to tell his side of the story."

While always willing to listen, Pop is firm in his convictions and his demands and is adamant about maintaining his authority, as Stephen Jackson, another young player, was to learn. "Jack," as he's known to his teammates, didn't always take kindly to Pop's "quick hook" when Jack went on a turnover binge, took quick shots, or became obsessed with what he considered an official's bad call. Jackson had been known to sulk and pout, stalk past the coaches and players as he left the floor, and distance himself from his teammates by sitting on the baseline. Pop let him know in no uncertain terms that such behavior would not be tolerated. He said, "I'd rather lose a game than give in on situations like that."

But Pop doesn't hold grudges. He gives players a chance to redeem themselves. And it was Jackson who, after being yanked in the early part of Game 6 in the Finals against New Jersey, came back to make key field goals down the stretch, as the Spurs pulled away to win that decisive game.

Pop's stance on such matters has solidified his stature with his players and in the Spurs organization. Pop credits working with Larry Brown for learning these values. "Larry showed me that persistence pays off, whether it's in drillwork, emphasizing the use of the proper pivot foot, or in striving for unselfish play among the players. You just keep at it, and don't back down—no matter what."

Pop's relationships with his assistants are just as solid. He has an excellent staff (P. J. Carlesimo, Mike Budenholzer, and Mike Brown), who work well together and to whom he delegates a lot of responsibility. He says, "I want the players to know that we [he and his staff] care about them beyond basketball. We feel a responsibility for doing that. In our staff meetings, I sometimes ask whether we've given enough personal time to a particular player, and suggest that perhaps it's time for someone on the staff to have a one-on-one with that player off the court. I want to develop a feeling of trust between us [coaches] and them [players]."

Pop recognizes the value of off-court communication as well, and to that end, he organizes team dinners and other social events for players, coaches, and their significant others to engender a family atmosphere. "I want the players to see the stability that we [coaches] have in our families, and encourage the same quality in theirs. We also try to demonstrate humility that comes from knowing how fleeting success is, and that we're privileged to have the opportunity that we have. We're not going to gloat over wins nor make excuses for losses."

And though he says it's not his objective, everybody likes Pop, from the Spurs affable owner, Peter Holt, to his players, his staff of assistants, the citizens of San Antonio, the media, and even opposing players and coaches. To be that well liked is a rare achievement for a leader.

Coach Pop's commitment to his job doesn't stop on the court. He involves himself in charitable work as well. In 1992, when he was an assistant coach, he and another assistant, Frank Martin, started a youth basketball league that required the participants to promise to remain drug- and alcohol-free, as well as to demonstrate good sportsmanship and fair play. By 2003, the league played in 75 locations in and around San Antonio, and more than 20,000 boys and girls, aged 7 to 16, participated in it. Through Pop's efforts, the league received President George Bush's Point of Light Award. Pop is also involved with other charities, including the Roy Maas's Youth Alternatives, the Kids Sports Network, the San Antonio Food Bank, and the National Youth Sports Coaches Association.

Pop makes sure his players give something back to the community as well. Everyone on the Spurs roster contributes to some worthy cause. Robinson, renowned throughout the league for his charitable extracurricular activities, founded the Carver Academy in San Antonio—a school for needy children—to which the Admiral has personally donated over $9 million. Steve Smith contributed $2.5 million for the construction of the Clara Smith Student-Activities Center at Michigan State University (his alma mater), in honor of his late mother. He also provided $600,000 in scholarship money to attend Michigan State for students at the high school he attended—Pershing High, in Detroit. Tim Duncan and his wife, Amy, started the Tim Duncan Foundation in November 2001, which focuses on health awareness and research, education, and recreation in San Antonio, Winston-Salem (where Wake Forest University is located), and the Virgin Islands (where Tim was raised). The foundation holds two fund-raisers a year—The Tim Duncan Bowling for Dollar$, which donated more than $350,000 for cancer-related charities, and the Slam Duncan Charity Golf Tournament, started in 2003, which raised more than $60,000 in its first year to help programs focused on breast and prostate cancer treatment and research. He also gives a block of 40 tickets to every Spurs home game to needy young people in the San Antonio area.

Coach Pop strives for the highest goals on and off the court, and is masterful at engaging those around him in that quest. Undoubtedly his experience at the Air Force Academy and as a second lieutenant contributed to that ability in him. But primarily, it's Pop just being himself, consistently demonstrating his skill at communicating with those around him, his work ethic, his demand that others work hard and together as a unified force, and his obvious care about his team members as individuals.

Phil Jackson

Phil Jackson, who has become known as a sort of coaching guru for his distinctive Zen-like approach to coaching and communicating, learned about extending the hand of leadership from another great coach: Red Holzman at New York.

At the beginning of his pro playing career in the NBA, Phil was a lanky 6–8 and weighed about 230 pounds, with wide-set shoulders and long arms. He seemed to be all elbows and knees when he ran. He played for Bill Fitch, later a long-time NBA coach, at North Dakota State where he averaged just under 20 points a game and grabbed about 12 rebounds. In 1967, he was a second-round draft pick of the Knicks and became a reliable bench player during his 11 years with the team. He was a very effective team defender and scored enough points to keep opposing defenses "honest." (He was the first big man I ever saw who would leave his own man to help pressure the opposing team's point guard while the ball was in the backcourt. He'd get back to conventional coverage when the ball crossed half-court. It was an effective tactic that took opponents out of the rhythm of their offense.) Jackson worked his way into the player rotation immediately, but missed the entire 1969–1970 season with an injury.

It was while he was on the disabled list that he grew close to Holzman and developed his interest in coaching. "I didn't travel with the team that season, but came to all the home games. There were no assistant coaches in those days, so after the players went out to warm up, it was just Red and me in the locker room for 15 or 20 minutes. Red would get a short glass of Dewers [Scotch whiskey] to sip on from [trainer] Danny Whelan, and we'd talk. He'd break down the other team's game and explain what the Knicks had to do to win. It was very interesting."

Later in that season, Holzman sent Jackson to scout opposing teams. Then he had Phil diagram plays that other teams used. Jackson recalled, "Red never drew up a play—ours or the opposition's—on a chalkboard or pad. He talked the play through and walked players through it, but never drew it up. After a while, he had me do that for the team."

Jackson returned to full-time playing with the Knicks the following season, was part of the championship team in 1972, and played five more years on Holzman's teams before being traded to the New Jersey Nets in 1978 as a player/assistant coach. He filled that role for two more seasons, became assistant in 1980, then did television work for the Nets for a season. By then his desire to coach was firmly planted. Red encouraged him to become a coach. But because there were no openings in the NBA at the time, Phil and a friend opened a health club in Montana. Had the club been a booming success, Jackson might never have had a coaching career. But the economy was soft, interest in health club memberships had waned, and the business wasn't able to support both partners. So when Jackson got a call to take over the floundering Albany, New York, Patroons in the Continental Basketball Association (CBA) midway through the 1982 season, he took it. The team showed some improvement, and Jackson was asked to return the following year—which he did. The CBA is as tough a coaching venue as a beginner can find, but Jackson was able to successfully incorporate his ideas of the game with his players and liked the challenge of it.

He coached Albany for five years, where his team won the CBA championship in 1984. He was named the league's Coach of the Year in 1985, then got a call from Jerry Krause to join the Bulls staff as an assistant to Doug Collins in 1987. Then when the Bulls lost to Detroit in the Conference Finals in 1989, Collins was fired and Jackson took over as head coach. And again, as they say, the rest is history.

For all his success today, Jackson still says that he learned the most from his mentor, Red Holzman. "Red insisted on team play. He also had a knack for handling players. He was harder on some than others, but he knew how to push the right buttons—and no one got away with anything. He was clearly the man in charge. I learned a lot just being around him."

Listen and Learn

The best teachers learn from their students. I've learned a lot about the game from many players. Jim Lynam was one of them. When Jim was a senior at St. Joseph's, I wanted to install an offense similar to St. Bonaventure's because I felt our personnel was well suited to it. We had spent weeks working on pass and cut moves, when Lynam suggested including a high post screener in the attack. I was skeptical at first because I thought it would clog the middle. Instead, I found that the screener freed up cutters with back-picks and gave us opportunities to score a lot of layups. It became part of the offense I used in college and in the pros.

The championship Portland squad of 1976–1977 included many with bright basketball minds. It was my practice when I took a new coaching job to meet with each player individually in his home, to get to know him personally and to give him an idea of the game we'd play and the role I expected him to play. My first meeting at Portland was with Bill Walton. We sat and talked for over an hour. He seemed to like the game I proposed and his role in it. But it was at the end of our session, as I got up to leave, that he said the thing I remember most vividly: "There's one thing more, Coach: Don't assume we know anything."

Bill, who had played for the legendary John Wooden at UCLA (University of California-Los Angeles) for four years, had seen how valuable Wooden's emphasis on fundamentals had been to those teams. He wanted that same kind of focus for this young Portland team, which at the time had never had a winning season, and so was suggesting that I take nothing for granted. I left his house elated. My feet hardly touched the sidewalk. To hear that concern about fundamentals from the team's best player assured me that we could be a great team. As soon as I got home, I called my assistant, Jack McKinney, to relate what had happened. He almost jumped through the phone.

There was a wonderful and unusual rapport among the coaches and players of that Portland team. We thoroughly enjoyed the time we spent together—on the practice floor, traveling, and playing the games. There was an open, almost lighthearted atmosphere, with time for laughs as

Long-Term Support: Bill Walton

To this day, Bill Walton continues to lift my spirits. For the past 10 years, there hasn't been a holiday—Christmas, Easter, Fourth of July, or Thanksgiving—that Bill Walton didn't call me to say, "I just want to say hello, thank you for all you did for me, and to tell you that we love you and Jean very much."

well as a serious, down-to-business attitude. (The Epilogue expands the idea of fun as an element of success.) I encouraged a free exchange of ideas. When they talked, I listened, then tried to incorporate their suggestions into our game plan. My feeling was that if the idea was sound technically, it had a stronger likelihood of success because the players had a personal investment in making it happen.

Usually, this approach paid off, as in an important, late-season game with Golden State. Rick Barry was defending Bob Gross and overplaying him hard. We had a backdoor sequence in our regular offense but we weren't getting to it. At a timeout, Gross said to everybody in the huddle, "Rick's really overplaying me. I can backdoor him." We came out of the timeout, ran the play, which started with a guard, Lionel Hollins, dribbling the ball toward Gross's wing position as if to pass to him. Gross came out wide luring Barry with him. But Hollins passed the ball to Walton at the high post, while Gross cut sharply to the basket. Walton delivered a perfect bounce pass to Gross for the layup. Listen and learn.

That team had four guards—Dave Twardzik, Lionel Hollins, Herm Gilliam, and John Davis—plus Larry Steele, who could play small forward or 2-guard; and it was impossible to apportion significant playing time to all. By the time we had played 50 games, I had settled on a three-guard rotation that left Davis and Steele with few minutes of backcourt action. I told the players in advance that was how I was going to play it, so it came as no surprise to them.

With about 20 games left on the schedule, Davis came to me before a practice and said, "I don't want to complain, but I think I can help the team if you can find a way to get me some minutes." I told him I'd try to work him in somehow—and I did. By the time we reached the playoffs, Davis had earned a chunk of playing time, and when Twardzik injured an ankle in the Denver series, Johnny became a key player in our championship run. Listen and learn.

I had coached Jack McKinney in high school and college. Later, he was my assistant at St. Joe's, and after I left to join the Sixers, he became head coach there. We were close friends. Jack had a very creative basketball mind and had just spent a year as Larry Costello's assistant at Milwaukee before joining me at Portland. "Costy" started the season with 30 to 40 different offensive plays for his team and added another 20 or so more during the season. Whenever the Bucks lost a game, Costy had a couple of new plays for them. McKinney knew them all. We blended a few of the Milwaukee options into our Portland game plan. Listen and learn.

Know What You Don't Know

Another important aspect of learning is to recognize your limitations. Few people can excel at all aspects of any endeavor. Thus, the wise student learns when to defer to others more capable. Two outstanding examples of that lesson in basketball are Larry Bird and Billy Cunningham.

Larry Bird

When Bird retired, Dave Gavitt, executive vice president of the Celtics during Bird's last two years as a player, wisely made him a "special assistant" with the franchise. Bird focused mostly on evaluating talent for the annual NBA Draft. But after five years of that involvement with the Celtics, and playing golf and fishing in Florida, Bird wanted to get actively involved in the game again. That word reached Pacers' president, Donnie Walsh, who was looking for a coach to replace Larry Brown, and a meeting was arranged. Walsh told me soon after, "I was shocked at how good a feel Larry had for the game. I was confident that he'd do well as a coach."

So in 1997 Bird became coach of the Indiana Pacers. Although he had no coaching experience, he knew what he didn't know, and he didn't try to mask the situation. At the press conference announcing his appointment, he said that the first thing he'd do was hire a defensive coach. He quipped, "You all know that I don't know anything about defense."

But his first hire was Rick Carlisle, a former teammate with the Celtics, to orchestrate the team offense. He then hired Dick Harter, at Carlisle's suggestion, to take care of team defense. After a meeting with Harter, Bird told him that he liked all the principles of defense that Dick was telling him, but added, "If you don't carry them out like you're telling me today, I'm going to fire you."

Carlisle and Harter worked well together and were thrilled with the responsibility that Bird gave them. I watched a practice where Dick and Rick ran all the drills while Bird watched from the sidelines. He interjected his thoughts to players from time to time, but that was all. At the end of practice, he brought the team together and spoke to them briefly before they left the court. Most NBA coaches have a difficult time delegating authority and are careful to demonstrate that they're in full charge of their teams. Bird was different. He not only delegated the major coaching responsibilities to his assistants, he willingly gave them credit for the team's success. During his first season with the Pacers, I asked him about the high quality of the Pacers' defense in a pregame interview. He responded, "You'll have to ask Dick [Harter] about that."

Later, when I asked him about that unique approach to NBA coaching, he explained, "First, I didn't have any ego in it. I'd already established myself as a player. Plus, I didn't have any experience in day-to-day coaching, so I let Rick and Dick do it. But I made sure we worked hard and that we were ready to play. We were in terrific physical shape that season."

The players liked the arrangement. They quickly realized that they were getting good instruction from the two experienced assistants and valued whatever Bird had to tell them. Reggie Miller told me, "We wish he'd talk to us more often." Bird became more vocal in the second and third years, but acknowledges that he should have been more communicative in that first season. "But things were going well . . . Rick and Dick

Always a Player: Bill Russell

Bill Russell was another great player who tried to transfer his winning ways to coaching, only to meet with frustration and unfamiliar defeat. I had tremendous respect for him as a player and liked him personally; I wanted to understand why he could not make the transition from player to coach.

I had been a Bill Russell watcher since his days at the University of San Francisco, where he was coached by Phil Woolpert, later a Hall of Famer. The Dons won back-to-back NCAA championships in 1955 and 1956, mainly because of Russell's intimidating defense. He played on the U.S. Olympic gold medal team in 1956 and had the same impact when he came to the NBA with the Celts, which won 11 championships in his 13-year career.

I got to know Russell casually after I joined the Sixers as general manager in 1966, then came to know him better as a coaching adversary after 1968 when he was player-coach with the Celts, and later when he was a bench coach at Seattle and Sacramento.

I knew he had undertaken a tough challenge in Seattle, which had finished with a 26–56 record in 1972–1973, the year before he took over as coach/general manager. The Sonics improved to 38–44 in Russ's first season, then had two 43–39 seasons, and dropped to 40–42 in his last season (1976–1977). Seattle made the playoffs in two of the four seasons that Russell coached them. Overall, I thought he did a good job of acquiring and developing talent that became the NBA champions two years later (1979).

Ten years later (1987), Russell took the coaching job at Sacramento, a year after he'd done some great work at my request with Sam Bowie, who was then going into his second season at Portland. I wondered how Russ would do with the Kings and hoped it would turn out well. It didn't.

The Kings were a bad team (29–53 the year before) and had below-average personnel who didn't fit well together. The team struggled from the outset, and when the record reached 17–41, Russell stepped down, turned the team over to assistant Jerry

(continued)

Reynolds, and moved into the general manager's office. Russ stayed in that position for only a season, then left the organization. He hasn't been active with any NBA team since then, although he's been a consultant for the Celtics from 1999 to the present.

What happened? Why had Russell, who had been such a winner all his life as a player, not been able to turn the same switch when he directed the action from the bench? Was he as competitive a coach as he had been a player? Was winning as important to him? Why had it all come apart at Sacramento?

As I watched his reaction to defeat during those years, it seemed to me that the game result wasn't as important to him as it had been when he played. As a player, he never, ever gave in. As a coach, he seemed at times resigned that his team couldn't win and appeared to pass it off lightly.

During a playoff game in Los Angeles in 2003, I had the opportunity to ask Russell whether my observations had been accurate. He answered, "I could have put more into it." But when I asked him to elaborate, he talked instead about what his teams had accomplished (in Seattle) and how he was restricted from making personnel decisions at Sacramento by the managing general partner, Gregg Lukenbill.

I did, however, get some insights from Reynolds, who coached when Russ was GM: "First of all," Reynolds said, "I thought the world of the guy. He was not easy to get to know, but once he knew you and trusted you, you couldn't have a better friend. And the players liked him a lot. He was gentler, softer, than the media pictured him to be, and some players might have taken advantage of that."

When I asked Reynolds what more Russell could have done to prevent the losing season, he answered with a chuckle, "He could have played. I watched him work out with Joe Klein and La Salle Thompson at training camp, showing them how to defend the post and help out, and he was still better than they were. He was still very quick—and he was 53 years old at the time. We just didn't have enough good players."

"Bill tried to make it work. He delegated authority to his assistants [Reynolds and Willis Reed]—kind of like Larry Bird did later at Indiana, but Larry had better players and it worked for him. But, like a lot of great players, Bill expected players to play like he did, even though they weren't at his ability level, and he couldn't get them there with motivational talks. It was very frustrating for him."

As the team struggled, the media and fans became critical of Russell, and he became more distant from them. Russ didn't like the media, didn't trust them. As the gulf between them widened, the criticism mounted.

"There were a lot of misconceptions about Bill," said Reynolds. "He worked hard when he was GM. But the team was understaffed. Bill had no assistant, and there was one assistant coach after Willis left and one scout. And he didn't have the support of the owners. They weren't willing to pay Otis Thorpe his salary [$2 million] and told Bill to trade him, although Otis was our best player and wanted to stay in Sacramento. Russ had worked out a deal to send him to New York, but the owners preferred to trade Thorpe to Houston, because we got two players [Rodney McCray and Jim Patterson] and the team saved $750,000 in salaries.

"Bill took defeat much harder than he showed. I could see it in his eyes. He still had great pride, but was frustrated by his lack of personnel and his relations with the owners. It wore on him. If he had the ownership the Kings have today [the Maloof family], and this [2003] roster, he would have done just fine."

I'm sorry it didn't happen that way. But I was glad to discover that Russ was essentially the same person as a coach-GM as he'd been as a player. He just didn't have the same talent level to work with. He didn't have Bill Russell playing for him.

were doing great jobs, and I didn't see any reason to change." Bird carried over his concentration on game preparation as a player to the job of coaching. He made sure the Pacers were ready for every possible situation before the season began.

Bird made a three-year agreement with Walsh to coach the Pacers. His teams won 147 and lost 67 (.687), won two Central Division titles, and reached the NBA Finals in 2000 (where they lost to the Lakers in six games). He was voted Coach of the Year in 1998. Near the end of his second season, I asked him how he liked coaching. "It's been a lot of fun, and I've learned a lot. But, Jack, you know I'm no real coach. I'll do one more year and that's it." And that's what he did. He knew himself, too.

Billy Cunningham

In contrast to Bird's transition to coaching, Billy Cunningham got into it by accident. He was doing television commentary for Sixers games the year after the team lost to my Portland team in the 1977 NBA Finals. Sixers management was unhappy with that loss, and when the team struggled early in the following season, Gene Shue was fired, and Billy went from the television booth to the coaching bench.

Cunningham hadn't coached a day in his life at any level. He had one resource on hand: Jack McMahon, a veteran NBA lifer who had played on the championship St. Louis Hawks team with Bob Pettit and had head coaching experience in the league. McMahon was head of the Sixers scouting system at the time. Billy then hired Chuck Daly, an excellent X-and-O guy, away from the University of Pennsylvania.

"I used the knowledge and experience of Chuck and Jack to get me started. I leaned on them heavily in the beginning, until I felt comfortable enough to make my own decisions. That's when I think my real leadership qualities developed." Billy added. "I literally looked myself in the mirror and asked, 'What can I do to make this team the best team it can be?' I started thinking about how I could utilize each player to the best of his abilities, how to get them to overachieve, and how to motivate them to play within the team game."

Cunningham became an outstanding coach. In eight seasons with Philadelphia, his teams won 454 and lost 196 (.698) in the regular season and won 66 out of 105 playoff games (.629). The 1983 Sixers won the NBA title with a 12–1 record, the only NBA team up to that time ever to go through the playoffs with a lone defeat. (The 2001 NBA championship Lakers had a 15–1 record.)

Learn about the Opposition

Throughout history, a high priority has always been placed on gaining knowledge of the practices and procedures of competitors. History has been changed by the development of special weapons, from the crudely sharpened stone arrowheads used by Native Americans to the sophisticated nuclear bombs and warheads of the modern military era. The producers of those weapons closely guarded information on the procedures of their production. Spy systems were developed to infiltrate the enemy to learn about those weapons and how they were produced. Military forces used stealth reconnaissance tactics to learn the position of the enemy, as well as their strength in numbers and weaponry.

When my unit, UDT 30, was preparing for the invasion of Japan, the Navy Seabees planted obstacles in the waters at our Florida training site at Fort Pierce similar to those that had guarded the beaches at the enemy-held islands at Tarawa and Tinian. The Japanese had used steel rails, concrete blocks, and wooden posts with barbed wire embedded in concrete in the sand, and pointed them seaward at a water level that hung up incoming landing craft. The job of the UDTs was to clear the beach of those obstacles so that troops could disembark on the shore. As part of our training, the staff staged mock invasion procedures similar to what we might expect at Japan. The first part was the reconnaissance. After being dropped into the water from speeding personnel carriers, we swam to shore from about 500 yards out in the early daylight, equipped only with shorts, swim fins, a face mask and a knife. We swam underwater as much as possible to reach the area of the obstacles. We reconn'ed the area, noted the kinds of obstacles, and wrote down their location, description, and number on small wooden slates that we carried around our necks. The boats returned at an appointed time to pluck us out of the water, again at high speed. The team then met to determine how much TNT and plastic explosives would be needed to blow up those obstacles, and to assign sections of the beach to platoons within the team. Then, under the cover of darkness, we swam back to the obstacles to plant and detonate the explosives, clearing the beach. We practiced those procedures until we could accomplish them with extreme proficiency. We were ready for the Big Event and were disappointed that the war ended before we had a chance to perform our specialty.

Likewise, in industry, great secrecy surrounds new product models before they are unveiled to the public. Gourmet chefs almost never divulge the ingredients of recipes that become their signature dishes. (Even my mother, Anne, a most gracious person who willingly shared just about everything, was vague when asked how she made her two dessert specialties: pineapple upside-down cake and blueberry cake. "I just mix in a little of this and a little of that" was her explanation to those who asked for the recipes.)

In sports, getting information on the opponent has always been regarded as important, but in recent years it has become a highly sophisticated process. Teams in all sports carefully guard their practices from prying eyes; but games are open to public viewing, and opponents have observers at those games. New technology allows teams to show videotape breakdowns of the first half of a game to players at halftime.

In the NBA, as soon as a game is completed, the rest of the teams in the league can get a videotape of that game to put on file for the future. Nevertheless, teams employ advance scouts who are constantly on the road to chart every play of opponents upcoming on their schedule. When I began high school coaching, I tried to see every future opponent play before my team met them, so that I'd have a feel for their strengths and weaknesses. I accepted that as part of the job of preparing my team for competition. It is a common practice among high school coaches now, but I seldom saw other coaches doing it then. I did the same thing when I coached in college and in the NBA. I'd get to the game site early enough to watch players warm up, and note every characteristic of their game that I could detect. When the game began, I'd chart their called plays, paying particular attention to the coach's tendencies—which plays he called when the shot-clock wound down, how plays were set up for the star players, and any characteristics in the defense that I thought my team could exploit.

In today's society of political unrest, terrorism, uncertain economy, and high technology in sports, every advantage—no matter how slight—

Scoutmaster: Jack Ramsay

Out of the hundreds of games that I scouted, a few stick out in my memory as being especially productive. At the college level, the rivalry between St. Joseph's and Villanova was highly volatile. Both schools were members of the Big Five, and countless avid alumni fans lived and worked in the Philadelphia area. Several Villanova grads lived on my street in Andorra, a section of the city located on the edge of Fairmount Park, and they never failed to let me know that they thought "Hawk was dead." The St. Joe's response—"Beat Villanova"—was a chant that I heard in my dreams.

St. Joe's managed to have good success against Villanova while the colorful Al Severance was its coach, but had greater difficulty against Coach Jack Kraft's teams. Kraft played an effective matchup zone defense during his tenure as coach of the Wildcats, and it perplexed most of their opponents. That defense gave every indication of being a 1–2–2 zone, but then the players matched up man-for-man and switched every player exchange. I watched Villanova play about 15 times a season before we played our annual game with them, which was usually scheduled late in the season. St. Joseph's played in doubleheaders with them at the University of Pennsylvania's Palestra. If they played the first game, I'd come early to watch; if they played the second game, I'd stay to see it. Most opponents passed the ball around the perimeter of the Villanova defense, penetrating only occasionally with passes to postplayers. That was ineffective. Then one night, I noticed that opposing players drove into the seam of the zone—considered a basic no-no—and created good scoring opportunities at the basket.

I experimented at practice with an attack that included dribble penetration and found that it worked out well. That tactic became a part of our game plan against Villanova; and St. Joe's had more success against them after that.

When I coached the Sixers, it was easy to take a train to New York or Baltimore to see opponents before they came to Philly. But I once went to a preseason game in Lake Havasu, Arizona, to see

(continued)

Chicago—our opening game opponent—play the Suns. I flew to Phoenix, rented a car, and made the three-hour drive to Havasu. I reached the arena early—in fact, I was there when both team buses arrived. When Jerry Colangelo and Cotton Fitzsimmons walked in and saw me, they both burst out laughing. Jerry said, "I was just saying to Cotton, 'There won't be anybody from the NBA here for this one.' I might have known that you'd show up."

I always thought that it was well worth the time it took me to scout opponents, but that game at Havasu paid special dividends. The Bulls had some new players that I hadn't seen, and I was able to observe how Coach Dick Motta used them in his finely tuned offense. The information I gathered from watching that game allowed me to prepare the Sixers for one of our best performances of the season several nights later in Chicago. We adjusted well to their offensive sets and kept most of them in check, and put some wrinkles into our offense that got us some easy hoops. After that game, Motta told the press that we had put on a "clinic performance."

Another memorable time that scouting really paid off was in my first year at Portland. Philadelphia played at Golden State two nights before they were scheduled to play us in Portland early in the 1976–1977 season. The Sixers had high-powered offensive personnel led by Julius Erving, George McGinnis, Doug Collins, and Darrell Dawkins, and they were overwhelming teams on their trip West. They were already being hyped as the early season favorite to win the championship that year, and they drilled the Warriors that night. I was impressed with their ability to score, but I noticed a casual looseness about their defense. They switched on most screens, but left gaps where the screener was open if he cut to the basket. I visualized Bill Walton making bounce passes to open cutters—a tactic already built into our offensive game. I also observed that they were slow in their transition defense, which made them vulnerable to our fast break.

I couldn't wait to go over those possibilities with my team the next day at practice. At our locker room meeting, I diagrammed the post "splits" that I was sure would work and emphasized the need for defensive rebounding to get our fast break going. Then we went on the floor and worked on those tactics, as well as our "help defense" that would give the matchup defender a backup against their one-on-one plays for Dr. J and Big George.

On game night, we blew them away. At one point in the second half, I looked up at the scoreboard and said to myself, "Are we really up by 40?" We were. That game was a huge confidence builder for the young Blazers and served us well in the NBA Finals, after we had fallen behind 0–2.

becomes significant. Knowing the competition is more valuable than ever before, and it's as true in basketball as it is in business or military preparedness. The basics of the game remain the same, but if rules change or one competitor finds a different way of playing that game and has success with it, every other team must either develop a tactic to nullify that strategy or discover how to do it better. Learning involves a change in thinking, acting, or relating. To reiterate the oft-quoted adage, the only constant is change—making learning a constant requirement.

Bask in the Light of Learning

A combination of numerous little things make the final result effective, but six guidelines can capture the main characteristics of a good coach: (1) Know the game thoroughly and develop a successful game plan; (2) teach the skills fitting the game plan; (3) set high standards and motivate your players to play that game; (4) be ready to make effective adjustments during the game when necessary; (5) know the competition; and (6) never stop trying to reach stated goals.

I began this chapter by revealing how ill prepared I was to coach when I took my first job at St. James. In addition, I discovered that I didn't know how to teach. So in my naiveté I had already violated the

Point Taken: David Stern

David Stern, who in 1984 was named Commissioner of the NBA, is regarded by many, myself among them, as the most successful sports commissioner of all time. I asked the commissioner to correlate my six steps to success in coaching. "They're good," he said, "but I would emphasize that the game plan must clearly lead to success, be fully supportable by your associates, and possess flexibility, so that, if changes are necessary, the plan is adaptable. And I've found it necessary to intensely research every aspect of my business. But those are good principles that bring success in my world as they do in coaching."

In summary, he said, "I never stop learning about some phase of my job. When I do, it will be time to leave [it]."

first two of the six characteristics. It was a bad combination of factors with which to begin a coaching career. But I have also related how I learned the game from as many sources as possible—and never stopped learning—to counteract that inauspicious beginning. Nothing stays the same in this world for very long, and although there are certain basics of life and sport, adjustments always have to be made to account for new factors that suddenly appear. On a grand scale, think how much the attitude of Americans changed regarding national security after September 11, 2001. That tragedy demanded an entirely different approach to defending our country than had ever been required before.

The ability to teach is the basis of good coaching or leading in any field. Teaching is demonstrating, telling, motivating, demanding, encouraging, correcting and criticizing, and showing approval. Learning is the product of teaching. If there has been no learning, there has been no teaching.

How does one know whether learning has taken place? In the classroom, testing programs measure the level of learning. In business, the results are visible in profits versus losses. The results of those may take time

Starlight: Kevin Loughery and Michael Jordan

One coach who saw the light of learning shine more brightly than most was Kevin Loughery, coach of the Chicago Bulls when Michael Jordan joined the team.

Michael recalls, "When I got to the pros, I fell back to lowest man on the totem pole again [after making the game-winning shot in the 1982 NCAA championship game against Georgetown]. What Kevin Loughery did for me, no other guy could have done at the time: give me the ball and let me go out and search for my individual talent. From that point on, I felt that I could really get to the elite class. Kevin gave me an opportunity to learn fast—and somehow I adapted."

Jordan "adapted" well enough to lead the league in scoring a record 10 times in a row, to hold the highest career average points per game (31.0 at the end of the 2002–2003 season), to play for a team (Chicago) that won six NBA titles, and to be named the NBA Finals Most Valuable Player on all six occasions.

to evaluate, whereas in sports, the results of individual and team performance are immediate. In track and field, the coach who works with a high jumper who improves his leap from 6 feet 6 inches to 6 feet 10 inches, knows there has been measurable improvement and that learning took place. In team sports, you get either a win or a loss for your efforts—and if you want to stay in coaching, you'd better get a lot more Ws than Ls. But there are also ways of determining the level of learning *inside* the game. In basketball, the coach who, after a strong emphasis on team defense, sees the field goal shooting percentage of opponents drop from 50 to 45 percent, knows that he's made progress in that important area of the game—and his players know it, too.

When teaching is successful, the result is palpable: A light comes on in the eyes of the student that actually radiates over that person's countenance. There is an instant communication of change. The student feels it, and the teacher sees it.

Looking back over my classroom-teaching career, only once did I feel satisfied that a whole group of students were learning on an exceptional basis. It took place when I was teaching English and social studies at Mount Pleasant Junior High, and coaching the senior high basketball team. One of my English classes was filled with bright, eager-to-learn students. Each day, I set aside time in class to work on expanding their vocabulary and improving their individual reading speed and comprehension. They entered into the activities with genuine interest and enthusiasm. I tested them periodically, and by the end of the year, every student had made significant strides forward. I never felt the same sense of achievement with any other class.

The basketball court was different for me. It became my best classroom and laboratory: There were tangible skills to be taught; I became able to teach them; and there were players eager to learn. You can't have a better teaching situation than that. And when the coach—the teacher—can show those players—students—that he can help them improve, the light of learning burns brightly.

Following Doctor's Orders: Tim Duncan and Jack Ramsay

Even though my official coaching days are over, when given the opportunity, I still take great pleasure in stepping back into my role as coach/teacher. Such an opportunity arose after the end of the 2001–2002 season.

After the San Antonio Spurs had won the 1999 championship, the next three seasons saw them struggle in the playoffs: In 2000, their star, Tim Duncan was hurt and couldn't play at all in the play-offs, and the Spurs were put away by Phoenix in the first round, 3 games to 1; in the 2001 playoffs, the Spurs were swept by the Lakers in humiliating fashion—by an average of over 20 points a game. And in the next year's playoffs, the Spurs and Lakers met again in the Conference Semi-Finals. Though the game scores were closer, the Spurs went under again, 4 games to 1. Duncan played well against the Lakers both years, but he wasn't able to dominate the Finals as he had done in 1999 against New York.

By the end of the 2002 season, it was apparent that the Spurs needed to retool their roster. They had too many unreliable shooters and too many who didn't want to shoot the ball in the clutch; and as great a player as Duncan was (at the time he was the league's MVP), I had spotted three areas of his game that he could improve.

I had done the radio broadcasts of many of those games for ESPN, and some wraparound television work as well. Moreover, Coach Gregg Popovich had allowed me to sit in on some of the team practices; and because I had done many interviews with "Pop" and his players, I came to know the team quite well. I found the Spurs to be as high quality a group of individuals as I'd ever come across in sports, and I felt their losses acutely. So following the 2002 playoffs, I told Coach Pop that I thought I could help Duncan improve and offered to spend some summer practice time with Tim. Pop talked to TD about it, and he was all for it.

First, although there was certainly no need to change Duncan's basic game, I was confident that by adding more diversity to his drives to the basket he could step it up significantly. Until then, when he received the ball at the post, he always turned to face his defender by stepping back and away from him, using the so-called Sikma move (named for Jack Sikma, the former Seattle star, who used the tactic to create space from his defender; this enabled him to hit countless jump shots during his career, but didn't create driving opportunities to the basket). For Duncan, who drove more than he shot jumpers, the Sikma move forced him to use the same pivot foot each time he faced his man, and thus he became very predictable. He needed to vary that move so that he could use either foot as his pivot—and make it easier to drive in both directions. Tim also had a tendency to drive to the middle too often from either side of the lane. He even drove there when defenders shaded him in that direction, instead of using a crossover step to drive to

(continued)

the open baseline side. I wanted to see Tim drive in either direction, from either side of the lane, then finish stronger at the hoop.

The second area of concern was when Duncan was double-teamed at the post. He sometimes turned to the baseline to attempt one-handed, cross-court passes. Those often were picked off by weak-side defenders and led to fast-break scores for opponents. The best passing postplayer I ever coached—Bill Walton—always turned toward the center of the floor, where he had full vision of the court, and always kept two hands on the ball when passing. I was confident Tim could do the same.

The third area I thought Tim could improve on was his transition offense. TD was excellent running the floor after the Spurs gained possession, but he generally ran up the middle of the floor, which limited his chances of getting a quick postposition. By running more to the weak side, he opened the lane for slash cuts to the ball or, if his defender denied that, could receive lob passes at the rim for dunks.

In mid-August 2002, Coach Pop set up two practice sessions for me to work with Tim. Pop and his staff were there, as were many of the other Spurs players. First, Tim and I worked at a side court on basic fundamentals—at which he already excelled. Next we focused on the foot moves, passing techniques, and, finally, on running the floor more efficiently. He listened intently to the things I proposed, worked at them, and proved to be a quick learner. We did some one-on-one work, after which Pop ran a controlled, 5-on-5 scrimmage, to give Tim opportunities to incorporate his new techniques. The results weren't ideal immediately, but we both felt we were making progress. The next day, we reviewed the work, followed by some full-court scrimmaging. I watched only Tim and made comments to him as I tracked the action. He was better the second day than the first and I felt good about his progress. After the practice, I made a list of the things we had covered and left it with him, along with a copy for Coach Pop. Tim assured me that he would have the skills mastered by the time training camp began.

I didn't see the Spurs play live that season until their Christmas Day game with the Lakers, but I had watched them on television several times. TD had improved in the areas we worked on: He was not as predictable on his drive to the hoop, he took the ball to the basket stronger—which got him to the free-throw line more often— and I never saw him throw a one-handed pass against the double-team again. He told me at the end of the season that our summer work had definitely helped him, and I felt good about that—especially after witnessing his Game 6 playoff performances against the Lakers and New Jersey. They were masterpieces.

Three-Pointer

Communicate, Communicate, Communicate

MOST PEOPLE WANT TO know where they stand. They want to do their job well, want recognition for their work, want to learn how to do the job better, and want to receive appropriate compensation for what they do. They also want the same ground rules to apply to everyone—from the most capable to the least. Telling people where they stand—on a team, in a relationship, in a family, at work—requires the ability to communicate effectively. Without it, success in any endeavor is hard to come by and success in a leadership position becomes virtually impossible.

Yet for all its importance, communication appears to be one of humankind's most serious shortcomings. How does positive communication begin? Simply enough: Eye contact, a smile, a handshake, a pleasant nod of the head, a simple "hello," or "how ya doin'" may be the start of something positive and enduring. Conversely, the lack of the same may forestall any communication at all.

Make Eye Contact

Eye-to-eye contact is the first and strongest bond that establishes good communication between two people. If the eyes are "the windows of the soul" as someone once wrote, then eye contact enables two people to look into the very depths of each other's being.

To that end, I made it a practice to speak to every player on my team each day that we met, which was almost every day during the season. I tried to make eye contact with them as well, and if that proved impossible, it was a clear sign that I had to try harder to communicate.

When Moses Malone joined the Trail Blazers at training camp in the fall of 1976, I welcomed him and told him how I thought he could contribute to the team. Moses listened, but kept his head turned away or looked at the floor. He nodded in agreement or gave short, one-word answers, but never looked directly at me. As we finished our meeting, I said, "Moses, when I talk to someone, I always look him in the eye. I'd like it if you'd do the same with me."

He responded—still looking away—"I can't look nobody in the eye. I've never been able to do that."

The Brows Have It: Jack Ramsay

In those days, I had bushy eyebrows; and I learned from Ron Culp, the Portland trainer (the team trainer is a great pipeline to the moods and genuine feelings of players), that my intense, direct look had come to be known as "the brows"—as in, "Did Jack put the brows on you?"—after I had a face-to-face meeting with one of them. In later years when we had chance meetings or gathered for reunions, the brows always came up as a topic of conversation. Each player would relate his particular experience, and the tales usually evoked varying degrees of exaggeration that resulted in howls of laughter.

I said, "Let's try each day to do it . . . all right?" He gave me a quick look in my eyes but couldn't hold it, and we both laughed. Then he added, "I'll try."

We weren't able to keep Malone at Portland because of salary issues, but whenever I see him, I always go up to him, greet him with a handshake, and look him in the eye. We still laugh about it, but he looks back now—right into my eyes.

Read Body Language

Like making eye contact, the ability to read body language is imperative for effective communication. The posture of a person speaks volumes. Those who stand or sit in a slouched position, facing away from the speaker are saying that they're neither happy nor comfortable being there. Arms crossed across the chest, feet set apart, and eyes narrowed impart a defiant attitude. Clenched fists signal anger or extreme nervousness or anxiety. Knowing how to read those unspoken signals and, then, how to put such people at ease can help defuse a potentially damaging situation. The following related incidents on the basketball court demonstrate the power of body language to first ignite, then defuse, anger.

The Blazers weren't known as a physical team and needed an intimidator. So when we acquired Maurice Lucas through the expansion draft in 1976, I wanted him to preserve the macho image he had earned following an incident in the ABA (American Basketball Association) when he knocked 7-foot Artis Gilmore, an acknowledged strongman, to the floor with one punch. That summer, Luke was working at Dave Bing's basketball camp in the Pocono Mountains of Pennsylvania, so when I returned to Ocean City, New Jersey, following the Blazers rookie camp in mid-July, I drove to the camp to have a meeting with him.

I told him that, initially, I wanted him to be as physical as possible— bang guys around and take hard fouls—and assured him that if he got in any fights, the team would pay the costs of the technicals. Luke agreed to the plan.

Consequently, in his first season with Portland, Lucas became a menacing figure as soon as he stepped on the court. He wore a perpetual scowl and frequently flexed his bulging biceps in a threatening manner and made maximum use of his elbows. Luke had most of his opposing matchups quaking in their sneakers before the game began, and he went through that season without an altercation.

In the second game of the NBA Finals, however, Luke and Philadelphia's Darrell Dawkins got into it. The Sixers had already won Game 1 and were handling us even more easily in Game 2. We used a pressure defense to try to get back in the game, and Dawkins became irritated at Bob Gross who had stolen the ball from him. He said something to Gross, and then took a swing at the nimble-footed Blazer. Gross deftly ducked under the blow, which went over his shoulder and hit Doug Collins, Dawkins's teammate, opening a gash under his eye. It was a comical sight and happened right in front of the Portland bench. We all broke up with laughter—which further aggravated Big Double D.

Shortly after, at a dead ball at midcourt, Dawkins and Lucas began jawing at each other and Luke threw a roundhouse right hand that hit Dawkins behind the ear. All hell broke loose. I sprinted from the bench toward the combatants to try to keep them apart. Fans streamed onto the court looking to do battle with anyone in a Portland uniform. Police and security personnel rushed to quell a potential riot, while the game officials did their best to stop the fight, get the fans off the floor, and protect themselves.

Luke and Dawkins were separated, both were ejected from the game, and order was restored. But the Sixers ended up kicking our butts again to go up, 2–0, in the series.

Before Game 3, played in Portland, Philadelphia players were introduced first. Then, as the Blazers were introduced, Lucas surprised everyone in the Coliseum by trotting over to the Sixers line of players to shake Dawkins's hand before joining his teammates. The Sixers—Dawkins in particular—appeared stunned by this gesture of sportsmanship, while the hometown fans roared their approval. Portland got off to a great start and never looked back. The Blazers registered a resounding 22-point victory, and went on to win the next three games. Lucas's communiqué may have been a key factor—and it took place without a word before the game began.

Get Personal

The door to effective communications opens wider when you get to know the people you work with—whether staff or players—on a personal basis. As a coach, in addition to talking directly with each player on my team every day, I took an interest in their families as well as their general well-being. And I gave players who weren't getting any playing time extra, personalized practice from me. I kept them longer to work on their game skills, so that they'd be ready to contribute if called on. I found that if players sensed they were benefiting from the work, they'd do whatever I asked of them, volunteer for more, and show appreciation for my interest.

A proponent of this approach is Coach Phil Jackson, who has had amazing success at both Chicago and Los Angeles, winning a combined nine NBA championships, six in Chicago and three (so far) in Los Angeles.

In 1989, when Phil Jackson became head coach of the Chicago Bulls, he took a unique approach to communicating with his team and achieving team unity. He had become closely associated with the Native American culture and used many of their unity concepts—like the human circle that stays in constant physical and spiritual touch—to bring his team together. He was a student of Zen Buddhist philosophy and brought the practice of quiet meditation to his players. He also took time to learn about their individual interests and bought books for them to read on those subjects or those he felt players needed to develop.

He gave his rookies a booklet put out by the Church of Scientology on ways to achieve happiness in life. ("It was all about living the good life . . . some Golden Rule principles, some on ways to get along well with others.") The premise for this approach was to tell the players: "We care about you; we want you to take care of yourselves." These were Phil's ways of showing a genuine personal interest in each player and enabled the Bulls to become a family as much as they were an NBA team.

By first treating them as individuals, it was then easier for Jackson to get his key players to buy into his team concept. That effort started with convincing Jordan to accept his role in Coach Tex Winter's Triangle offense. At first, MJ resisted this strategy, unable to see the wisdom of the passing and screening that was required of him. But more than anything, Michael wanted to win, and he saw in the system a method of finally getting past the dreaded Detroit Pistons, the team that had taken the Bulls out of the playoffs the previous two years. Phil assured Jordan that the triangle was the best opportunity for the team to win, that he'd still be able to score as much as he had previously, and that he'd have less wear and tear on his body. Once MJ agreed and was onboard, the rest of the players followed suit. Though the Bulls lost again to Detroit in the Conference Finals in Jackson's first year, they then won three titles in a row. Jackson, with his unique approach, was on his way to becoming a special coach in the NBA.

When Jordan left the team to try his hand at baseball in 1994 and 1995, Jackson maintained his same persona, and the Bulls remained a competitive team (55–27, 47–35), but were no longer championship caliber. Michael returned to the team for the final 17 games of that second season, but Orlando eliminated Chicago in six games in the playoffs. That summer, Jordan dedicated himself to intense workouts to regain his previous level of play, and the Bulls won three more titles.

After the 1998 championship, the "two Jerrys"—owner Reinsdorf and general manager (GM) Krause—decided that the Bulls were getting too old and costly, and dismantled the team. Jackson took a sabbatical from basketball and returned to his home in the Montana hills; Jordan retired (again); and the rest of the players were dealt to other teams. (Since then—1998–2003—the Bulls have compiled the worst record in the NBA, a combined 96–282. At the end of the 2003 season, Krause resigned. He was replaced by former Bulls guard John Paxson, whose long-distance shooting won many a tight game during the Bulls first championship run.) During that year off, Jackson received queries from many NBA teams that wanted the benefit of his services. But Phil wasn't interested in a rebuilding project or any team that didn't have championship potential. Then the Lakers called; in them he was interested.

The Lakers had Shaquille O'Neal and Kobe Bryant, and had compiled winning records, but weren't getting anywhere in the playoffs. In 1997, under Del Harris, they were 56–26, beat Portland (3–1) in the first round, but were sliced and diced by Utah, 4–1. In 1998, the team was a gaudy 61–21. The Lakers beat Portland, 3–1; Seattle, 4–1; but then were swept by Utah. In the 1999 shortened season, Harris was let go after a sluggish (6–6) start, and Kurt Rambis coached the team to a 31–19 finish. In the postseason, the Lakers beat Houston, 3–1, but were then swept by San Antonio.

Enter Phil Jackson. In typical fashion, his first player meeting was with Shaquille O'Neal. Shaq, about to begin his eighth NBA season, was the most dominant player in basketball, and Jackson likened his current status to that of Wilt Chamberlain's early career. Jackson challenged Shaq to play a Chamberlain-type of game (when Wilt played for the championship Sixers). Jackson explained to Shaq that the offense would run through him at the post, where he'd have the opportunity to display his scoring and passing skills. Jackson also told Shaq that he'd need to be more dominant on defense than he'd been in the past—more like Wilt as a rebounder, shot-blocker, and intimidator. Shaq bought in.

Phil's next quest was Kobe Bryant, who proved to be a more difficult sell. Kobe also wanted a ring, but he preferred to play an up-tempo game that better suited his skills. Jackson told him that there would be occasional fast breaks, but most of the offense would be in half-court, focused on playing through Shaq at the post. In the end, Kobe agreed, with some reluctance, to a slower-paced game plan. Although it wasn't a perfect fit for him—and there were times during the season when he was openly at odds with both Jackson and O'Neal—Bryant stayed in the team concept and the Lakers thrived. They finished the season (1999–2000) with a 67–15 record, then squeezed past Sacramento 3–2, in the opening round of the playoffs. They then beat Phoenix, 4–1; narrowly got past Portland, 4–3; and downed Indiana, 4–2 in the NBA Finals. Jackson had done it again. He had taken a group of talented players, made them play team-first basketball, and took them to the top. He allowed his players to work through difficult experiences and to find their own solutions. He gave them a game plan and let them play it, looking on with something akin to parental pride as the team matured and grew in stature.

In the end, everybody benefited. Everyone in the organization—coaches, players, management, and staff—experienced the joy of winning an NBA championship. Jackson proved he could win without Michael Jordan—a criticism sometimes heard from those who searched for flaws in his success. He again demonstrated how best to use the skills of outstanding players. The Lakers stayed with the Triangle Offense, averaging about 101 points per game while allowing 92 (a league-leading positive point differential of 8.5). They also led the league in field goal percentage defense (.416), the most telling statistic regarding defensive quality. Individually, O'Neal led the league in scoring and field goal percentage, and ranked second in rebounding and third in blocked shots. He was named the league's Most Valuable Player. Bryant raised his career averages in points (22.5), rebounds (6.3), and assists (4.9).

Say It Straight

Alex Hannum, my predecessor at Philadelphia, had great rapport with his players, and was a stand-up guy. Though he'd had only modest success as an NBA player career (averaging 6 points per game over nine seasons), he had a great sense of the game as a coach. Known as "Sarge" for his no-nonsense approach with players, he was widely admired by players throughout the league. As general manager of the Sixers for the two years Alex coached them, I was able to listen in at team meetings. When he spoke of the strengths and weaknesses of his team, he indicated which players were doing enough and which needed to contribute more. He was direct; he told it like it was. He also invited comments from the players, which they often accepted. Everything was out in the open. They were good meetings.

When Alex left, I took the coaching job, with many of the same players. In contrast to Alex's style, my habit was to speak in more general terms in my critiques about the team—"We're not getting back on defense," "We're not moving the ball," "We're not rebounding"—then would talk later with players individually about what they needed to do. Early that season, Hal Greer, an All-Star 2-guard, said to me, "Coach, I think it's better if you name names at the team meetings—say *who* isn't doing the job. That's the way Alex did it and everybody knew who he was talking to and what each of us had to do."

Greer's point was well taken. Not that I would try to be Alex Hannum, but becoming more direct was a method of communication I could easily work into my approach to my players, and I did.

Crystal Clarity: Walter Kennedy

Walter Kennedy was one who adhered to a cut-to-the-chase style of communication. He was commissioner when Dick Motta and I started coaching in the NBA. It was one of those years when the annual league meeting was held at Kutcher's, a resort in the Catskill Mountains of New York, and Kennedy called for all coaches to be in attendance for a special session.

There were only 11 teams in the league at that time (1968) and all the coaches were at the designated place for the start of the meeting. When Kennedy walked into the room, he stood for a moment, fixing the group with a narrowed stare.

"All right you bastards," he said in a loud voice. "I just want you to know that this is the year of the coach in this league . . . and the first one of you sons of bitches that gets out of line with officials is going to get hit with a heavy fine. I'm sick and tired of all the bitching that went on last year, and it's going to stop."

As he paused to let that sink in, I looked across the table at Motta, a Mormon, and fresh from Weber College. His eyes were wide and he shook his head incredulously.

Kennedy wasn't through. In another profanity-laced tirade, he added that there'd be no more debating calls or moving from the bench area to challenge referees. "You've been warned. This is the year of the coach!" With that he strode from the room.

Johnny Kerr, who was coaching the Bulls at the time, looked over at Motta and me and said, "Welcome to the NBA, you guys."

Make Your Point

My first team meeting as coach of the Portland Trail Blazers was set for 7:00 P.M. before the opening day of training camp. Everyone was there at the designated time—except three key players: Bill Walton, Maurice Lucas, and Herm Gilliam. They strolled in together at 7:05. I knew my authority was being challenged. I pointedly checked my watch, then announced that the three players—and I named them—who were five minutes late would be fined $5 a minute, an accepted rate for tardiness in those days. I added that, henceforth, starting times for all team events would be observed to the second and that any stragglers would be penalized.

Years later, Larry Steele, a reserve swingman on that team, observed that fining those three players was my most significant act in getting the team off to a good start. He said that it established team unity and made it clear that everyone would be treated the same.

One who seems to know innately how to communicate pointedly is Avery Johnson. When the San Antonio Spurs won the NBA title in 1999, Tim Duncan was their major cog but Avery Johnson was the floor leader. Johnson, only 5–11, 180 pounds, was the coach on the floor; the one who understood Coach Gregg Popovich's game plan and was determined to see that the team carried it out. Avery, with his distinctive twang, was very direct when talking with teammates about the way they played. They all accepted his criticism because they knew his words came straight from the heart and were in the team's best interests. Avery developed a special relationship with David Robinson and referred to him as "Faave-oh" (50)—Robinson's uniform number.

As a broadcaster of many of their games in the Spurs championship season, I was an interested observer of "little" Avery's generalship. While he was smiling and gregarious most of the time, he was all business on game day. Coach Popovich ("Pop") told me that, beginning with day-of-the-game shootarounds, Johnson had on his game face and had no time for joking or small talk.

In 1999, the year of the lockout (which was finally resolved in time to play a 50-game season), the Spurs were considered a contender but got off to a slow start and had a 6–9 record before turning their season around. It was during the early season struggles that an incident took place that helped galvanize the Spurs into a championship team.

According to Coach Popovich, the Spurs were struggling through an ugly first half at Minnesota and were getting hammered on the boards. David Robinson was doing little to hold off the Timberwolves' big men. As the teams left the floor at half-time, Pop, walking alongside Johnson, said to his point guard, "Do you want to get him [Robinson] or shall I?" Johnson replied, "I've got 'im, Pop . . . I've got 'im."

Once in the locker room, after the players had settled in with their water or energy drinks, Pop started his half-time critique. He hadn't finished his first sentence when Johnson interrupted, "Excuse me, Pop, but there's something I've got to say." Turning to Robinson, Avery continued, "Faave-Oh, are you going to keep dilly dallyin' around out there and waste all the hard work all of us have done in the off-season or are you gonna start playin' like we know you can and do some reboundin' so that we can win this game?"

Robinson just sat in his stall with his head down, so Avery left his locker, went over to where Robinson was sitting, and bent over so that he could look Robinson in the eyes and Robinson had to look directly at him. "Are you gonna get it goin', Faave-Oh? Are you? It's the only way we can win, Faave-Oh. Are you gonna give it to us now?"

Pop said that the other players sat transfixed, watching this scene. Robinson nodded in assent, Johnson went back to his place, and Pop finished his talk. The Spurs went out in the second half, and led by Robinson's inspired play, came from behind to win the game. As the teams left the floor, Johnson trotted past Robinson, smacked him on the backside and said, "That's what we need from you, Big Fella."

Unlike Avery Johnson, and like most of the rest of us, Billy Cunningham had to learn his way to communicating successfully, both as a player and a coach. Cunningham spent most of his career with Sixers, except for a two-year interlude with the ABA's Carolina Cougars. When the Cougars moved to St. Louis, he returned to Philadelphia to finish his career in the NBA. Larry Brown, his coach at Carolina, told me recently that, in his first year with the Cougars, Cunningham played better than any player he ever coached—a strong statement considering all the great players that Brown has coached including David Thompson, Dan Issel, David Robinson, and Allen Iverson. Brown recalled, "Billy did everything: he scored, rebounded, assisted . . . he was great." (A check on Billy's stats supports Brown's recollection: In that season, Cunningham averaged 24 points, 12 rebounds, and dished out 6 assists on a team that won 57 games and finished first in the ABA Eastern Division.)

But when communicating as a team leader, Cunningham had the disturbing practice of carping at his teammates during games. (During my coaching tenure at Philadelphia, he had done that often enough that I had resorted to fining him for inappropriate conduct.) Brown remembered the same thing at Carolina: "Most of the players accepted it because he was from the NBA, and they respected him for that; but Joe Caldwell, also a former NBA player, didn't like it and let him know about it. It was a tough spot for me because I had played with Billy at UNC and that was my first coaching job."

When I talked with Cunningham recently, I reminded him of his habit of criticizing his teammates. He said, "I was wrong doing it that way. I was trying to get players to play up to a higher level and often told them privately of my intention later, but it wasn't the right way to go about it."

Cunningham learned more about communicating after he became the coach of the Philadelphia Sixers in 1977. His 1983 championship team had some great players—Moses Malone, Julius Erving (Dr. J), Bobby Jones, Andrew Toney, and Mo Cheeks were the mainstays. Cunningham found that he got the best performance from them by dealing with each as an individual. "Some I could criticize in front of the team; others I did in private."

Erving was one who needed private treatment. Two years before the championship season, Erving was in somewhat of a slump as the season wound down, and it continued into the playoffs. The Sixers had gotten past Indiana and Milwaukee without Dr. J playing at his best, but Billy felt that Erving had to lift his game to get the team past Boston in the Eastern Finals. "My soft approach hadn't worked, so I decided to get on him hard—something I had never done before." It didn't work. The

Doctor didn't respond to Cunningham's treatment, and the Celtics edged Philly in seven games and went on to defeat Houston for the NBA title.

After the series, Erving let it be known to the Philadelphia press that he felt Cunningham didn't like him as a player and thought that he would probably be traded before the next season. Cunningham was startled by Erving's remarks and immediately set out to clear the air. He explained to Dr. J that he had tried to motivate him to a better performance level that he felt the team needed to beat Boston—and that was all. He told him he still valued him as a key player, that he had no plans to trade him, and looked forward to the next season with him.

The explanation helped Erving understand why Cunningham had acted the way he did. The breach was mended, and Cunningham had laid a foundation to be a bit more critical of one of his stars when necessary. The Sixers went to the NBA Finals in 1982 and then won in 1983.

Hear Yourself Speak

Adjustments are almost always necessary in any leader's communication, to account for changes, especially in personnel. Two episodes from my coaching career stand out in my mind.

In my third season at Portland, after many personnel changes, we were no longer a championship team. I was exasperated with the way we were playing and communicated that emotion to anyone within hearing distance. I often became angry on the sidelines and at times chewed out players for their mistakes. Soon, team morale was sagging, and I tried to turn things around by calling a team meeting before the next practice. At the meeting, I went over the areas where we needed to improve, told each player where and how I thought he could upgrade his performance, then asked what I could do to help him achieve the new level of play.

Maurice Lucas was the last to respond. He said that I should calm down, that the players were getting negative vibes from my conduct on the sidelines, and it was hurting their confidence. Instead of jumping all over players at timeouts, Luke suggested, "Just tell us we fucked up, and let it go at that." With that, everyone in the room, including me, broke up laughing. I agreed to be more patient, but said that I still wanted each player to lift his game. There was a united nodding of heads, the meeting ended on an upbeat note, and our play picked up after that.

It was in my first year coaching the Sixers that I learned another lesson about the importance of clear communication. That season Archie Clark joined the team, along with Darrell Imhoff and Jerry Chambers, in the trade that sent Wilt Chamberlain to the Los Angeles Lakers. Clark was a point guard with excellent scoring skills who could get his own shot—often using a dynamite crossover dribble, then a step-back jumper that he called his "stinger." He was also a good defender and played hard every game. But Clark was not a playmaker.

The Sixers already had an excellent floor general in Wally Jones, who had been a key member on the 1967 championship team, and Hal Greer was a fixture at 2-guard. I tried alternating Jones and Clark at point guard according to matchups with opponents, but it didn't work out. After about 10 games, Archie suggested that Jones start, and that he'd accept coming off the bench. I liked the idea because I felt our team play was better in the opening minutes with Wally. So I settled into a rotation in which Jones started and Clark came into the game when we needed scoring spurts, and often played the closing minutes because of his ability to beat his man. We had a pretty good season, winning 55 games but lost to the Celtics in the playoffs, while Clark and Jones shared minutes. The season had gone generally without incident, although I had registered the dark looks Archie shot in my direction after games when he was unhappy with his playing time.

The situation worsened in the second season. Clark wanted a starter's minutes, but I did what I thought was best for the team and didn't give them to him; as a result, there was constant tension between us. It erupted following a great playoff win in Milwaukee. Jones was having an outstanding game so I stayed with him down the stretch, limiting Clark's minutes. The Sixers had just tied the series 1–1, and were going to Philly for Games 3 and 4; we were elated and the postgame locker room vibrated with the sounds of celebration. Then, through the sounds of joy, I heard

Clark blast out, "You can trade me! You can just trade me!" He was looking menacingly in my direction as he was taking off his uniform.

Caught up in the euphoria of our biggest win of the season, I was at first stunned, then angered by his outburst. We got into a shouting match that almost came to blows. I tried to clear the air the next day at the team meeting, but the team's high spirit was deflated, and the Bucks blew us away in Game 3, then won the next two to end our season.

In retrospect, the Clark incident was an example of poor communication and personnel management on my part. I had ignored the warning signs. I should have tried harder to find a solution to the problem, to find more personal one-on-one time with Clark to reach a common ground. It was a lesson I learned the hard way in my first years of NBA coaching. Perhaps nothing would have worked, because Clark had such a strong, self-centered personality. But I hadn't done my job well, and that bothers me to this day. Philadelphia later traded Clark to Baltimore for Kevin Loughery and Fred Carter.

Have the Last Word: Respect

One of the best at successfully communicating with his players —with the championship rings to prove it—was legendary Celtics coach Red Auerbach. When the old Boston Garden was being razed in 1995 to make way for the upscale Fleet Center, *Courtside Magazine* asked me to write a piece on Red, who was 78 years old at the time, but whose recollections were amazingly clear.

During our conversation, I complimented him on the marvelous rapport he had had with his players, evidenced by the way they all talked about him. Whenever any of those players spoke of their unique reign of championships—8 in a row, and 9 in 10 years with Red as coach—they always mentioned Auerbach prominently—most often prefacing some story about their involvement with the Celtics with "Red said this" or "Red did that." Many of them played their entire careers with Boston: Bill Russell, Bob Cousy, Tom Heinsohn, John Havlicek, Sam and K. C.

Jones, Satch Sanders, Frank Ramsey, and Bill Sharman were among those who wore only Celtic green during their pro basketball lives.

I asked Red how he had handled so many star players so well. "First of all," he said, "you don't *handle* people. You handle animals; you treat people like human beings. That was always the most important thing with me." And that's what Red did. He treated each player with respect and got the same in return.

Taking Possession

Job Readiness

JOB READINESS—WHETHER ON a basketball court, in a classroom, on a production line, or in a corporate boardroom—means that you know the job requirements, possess the ability to do the job, and have the determination to get it done. Being ready comes from hours, days, months, and years of hard work. Over and over, I've heard the greatest players and coaches in basketball say how important job preparation was to them. And these achievers are never satisfied with their level of accomplishment. What they've done is never enough—they want more and more.

As an NBA coach, I received a flood of letters each year from players who claimed that they had the ability to play for my team and only needed the opportunity. One young man wrote that although he had never played organized basketball at any level, he worked out daily at the local YMCA courts and was an excellent ball-handler and deadly accurate shooter. He said he was ready for NBA competition. He had no idea what that meant.

Everyone I know who has attained success at a chosen endeavor has prepared diligently for it. But they were realistic about their performance and tested themselves repeatedly to be sure that they had acquired the necessary skills for the designated task. The so-called lucky breaks that are sometimes ascribed to high-level achievers are most often a case of being job-ready when an opportunity comes along.

Cultivate a Work Ethic

The adage "The harder I work, the luckier I get" applies universally, but not everyone subscribes to that saying. There are those who try to short-cut preparation or are just too lazy to do their job at their highest level. Motivating such people is tough, but if you're in a position of authority, you must try. Most athletes with whom I've had contact are workers who want to improve their skills. The coach simply points the way. We say that they have a "solid work ethic." In contrast, other players do just enough to get by. They do the minimum required, are satisfied with their status, and drift along as inadequate contributors to the group. Left on their own, they're the last to arrive at practice and the first to leave. What can you do to improve the productivity of those people? How do you motivate them to seek higher goals and achieve greater performance levels?

The best procedure that I found is to let that person know his present level of preparation is unsatisfactory. Next, give him extra attention: Bring him to practice early and keep him late for personal drillwork to improve his skill level. If he's a fringe player, impress on him the need to get his act together if he wants to stay on the team. If he's in the playing rotation, make him understand that the team needs more from him than he's giving and that improving his contribution would enhance the team's success.

I got favorable results with that approach most of the time, especially with end-of-the-bench players. On most teams that I coached at the various levels, I tried to create a "special team" approach similar to that used so well in pro football. I developed a pressure defense unit that could be inserted into the game for five- or six-minute segments of the game to upset the tempo. We drilled hard with those players on the practice floor, and it gave everybody on the squad the opportunity to be a team contributor. Occasionally those units had game-decisive input. It was great for team morale.

But some players resisted my best efforts. Geoff Crompton was a large, 6–10, 300-pound center who had played college basketball at North Carolina. As a concession to Dean Smith, the fine Tar Heels coach, the Trail Blazers brought Geoff to Los Angeles to play in the summer league, with a chance to make our regular roster in the fall. He had some decent parts to his game, but needed conditioning to lose weight and increase his speed and vertical jump. Our team doctor, Bob Cook, set up a nutritional program for him, and the coaches worked hard on his conditioning and game skills, but by the end of each day, Geoff was physically exhausted. He was also unable to discipline himself to adhere to the diet that Dr. Cook had advised. He ate the meals set out for him, but then consumed extra fatty foods in his room in the evenings. Crompton played in six games for Portland that season, then saw limited service with three other teams before ending his NBA career.

In stark contrast was Kermit Washington. Kermit was a 6–9 big forward who was built like a brick outhouse. He was an incredible rebounder and never gave ground as a defender; but he had no shooting touch and lacked confidence in his passing skills. At one point in his career, Kermit, although an almost gentle person off the court, had been overly aggressive on it. But after throwing a much-publicized blow that shattered the face of Houston's Rudy Tomjanovich, he played very much under control. He came to Portland in a trade that sent Bill Walton to the LA Clippers.

At Washington's first practice with his new team, he told me that he knew his game needed work, but was willing to come early and stay late so that he could contribute to team success. That attitude didn't go unnoticed by his teammates. His extra efforts made everyone else work harder.

We worked on Kermit's short-range shooting and interior passing on a daily basis. Kermit was never going to be a great assist man or possess a satin-smooth shooting touch, but he made progress, and his overall game improved. It was Washington who made the pinpoint pass to Billy Ray

Bates that won a game for the Blazers against Philadelphia later that season. In that particular situation, the Blazers had two timeouts to plan the play. I wasn't sure that Kermit had enough confidence to make the critical sideline pass to the basket, so on the first setup, another player was designated as the passer. After Philadelphia saw how we were aligned, Sixers coach Billy Cunningham called timeout to set his defenses. When the Blazers returned to the huddle, Kermit leaned over to me and said, "Coach, I can make that pass." I then rearranged the players on the floor and designated Kermit as the sideline passer. True to his word, he delivered the perfect pass.

Some observers have a mistaken impression that NBA players don't require coaching. Nothing could be further from the truth. NBA players not only need coaching, they want it. Even the greatest players of all time have to work hard to make adjustments to their games to reach satisfactory levels of performance. Why? Because the game is different from that played anywhere else in the world. The rules are different, there are more games to be played, and the players are the best anywhere. Players coming out of high school, college, or from international experience must make huge adjustments. Two players who took different routes to make those adjustments were Earvin "Magic" Johnson and Clyde Drexler.

Magic Johnson

When Magic Johnson came into the NBA in the 1979–1980 season, my former assistant, Jack McKinney, was his coach with the Lakers. I had watched Magic's Michigan State team win the NCAA championship the previous spring, and thought his position in the NBA would be at small forward, so when McKinney told me that he planned to make Johnson his point guard, I expressed surprise; moreover, the Lakers already had Norm Nixon at the point. But McKinney said, "You'll see; he's going to be a great one."

McKinney was right. Magic became arguably the best point guard of all time. But Magic's transition to superstar NBA point guard didn't take place overnight. Nixon, the Lakers' incumbent playmaker, wasn't about to hand over his position to the young rookie. And at training camp,

Magic deferred to the veterans too much. He didn't push the ball on the break, didn't penetrate the defense, and in general played too passive a game. It was not the floor leadership McKinney envisioned. One day, following a lackluster practice session, McKinney pulled Magic aside and said, "Kareem wants to know when you're going to start taking over this team? I told him all this good stuff about you, and he asked me when you were going to start doing it." Magic's eyes widened. "Did Kareem say that?" he asked.

Kareem, in fact, hadn't said it, but McKinney needed to jump-start the rookie's game and knew that Magic was in awe of the great center. So McKinney said, "He sure did—so you'd better get your butt going." That was all that Johnson needed: the green light from the player he revered. Magic immediately became more assertive and soon became the floor leader. He retained that role after McKinney had a near fatal bike accident early in that same season and his assistant, Paul Westhead, took over as coach.

Johnson became the driving force that led the Lakers to a championship that season (1980), and was named the NBA Finals MVP. The Lakers led three games to two in the NBA Finals that year, with Game 6 to be played at Philadelphia. But Abdul-Jabbar had a badly sprained ankle and didn't accompany the team on the trip east. Westhead had a contingency plan and made a prophetic statement to his team: "Never fear, EJ is here." Westhead inserted Johnson into Kareem's center position, and the rookie went to work to dominate the game. Displaying his complete array of skills, Magic scored 42 points, grabbed 15 rebounds, and handed out 7 assists in a sensational performance, as the Lakers routed the Sixers, 123–107 for the title. Magic Johnson had arrived.

Johnson's career blossomed fully under Pat Riley, who replaced Westhead early in the 1981–1982 season. Riley organized the "Showtime" game that featured Magic leading the fast break. The Lakers were the dominant team of the 1980s, winning five championships and losing in the NBA Finals three other years. Johnson averaged 7.45 rebounds, 11.1 assists, and just under 20 points a game in that 10-year span. He was a one-man force, often rebounding an opponent's missed shot, driving the ball into the front court, then delivering no-look passes to James Worthy,

Byron Scott, or Michael Cooper for layups. In the half-court, Magic took time to set up Abdul-Jabbar at the low post for his patented skyhook. Using Riley's well-organized principles, the Lakers were strong defensively and almost impossible to stop on offense.

Magic was a student of the game and carefully critiqued his own performance to define areas that needed improvement. In his rookie year, he didn't have full control of his left-hand dribble. I coached Portland at that time and made sure we kept Magic going to his left. In one game, he had nine turnovers. That strategy never worked again because during the summer following his first season, he worked hard on being equally adept dribbling in either direction. Each year, Magic added a dimension to his game. He was a marginal perimeter shooter when he first came in the league, but in a few years he became a dangerous three-point threat. Later on, he added a wheeling hook shot—not unlike Kareem's—to his scoring arsenal. There was always a positive addition to Magic's game each year, and it was no accident. Those changes took place because Magic was never satisfied with his level of play, took the time to focus on some area that wasn't up to his expectations, then worked hard to improve on it.

Clyde Drexler

Clyde Drexler was a great athlete who became a great basketball player. Clyde had played at the University of Houston with Hakeem Olajuwon on a team that reached the NCAA Finals. Clyde was Portland's first-round pick in 1983 and played 2-guard or small forward. He had great speed, athleticism, and leaping ability, but didn't like to practice. He had joined a pretty good Portland team that had finished with a 46–36 record the year before and had two very good players—Jim Paxson and Calvin Natt—at the positions he played.

Clyde had never sat on the bench before and couldn't understand why it was happening to him in the NBA. We talked frequently about his situation, but he wasn't satisfied with conversation—he wanted to play. His practice habits, however, continued to be less than satisfactory. He arrived on court seconds before practice started and would leave promptly when it was over unless I kept him for extra drillwork—which

I did. Clyde did everything I asked of him in those workouts, but his body language told me that he was only doing it because he had to.

As for me, I didn't care what he thought. My job was to be sure that he got the work that I thought was necessary for him to help his team and for him to become an outstanding NBA player. We had many confrontations during the years that I coached him at Portland, but he worked his way into the starting lineup before his second season ended, and later became an All-Star player. After I left the Blazers, Drexler played on two Portland teams that reached the NBA Finals. Then after being traded to Houston, he played on the Rockets championship team of 1995.

ESPN did the radio broadcast of those Finals, as well as pregame and postgame television coverage. I was involved in both, and had the opportunity to interview Clyde following the final win in their four-game sweep of the Orlando Magic. As he came over to our broadcast site, he was absolutely beaming with joy. I started the interview by asking, "Remember all of those drills that I had you do in Portland? The ones you hated to do? Those were done so that you could have a night like this."

Clyde laughed and said, "I know that now."

Stay Physically Fit

Whether you sit behind a desk or in front of a computer all day or play point guard in the NBA, to do the job well requires staying physically fit and mentally alert. It means finding enough time in a busy schedule for adequate rest and an exercise routine, eating a sensible diet of nutritious foods, and drinking an adequate amount of fluids—but abstaining from or restricting your consumption of alcohol to a moderate level. And there's no place for habit-forming drugs if you want to be at the top of your game. Lace 'em up tight!

Achieving and maintaining a top level of physical conditioning has been a necessity for athletes since the Olympic Games in ancient Greece; but today's athletes (professional, amateur, and "weekend warriors" alike) have expanded on previous methods of improving their skills. Athletes' use of performance-enhancing drugs and steroids appears to be diminishing in

Pacesetter: John Havlicek ("Hondo")

During a radio interview many years ago, Hondo, the greatest sixth man of all time, gave me some clues for his incredible stamina and success in coming off the bench: "When I was a kid, all my friends had bikes. I didn't have one, so I had to run to keep up with them. From early on, I learned I could run a pretty good distance without getting tired."

"When I go into a game, I just run, run, run. I run down the sideline, cross under the basket and out the other side. Then I'll back-cut and take my man through again. Then I pick him up deep on defense. I do that over and over until I start to get a little winded—then I turn it up a notch. I know that the guy playing me—who's usually not as fresh as I am—has to be exhausted. That's when I do some of my best work."

It didn't hurt that John never looked like he was sweating either.

many sports, whereas training techniques to improve their speed, stamina, and strength continue to escalate. Today, the NBA prohibits the use of illegal drugs. In addition, it has instituted an effective plan for educating its personnel on the dangers of drugs and on the prevention of their use, as well as a treatment program, if necessary, for those who violate this restriction. Unfortunately, not everyone hears the message.

Weight training is a popular technique today. When I was a teenager, weight lifting was for bodybuilders, boxers, and interior linemen in football. Basketball players completely avoided the practice because it was believed to make them muscle-bound and thus inhibit the fine touch needed for shooting accuracy. Supposedly, the ideal build for basketball was long and lean, so players could be lithe and agile. Then, when I was coaching at St. Joseph's in the early 1960s, I read an article in a coaching magazine by Bucky O'Connor, the basketball coach at the University of Iowa, about his use of a weight-lifting (isotonic) program to improve the vertical leaping ability of his players. They did a series of

Weighty Transition: Bob Pettit

Bob Pettit was a gangly, awkward teenager who didn't make the basketball squad in his first two years at Baton Rouge (Louisiana) High School. His goal then was merely to earn a varsity letter by his senior year. He achieved that goal and played well enough as a senior to receive a scholarship from Louisiana State University. At LSU, Pettit developed into a skilled center, and became an All-American, averaging 31 points and 17 rebounds in his senior year. The Milwaukee Hawks drafted him in the first round in 1954, and Coach Red Holzman switched him to the big forward position. Pettit was named Rookie of the Year that season, averaging 20 points and just under 14 rebounds a game.

The Milwaukee franchise moved to St. Louis the following season (1956), where Pettit led the league in scoring and was named the league's MVP. In 1958, he led St. Louis to the NBA championship by defeating the Boston Celtics in a hard-fought, seven-game series. (The Hawks reached the Finals twice more during Pettit's career, but lost to the Celtics each time.)

Pettit was an All-NBA first team selection 10 consecutive years—starting with his rookie season—and was voted to the second team in 1965, the last year he played. Pettit was a fierce competitor and is still regarded by many as the greatest big forward ever to play the game. In a quote that appeared recently in the Atlanta Hawks' *Hawk Talk* magazine, Celtics great Bill Russell noted at Pettit's retirement, "There's no greater competitor in sports. He's a winning ball player who made the expression 'second effort' a part of the sports vocabulary."

It was a remarkable transition, from a high school player who just wanted to get a varsity letter by his senior year, to being selected as one of the 50 Greatest Players in NBA History. I asked Bob how it happened.

"I just set goals for myself and never stopped working until I reached them," he said. "First I just wanted to get that green and gold letter from Baton Rouge High School. Then when I got to

(continued)

LSU, I wanted to be an All-American. Then, after I was drafted, I wanted to make it as a pro player. Then I wanted to be the best player in the league . . . then in the world. I was never satisfied with where I was. I wanted to keep getting better and worked very hard to keep improving."

One of the ways he improved himself was by getting into weight training when no one else was doing it. "In my early years in the NBA, I was on the lean side: I weighed about 215. I wanted to get stronger, so I went to a strength coach, Alvin Roy, who was recognized for his success in building strong football players at LSU and later in the NFL."

Roy told Pettit that, under his regimen, he'd increase his strength without bulking him up or limiting his flexibility. Bob remembers that the added strength had an enormous impact on his game. He was able to hold position better, and it especially improved the strength in his hands. He recalls that he became a more efficient scorer in the paint and a stronger rebounder.

squats and toe-risers while supporting enough weight to limit their repetitions to 10. O'Connor reported an average increase of two inches in his players' leaping ability.

Then I read where future Hall of Famer Bob Pettit, then a player for the St. Louis Hawks, had done isometric exercises that improved his jumping ability, overall strength, and stamina. I researched that technique with the York Barbell Company, York, Pennsylvania, and received a program of eight isometric (the exertion of force against an immovable object) exercises. I chose the five exercises that seemed most applicable to basketball and had the necessary apparatus set up in an unused room of the field house. I then put myself through the program. I was 36 years old at the time and still in good enough shape to scrimmage with my teams, but I was a below-average leaper. By the end of a six-week period, I had increased my vertical leap a startling seven inches! I was above the rim for the first time in my life—a great feeling. My players, who had watched my progress, were eager to see what results they could achieve, so isometric exercises became a part of our conditioning routine. No player increased his leap as much as I did—but none started from where I had either.

Weight training is now an accepted part of conditioning for athletes in all sports. Every NBA team has its own strength and conditioning coach. They not only focus on gaining strength, but also have techniques for improving agility, speed, quickness, and stamina. There is an accepted theory that strength plus quickness equals power, and power translates into improved performance in every sport.

Extend Your Reach

I was coaching Portland and was in my early 50s when I became interested in triathlon competition. I had watched with fascination television broadcasts of the Iron Man competition from Hawaii, and I marveled at the skill and stamina of the participants. Then I became aware of a modified triathlon series that was starting up in several cities in the United States, Portland being one of them. A writer friend of mine, John Strawn, with whom I sometimes worked out, urged me to enter the race with him. The distances of the event were 1-mile swim, 25-mile bike, and 9-mile run. It was March when Strawn called me and the race was not until August. That seemed like enough time to get in shape, so I agreed to enter the race and set out a training program for myself.

I lived in Lake Oswego, a quiet community about eight miles outside Portland, and a perfect area for training. Our house sat on a bluff above the lake; there were little-traveled, hilly roads on which to run and bike, and I was not far from the high school, which had a running track open to the public. Because the Blazers were still in their season, I did my workouts before practice, between 6:00 and 8:00 in the morning.

Tender Achilles tendons had been a problem for me since I was a player, and I had stopped distance running altogether, so my first objective was to see if I could run without aggravating those tendons and then to build up some endurance. I started by jogging a quarter mile to a nearby convenience store to pick up the morning papers. I stretched before and after that run and found I could do it pain-free. I then increased the distance gradually, still running at a moderate pace, until I was logging about five miles each day—still without pain. The next step was to increase my speed. I had met a running coach in the area, Roger Smith, who had helped coach U.S. teams in international track competition and was an advocate of special drillwork to improve the form of his runners. He showed me several drills that improved my form and ultimately my running speed. I devoted one running workout a week to speed drills, sprinting the straightaways and jogging the turns at the high school track. My running improved, with no Achilles problems.

I had been doing a lot of biking on a rugged Schwinn model that was fine for riding to and from practice, but as it turned out, was too heavy for competitive use. That was a costly error in judgment, since most of the time in triathlon competition is spent on the bike. But I rode the hills near my home and increased my distances until I was covering the 25 miles required in the race in about an hour and a half. I thought it was good time, but found out on race day that the superior performers were finished in about an hour.

I got into a routine of swimming in the lake, running the nearby hills, then biking, each for about a half an hour. My stamina and speed began to increase in the run and the bike, but my swim time was slow. To help that, I talked to one of my neighbors, Don Schollander, a former U.S. Olympic swimming great. In the Navy, I had become reasonably proficient in the swimming techniques used by the underwater demolition teams (UDTs), but they were designed to keep hands and feet from breaking the water's surface, and relied on swim fins for speed. Triathlon swimmers used an overhand, freestyle technique—and, of course, flippers were not permitted. My stroke technique needed a lot of changes and Don suggested that I call Tye Steinbach, an area coach who had taught him as a teenager. Tye agreed to work with me at his downtown swim club, and I went there three days a week on my way to Blazers practice. Tye was an excellent teacher. He improved my kick, which enabled me to swim more on the surface of the water, and improved my stroke speed by quickening the rhythm of my breathing.

By race day, I felt in good shape, and had bettered my performance in each of the three parts of the triathlon. But my friend Strawn, who had aroused my interest in the event initially, had strained a hamstring while training and was able to take part in the event only as a biker on a three-man team. The race was held in Forest Grove, a community about 25 miles outside Portland. There were about 300 entrants, including Dave Scott, who was soon to become recognized as the king of Iron Man competitions. For Scott, this was just a workout day. He rode his bike out to the event from Portland, won the race, then biked back to his hotel.

I finished the race in the middle of the pack, third in my 50–54 age group, but feeling good physically; and I was determined to do better the next time. I was impressed by the competence of so many men and women as well as by their spirited and upbeat attitudes. It was an exhilarating experience.

I upgraded my bicycle and did at least one triathlon competition a year for the next 20 years. I also competed in many road runs of half-marathon, 10K and 5K distances, and ocean swims of up to 3 miles. I had learned the importance of top-level conditioning and liked how it made me feel, both physically and mentally.

I also learned a lot about my body, competitive spirit, and the will to endure physical stress. I found out how to keep going when race conditions were less than ideal. In a couple of races, the frigid water reduced my body heat to the point where I was shaking from head to toe so badly that I could hardly get on my bike for the second stage of a triathlon. There were times on the bike segment when steep hills or headwinds reduced fast, forward progress drastically and increased the stress on my quads until they felt like two bags of wet cement—with the run yet to come. And there were times when the run was completed in temperatures of over 100 degrees and the humidity was so stifling that my run became a walk.

But I discovered that the human body, even at the point of exhaustion, can be pushed further yet. I can remember sprinting the final 200 hundred yards of a triathlon in Chicago in blistering heat to finish ahead of a competitor who at the start of the run had a half-mile lead on me. The body is an amazing piece of machinery, and your will can push it to unexpected results. That experience became an integral element of my approach to coaching. By successfully driving myself beyond what I

Air Quality: Michael Jordan

Michael "Air" Jordan is a relentless worker at his craft and a fanatical conditioner. After he took his hiatus to try his hand at baseball in 1993 and returned a year and a half later to play the final 17 games of the season, his game had some rust on it. I saw him in a late-season game in Miami and asked him if the return was more difficult than he had expected.

"It is. I thought it would be like riding a bicycle—you jump back on and start going. It's not that easy—but I'll be ready next year," he warned. The Bulls lost to Orlando that season in the second round of the playoffs.

Jordan worked all summer to sharpen his game and hired a personal trainer, Tim Grover, who worked him out during the summer and for an hour *before* practice during the season. Grover told me that the workouts weren't basketball drills, but stretching and strength workouts designed to promote stamina, power, and flexibility. In the last "running of the Bulls" (from 1996 to 1998), Jordan started what became known as the Breakfast Club, whose members, in addition to MJ, included Scottie Pippen and Ron Harper. They met each morning when the team was in Chicago to participate in Grover's workout regimen before they went to the Bulls practice. Michael and the Bulls came back to win three more straight titles, their second "threepeat."

thought were my physical limits, I was able to call on my team to play through fatigue and push themselves to maintain a high level of performance. I had done it myself and knew they could do it, too.

Eat and Drink Right

Perhaps the greatest lesson I learned from those triathalon competitions was the importance of sound eating and drinking habits. Triathletes burn a lot of energy, and must consume food and liquids that enable them to perform well. The first book I read on the subject was *Eat to Win*, by Dr. Robert Haas (New York: Rawson Associates, 1983). Haas broke down the nutritional requirements of high-performance athletes to about 70 percent carbohydrates, 20 percent protein, and 10 percent fats.

At one time, I had been a high-level consumer of bacon and eggs for breakfast; cheeseburgers at lunch; and steak, roast beef, and other meats at dinner. I drank whole milk, used butter on toast and sandwiches, and slathered it on baked potatoes. I loved cheese and nut snacks, and ate ice cream, cake, pie, and cookies for dessert. I can recall drinking a blended mixture of orange juice, four raw eggs, a tablespoon of honey, and two tablespoons of wheat germ before my morning workout. I thought I was providing my body with energy when I was actually helping to clog my arteries with cholesterol! I was exercising a lot so I didn't experience any weight gain, but a physical exam showed my total cholesterol level to be 270.

I abruptly changed my diet to include broiled or baked fish and chicken, green veggies, cereals and other grain foods, salads, and fruits, and I limited my intake of sweets. I felt better physically, more alert mentally, and my competitive performances improved. I drank water, fruit juices, tea, skim milk, decaffeinated coffee, and a glass or two of red wine with dinner each day. I supplemented that intake with a daily combination of 15 vitamins and minerals.

I've stayed with that regimen for more than 20 years and have enjoyed it thoroughly. I continue to work out on a daily basis, although I don't do competitions any longer. My usual daily routine is to run a couple of miles, swim a half mile, and then do some upper-body work with hand weights ranging from 20 to 50 pounds. Because I live in Naples, Florida, on the Gulf of Mexico for eight months of the year, and in Ocean City, New Jersey, on the Atlantic Ocean for the other four, I can always do my swimming in open water. The beaches are ideal for running. I keep a set of weights in each of my residences. The workouts take about an hour, and I get them done before breakfast in the early morning (my favorite time of the day). Then I feel physically and mentally ready for whatever the day demands.

Heart of a Champion: Darnell Valentine

Many of the players I coached who weren't among the team's most gifted players were the hardest workers and made maximum use of their skills. Darnell Valentine, a point guard that I coached at Portland, was perhaps the most self-disciplined player I ever dealt with.

DV—who had watermelon-sized quads, a strong upper body, and excellent quickness handling the ball and defending—worked fanatically on his conditioning. He was on the floor an hour before practice, working on his defensive footwork, pull-up jumpers, or full-court drives to the hoop. Then he would stretch for about 15 minutes, before the team practice began.

He was also extremely careful about his diet. He ate primarily foods high in carbohydrates and supplemented them with enough protein and fat to fuel his extraordinary energy level. Valentine even brought his own food blender with him on road trips and often boarded the team bus carrying large bags of fruits and veggies, which he offered to everyone.

In addition to his fierce work ethic, relentless self-discipline, and powerful will to win, he always wore a smile and was one of the best team players I ever coached.

I have no doubt that my attention to diet and exercise helped me to withstand the physical and emotional demands associated with coaching over 20 years in the NBA, and then allowed me to continue in the communications media for another 14 years.

Exercise Your Mind

Physical activity and good diet also facilitate and strengthen the mental process by increasing blood flow to the brain. Ancient Greeks advocated a strong mind in a strong body, and medical authorities have long subscribed to the idea that physical stress to increase the heartbeat generates improved blood circulation to all parts of the body. Scientists have recently discovered that this is especially helpful in slowing memory loss among the aging.

The mind is like the body in that the more it is used, the more efficient it becomes. Muscles become stronger with use and atrophy when neglected. So does the mind. The mind needs daily workouts too. Thinking, planning, recalling, and problem solving are all mental gymnastics that help keep the brain sleek, agile, and quick-reacting. Therefore, in addition to promoting blood flow to my brain through exercise, mental activity is necessary to keep it functioning smoothly and effectively. To that end, I do crossword puzzles, cryptograms, and word puzzles while I am eating my breakfast.

Get a Physical

One of the advantages of coaching in the NBA is that each year there are mandatory physical examinations for all playing and coaching personnel. A former player, Barry Clemens, and a close coaching friend, Jim Lynam, both were discovered to have testicular cancer through annual team physicals. Both have recovered well, but had the cancers not been discovered when they were, the results could have been fatal. Physicals have identified many players with heartbeat irregularities that required medication for them to continue in their playing careers. And, in the shot heard around the world of professional athletics, Magic Johnson was discovered to be HIV-positive. Magic immediately went on a program of intense and effective medication that, along with a vigorous exercise regimen, keeps him alive and active to this day.

When I left the NBA, I continued to get those annual exams on my own. I carefully watched my cholesterol levels, readings on EKGs, and monitored my PSA findings (a barometer for prostate cancer). I knew I needed to keep a lid on my fat intake because my body apparently manufactures a higher-than-normal level of cholesterol, and even with careful dieting and continued exercise, my LDL remains comparatively high. However, my HDL—the "good" cholesterol—is also above the norm, so the ratio keeps me in the safe area for potential heart problems.

Survival of the Fittest: Magic Johnson

When Pat Riley left the Lakers in 1990, Mike Dunleavy took over as coach. The Lakers reached the NBA Finals again, but lost to Michael Jordan and the Chicago Bulls in the first of their three straight championships.

In the following preseason, the Lakers were in Paris, France, to play in the McDonald's Open. I was there to help put on coaches clinics for the NBA. I sat in on a Lakers' practice one day, watching how Magic directed his teammates and controlled the flow of play. He was like a coach on the floor. When I expressed my admiration of Magic's play to Dunleavy after the practice, he acknowledged how great it was to coach a player of Johnson's skills and team attitude, but added, "Magic's not feeling up to par, though. We're going to have him checked out when we get home [Los Angeles]."

Soon after that came the shocking diagnosis that Johnson was infected with the HIV virus, followed by the announcement that he would retire as an NBA player. The devastating diagnosis didn't dampen Johnson's trademark enthusiasm or determination, however. Pat Riley recalls that Johnson called him before making the announcement publicly, and while he (Riley) was reduced to tears—at the time, an HIV diagnosis led to AIDS and was regarded as a death sentence—it was Magic who buoyed the spirits of his former coach. In a strong, firm, confident voice, Magic stated, "Don't worry, Coach, I'm going to beat this thing. I'll be all right."

Johnson learned what he had to do medically and followed those directions carefully. He also engaged in vigorous physical workouts while he reorganized his life. With the disease under control, Johnson returned to the Lakers as coach at the end of the 1994 season, but resigned that post after the team won only 5 of 16 games. He came back to play again in the 1995–1996 season under coach Del Harris. But at the age of 35, he was unable to perform at his previous skill level, and retired for good at the end of that season. Johnson was included among the 50 Greatest Players in NBA History in 1996, and in 2002, he was inducted into the Naismith Basketball Hall of Fame.

Today, Johnson's HIV infection is still in abeyance. "I feel good," he says. "I'm probably healthier now than when I was a player. I follow a better diet and have a consistent aerobic and weight work routine. There is more and better medication available now for the disease than when I was first diagnosed. My family [the Johnson's have three children] has been wonderful. Cookie [Magic's wife] and I adopted a strong attitude right from the beginning that we were going to beat this thing—and so far we have. I feel good when I get up each day. God has blessed me."

Though basketball continues to be a big part of his life, Magic plays on a much bigger court these days, as head of the four-entity Johnson Development Corporation (more on this in Chapter 10). It's a life as full and rich as when his trademark smile lit up NBA courts all over the country.

Several years after I had finished active NBA coaching, I noticed that my PSA readings were slowly increasing, although still in the normal level. Then, three years ago, in the fall of 1999, those readings rose to a level that indicated cancer in my prostate. Biopsies confirmed the cancerous presence, and I had choices to make about treatment. After extensive conversations with my doctors, I felt fairly confident that radiation therapy would be effective. I didn't want to worry my family members unnecessarily by telling them about the diagnosis, and I was aware how the media jumped on news of a sports figure with cancer; I didn't want any of that.

So, without telling anyone, and with assurances of confidentiality from the medical staff, I began treatments that entailed radiation five times a week for six weeks and culminated in an outpatient seeding procedure of the prostate about two weeks later.

I was doing television work for the Miami Heat at the time and managed to keep all of the radiation appointments without missing any games. On home-game days, I received my treatment in the morning, drove to Miami to do the game broadcast, and then returned to my home in Naples, Florida. Road games required some maneuvering with flights, but the radiation center was flexible with my appointments. I could take a radiation treatment, go immediately to the airport, fly to the game site, do the broadcast, fly back after the game on the team plane to Miami, then drive home to Naples. In that way I was available for my scheduled treatment the next day.

I was curious about the effect the radiation might have on me physically, so I maintained my daily workout schedule of running, swimming, and weight work. Although I wasn't exactly brimming with energy, I was able to complete the workout each day without ill effect, and I was able to maintain my physical strength. It made me marvel all the more about the capacity of the human body. It appears that the more that is asked of it, the more it responds.

By the time I had finished the radiation treatments, the NBA season had reached the playoffs and my luck in scheduling ran out. The appointment for the seeding procedure had to be made several weeks in advance, and it happened to fall on a day when I was scheduled to do a radio broadcast of a Knicks game in New York. I told ESPN radio executive producer John Martin that I had a medical appointment in Naples that I had to keep and needed the day off. He gave me that consideration without inquiring too much, and I was able to have that work done and return two days later for the next playoff game.

The rest of the playoffs went without incident for me, and I was able to enjoy covering the Pacers-Lakers NBA Finals for ESPN radio and television. (The only real inconvenience was that I had to dash quickly to the men's restroom at the end of the half and after the game to relieve an uncooperative bladder!)

I have now completed my third year of recovery and have had checkups every six months. So far, the procedure has worked out well. My PSA readings are at an all-time low and the dreaded digital examinations show no irregularities in the shape and feel of the prostate. My doctor, Bruce Nakfoor, tells me that those whose PSA readings are under .5 three years after the seeding process, have a 95 percent chance of full recovery. My most recent reading (May 2003) was .23. God is good.

None of that—the discovery of the cancer, the ensuing treatment, and the improved condition of my prostate gland—would have happened without the annual physical examination.

Share the Health

Those who eat right, exercise consistently, and are blessed with general good health have the desire to share their euphoric feelings with others. I've been described by some as a "fitness freak"—and I don't object. And my friends say, somewhat in jest, that they hate to eat out with me because they feel uncomfortable eating other than wholesome foods. So I don't make an issue of it when they have bacon, eggs, sausage, and buttered toast for breakfast.

But the fact is that two of my friends and working associates, Jim Durham and John Martin, both ate without restriction for many years, then recently experienced heart problems. Both are on the mend and are following a healthier diet regimen.

When I was still coaching, I recommended healthy, high-performance diets to my players. I had nutritionists speak to them and their wives regarding good foods and proper preparation. Not everyone was interested, but I think most players tried to adhere to a high standard of overall fitness. Although there are still athletes who battle weight problems and ignore advice on proper diet and conditioning, there appears to be a greater concern among athletes today about the relationship between effective conditioning and their intake of food and beverages. Many subscribe to a regimen similar to that advocated by Dr. Haas and are careful to maintain a good fluid level in their bodies when competing.

Dr. Haas's basic premise—"the right foods provide energy for optimum performance"—stands up over time. Athletes in all fields benefit from a diet that provides the fuel for the energy they burn. Duration events, like the triathlon, demand the highest source of proficient and long-lasting energy. The best athletes—and leaders—in their fields pay close attention to what they put in their bodies, enabling them to make the most of the opportunities that come their way.

Fast Break

Maximizing Opportunities

IN GENERAL, I DON'T believe that our lives are preordained; we make our own breaks. But there are times when we just seem to be in the right place at the right time, and when those moments occur, it's important to take full advantage of them. Throughout our lives, we are presented with choices and opportunities. We choose one path instead of another, select one course of action over another, or elect not to act at all. Those choices often have a profound influence over what follows in our lives; even when we make the wrong choice, we have the opportunity to learn from our mistake.

I've heard and answered the knock of many opportunities, sometimes when I least expected them. And—just as important—I've never forgotten the people who ushered those opportunities through the door.

Knock, Knock

When I was a senior in high school, an unlikely circumstance provided such an opportunity. A young doctor, who was a St. Joseph's College graduate, was attending my mother for a colon condition (which was later to become cancerous). My mom apparently talked so much about her son's basketball ability that the doctor arranged a meeting for me with Bill Ferguson, the St. Joe's coach. From that meeting, I received a tryout that led to a four-year scholarship. Had it not been for my mom and the doctor, I would have gone to another college and my life would surely have been different. And as it turned out, that was only my first serendipitous opportunity at St. Joe's. The second was of a more personal nature.

I met my wife Jean at a Halloween dance given by the St. Joseph's College Evening Division, where she was a student. Two of my team-mates, Ed O'Halloran and Joe Wesner, were going to the dance and urged me to join them. Jean was one of the organizers of the dance and was standing across the dance floor when we walked in. Wesner and I saw her at the same time. He said, "I see the girl I'm going to ask to dance." When I saw he was looking in Jean's direction, I made a fast break and beat him to her. We danced and seemed to have an immediate feeling for each other. We dated, became engaged, and married a year and a half later. That union led to the births of 5 incredible children, and their marriages have produced 13 grandchildren as remarkable as their parents. We have indeed been blessed. Marriage is seldom a smooth path, and ours has had its uneven moments, but Jean and I have weathered the storms along the way. Now we are sharing our 53rd year together—all because I went to that Halloween dance at St. Joseph's College and was faster on my feet than my friend.

A professional opportunity at St. Joe's also came because I was in the right place at the right time. I was teaching and coaching at Mount Pleasant High School in Wilmington, Delaware, and during the summer of 1955, I worked at the high school with a maintenance crew of teachers. (I took that job to be near home because Jean was anticipating the birth of our third child, Sharon.) One of the crew, the athletic director,

Howard Parsons, had a friend in advertising who had access to tickets to Phillies baseball games. One afternoon, Howard announced that he had tickets for the Phillies game that night for any of us who wanted to go. I was among those who said yes.

At the seventh-inning stretch in that game, I recognized Father Joseph Geib, SJ, the moderator of athletics at St. Joseph's, standing up several sections away from mine. I immediately went over to say hello. We knew each other, although Father Geib arrived at St. Joe's after I had graduated. I had done six years of high school teaching and coaching since then, so we had a lot to talk about.

We got into a discussion of the Hawks' teams, which had been having mediocre success, then about my teams at Mount Pleasant, and my playing experiences in the Eastern League. We chatted about 15 to 20 minutes, and I left with two impressions: First, Father Geib wasn't pleased with St. Joseph's basketball; and, second, he seemed interested in me as a coach.

When I got home from the game, I told Jean that I had bumped into Father Geib and that I thought St. Joseph's might make a coaching change. I added that if they did, I thought I had a chance for the job. Two days later, Father Geib called me to say that they were indeed considering a coaching change and asked if I would be interested in the job. I nearly jumped through the phone! We arranged a meeting for the next evening.

Father Geib and I sat outside his residence hall and talked for about two hours. He asked about my coaching philosophy, how I conducted practices, and about the talent on hand at St. Joseph's. I knew many of the players; two of them—Jack McKinney and Bill Lynch—had played for me at St. James High School. At the end of our discussion, he offered me the job. I said I'd take it—without even discussing salary. I later learned the job paid $3,500, $2,000 *less* than I was making at Mount Pleasant. I didn't care. I knew I could get other work to supplement my income. I just wanted to coach at the college level—and at my alma mater to boot. I was in hog heaven. Probably none of that would have happened if I hadn't gone to that Phillies baseball game that summer's night.

Opportunity Abroad: Jack Ramsay

Shortly after leaving the Pacers in 1988, I received a phone call from Michael Goldberg, legal counsel for the NBA Coaches Association, with whom I had a long association as its president. Leon Wandel, the organizer of the Belgium national basketball team, had contacted Michael about my availability to help that team prepare for an upcoming qualifying tournament in Portugal in April 1989. Belgium had never had much success in international basketball competition and it appeared to be an interesting challenge. And, since my wife was interested in spending some time shopping in Brussels, we agreed to go.

The beginning workouts were held in a college gymnasium in Brussels. We had about two weeks to get ready for the tournament. My job was to assist the young head coach, Tony Van Den Bosch, in any way I could. Our first task was to select a 12-player squad from a group of 20 candidates, all national citizens, who made their living playing in the Belgian professional league. They ranged in age from early 20s to mid-30s and compared favorably in ability with players at a good Division II college in the United States. French is the national language of Belgium (although those from the northern sector speak mostly Flemish), but all except one of the players spoke English, so there was no major communications barrier. (I did, however, finally get to make use of the French I'd learned in high school and college in the hotel, restaurants, and local shops.)

There weren't any NBA prospects among the Belgians, but there were enough players who understood the game and knew how to play to convince me we could have a good team. I liked Coach Van Den Bosch very much. He ran the practices, but allowed me to stop the action at any time to make corrections and suggestions. Together, we became an effective team. We made our squad selections after several sessions, and the team made solid progress over the next week. The players were attentive and receptive, and Coach Tony gave me plenty of opportunity to teach. I especially liked the team's center, Rik Samaey, and the point guard, Ronny Bayer. Rik was an experienced European player with a solid inside game, although he was only about 6–8. Ronny was a quick, aggressive point guard who was a fierce competitor.

Wandel had scheduled two pretournament games with France, both to be played in Belgium. France was reputed to have a superior team and didn't have to go through the qualifying procedure that Belgium did. There was high interest in the games—in part due to the historic animosity between the two countries. Unexpectedly, Belgium ended up decisively beating the French in both games.

Suddenly, there was a stirring of interest in the national team, although no one gave us much of a chance in the upcoming tournament. Our first opponent was top-seeded Israel, which had gone to the Final Four in the last competition (the other teams included Iceland, Hungary, and Portugal). One of the journalists who had been covering the team in Brussels told me that he wasn't going to the tournament because it made him feel too sad to watch Belgium lose all the time in international competition.

The team made the trip to Lisbon, Portugal, by air, then bussed to Anadia, a small town in the mountains where the tournament was to be played. We had one day of practice and looked sharp. I didn't know anything about the Israelis, but I sensed that our team was playing well and should be able to at least hang in the game with them.

To the surprise of everyone there, we beat Israel. When the tournament began, there were no spectators from Belgium at the games. But after the victory over Israel, the fans started to appear. They made the drive over the mountains into Portugal, then up to Anadia. By the time the tournament ended, about 100 Belgian fans had traveled to the mountain town to see the final game. We made their trip worthwhile, because we beat Israel, Iceland, and Hungary in succession and, finally, Portugal in the Finals. We won four straight games in four days. Samaey was marvelous—playing through the pain of aching knees—and Bayer was not to be denied.

Helping the Belgian team was one of the most enjoyable experiences that I ever had in the game of basketball. Leon Wandel, a wonderful patriot who personally financed most of the expenses,

(continued)

was ecstatic. The players were equally thrilled, and Coach Tony and I were flat-out elated.

At the conclusion of the dinner following the championship game, the players and their fans began singing their victory song, and when quiet had been restored, they began a chant of "Ramsay, Ramsay, Ramsay." It was an emotional moment that I still feel deeply. I rose from my seat at the table and simply told them how happy I was to have been a part of their great success. It was an experience that I'll never forget.

I returned four more years for brief periods with Wandel, Van Den Bosch, and the team, and while each time was enjoyable, we never duplicated the magic of that first year.

Eleven years later, in the summer of 1966, I again heard the distinctive knock-knock of opportunity when Irv Kosloff called me about the Sixers job. I was ready to make a change in my professional life, as I was concerned about the loss of vision in my right eye (from a stress-related edema on the retina following the 1965–1966 college season) and needed to step away from coaching. Koz's call couldn't have come at a more opportune time, and it led to an enduring association with the NBA.

Likewise, at the conclusion of my coaching career, when one door was closing, another opened. My retirement from coaching coincided with the beginning of Commissioner David Stern's program to expand the influence of the NBA around the world. He planned to use current and former NBA coaches and players to teach the game of basketball by giving coaching clinics and asked me to head up the program. That led to the wonderful experience of working with coaches and players in Europe, the Near and Far East, and South America to help improve their knowledge of basketball and their game skills. The association with others on the clinic staff—especially core members Hubie Brown, Bill Walton, and Calvin Murphy—was priceless. All who participated in those clinics take pride in the number of players from outside the United States who are on NBA rosters today.

The People Factor

No leadership lesson is more critical to learn than how essential other people are to your success in any endeavor. Indeed, the right people can ensure that you turn a nice opportunity into a grand success; the wrong people can make the chance of a lifetime seem like a bad choice.

With few exceptions, I've had the right people on my team, both on court and off. When I took the job at St. Joseph's, I had the right people. I inherited a squad of good players who had struggled through two seasons with modest success, but who had gained valuable experience in the process. By the time I had a chance to work with them, they were ready to win. They just needed to be shown how.

I was 30 years old, still young enough to go on the practice floor and teach in a hands-on manner. The players liked that approach, and it established a strong rapport between us. Years later, Joe Ceremsak, one of the reserve players on that team, told me how the players hated to have me match up with them in drillwork or scrimmages. "You were so aggressive," he said. "But it was good for us. It made us a tougher team."

I remember those players as if it were yesterday. Mike Fallon, the lead guard and team captain, was almost as old as I was, having spent time in the seminary and in military service. Dan Dougherty, Fallon's backcourt mate, was powerful and a fierce competitor. Bill Lynch, my former high school player, was the center; and Kurt Engelbert and Ray Radzisezewski were the forwards. Engelbert's play was smooth and seemingly effortless; at the end of the game he was usually the leading scorer. Ray Radd was the team's enforcer with his hard play around the basket, and Al Juliana, a left-handed jump shooter with a knack for hitting big shots, was the leader off the bench. McKinney, Ceremsak, Jim Purcell, Jack Savage, and Steve Idzik were other reserves who made contributions—big and small. They were a mentally tough, resilient bunch, good enough to win the Big Five championship and finish third in the NIT.

As good as they were as players and team members, I remember them most for their admirable qualities as people. Each one displayed high integrity, was earnest and hard-working, and had a great sense of loyalty and teamwork. Some have passed away, but many I still see on occasion. The strong bond that was established in 1955 is still evident today.

The championship Portland team of 1976–1977 was also a special group of individuals. Like the St. Joseph's players that I coached my first year there, the Blazers on the 1976–1977 roster hadn't had team success either. None of the holdovers from previous Blazers teams (Bill Walton, Bob Gross, Lionel Hollins, Larry Steele, and Lloyd Neal) had been to the playoffs—in fact, none had played on a .500 team. Of the seven new players, only Herm Gilliam had been on a playoff team (at Seattle, the previous season). Three players (John Davis, Wally Walker, and Robin Jones) were rookies; two from the ABA (Dave Twardzik and Maurice Lucas) had played on losing teams there, and Corky Calhoun, signed after being

Winners and Still Champions: Portland Trail Blazers

The 1976–1977 NBA champion Portland Trail Blazers have held two reunions: one to mark their 20th anniversary, and a second their 25th. Both were well attended by the players and coaches of that team and were huge successes. Portland fans came out in strong numbers to share the memories of that season and to relive an event that remains as the most dramatic sporting event in the history of the city.

The first was held in conjunction with a Blazers game at which the championship team was introduced at half-time. There was also a dinner, and a question-and-answer session involving the fans—complete with reminiscences that, over the intervening years, had entered the realm of exaggeration. It was great fun.

The second was a golf weekend held at a Native American resort (Wildhorse Resort and Casino) near Pendleton, Oregon. Maurice Lucas organized it, and all the players except Wally Walker and Robin Jones, a stroke victim with limited mobility, were there. At this reunion, the players and their wives had more time to be together, and the team seemed to grow closer than it had ever been—a remarkable trait after 25 years.

waived by the Lakers, hadn't played on a winning team during his four-year tenure in the NBA. They were all good players, but they just hadn't been in the right place at the right time. Thus, they were hungry to win and were willing to put personal achievements aside so that the team could benefit. And they took pleasure in doing it.

The team defense was tough. Perimeter defenders put pressure on the ball; there were always weak-side defenders in the lane to plug driving lanes and take charges; and the big men, Walton, Lucas, Neal, and Jones, blocked shots and controlled the backboards.

The offense, which I designated as the Turn-out, had a built-in, multiple-pass, screen-and-cut system. It took a fair amount of discipline to make it work, but the Blazers did it willingly. I never had a group of players like them in the pros before or since. I looked forward to every practice session as much as I did the games. Road trips were always enjoyable. We had two great years together until injuries and contract dissatisfaction broke up the team. At reunions over the years, those players repeat over and over what a unique group we had and how much each enjoyed the experience.

Beginnings in Endings

In 1978, after the Blazers had been eliminated from the playoffs, the station that telecast the Sonics games asked me to do game analysis for their series with Denver. I knew the play calls of both teams from having coached against them during the just-completed season, so I was able to tell the viewers what was coming before it happened. I found it very enjoyable and my prescient calls had the TV staff thinking that I was clairvoyant. The program director later told me that following the game, the station switchboard lit up with calls praising my work. I only did a couple of games, but it was enough to whet my appetite for television work. Little did I know that it was my first experience of what was to become, some years later, my next career: telecasting basketball. More important, I learned that something good (the chance for a new career) could come from a negative event (elimination from the playoffs) if one is ready for it.

Man in the Media

After I had given up active coaching in 1989, Jim Barniak, sports director for Prism, a cable television network in Philadelphia that aired Sixers
games, gave me my first job as a telecaster: working Sixers games.

My first broadcast (Milwaukee at Philadelphia) turned out to be less
than spectacular. First of all, I almost missed the game (see sidebar); then
I didn't project my voice fully during the game and was often drowned out
by the crowd noise. The television critic for the *Philadelphia Daily News*
roasted me in the next-day's edition for my inept performance. I hadn't
read the review, but Barniak was on the phone that morning to tell me
about it. He said that he and Sam Schroeder, who was in charge of production, would be at my Ocean City, New Jersey, home that afternoon
and would bring a videotape of the game that we could review.

They arrived in the early afternoon. We had lunch and then watched
the game tape. When I heard my voice level, I could understand why I
had been criticized. A band had been set up near the courtside location
where we did our pregame stand-up commentary. I had used my normal
speaking voice, so the band came through louder than my comments. As
the game unfolded, although I made pertinent observations, the viewers
sometimes couldn't hear them. There were also times when I "stepped
on" Barniak—spoke while he was speaking—a no-no for an analyst.

All in all, it turned out to be a very productive meeting. It helped me
to become better at my job. After that, I taped the games that I did and
replayed them when I got home. It became a great tool for evaluation,
which I continue to use in both television and radio work.

In 1992, after I had already agreed to a new contract with Prism to
do Sixers games, I got a call from Billy Cunningham, then a minority
owner with the Miami Heat, asking if I'd be interested in doing their television broadcasts. I told him that I was already committed to the Sixers, but he offered to speak to owner Harold Katz about letting me out of
the agreement. Billy and Harold were good friends, and Katz agreed to
let me go if he could find an adequate substitute. They tried out my old
friend, Jack McKinney and liked him well enough to allow Jean and me
to move to Florida.

Lockout: Jack Ramsay

It is probably not surprising that my first telecast for the Sixers was not my best performance. In addition to my inexperience, events leading up to the opening home game against Milwaukee in the 1989–1990 season were inauspicious. I had made an earlier commitment to attend a physical fitness event known as the Tyler Cup held in Dallas, Texas. When I informed the organizers of that event that I wouldn't be able to be there that day because of the Sixers game on the same night, they offered to fly me back to Philadelphia in a private plane to be in time for the game. I couldn't refuse and flew to Dallas the night before. When the event wrapped up about noon the following day, I was whisked to the airport, I hopped onboard an awaiting plane, and I was back in Philly by midafternoon.

It was too early to go to the Spectrum, so I drove my car—a new Ford Thunderbird that I had owned only a week—to a motel near the arena to have a bowl of soup in the coffee shop there. I took the keys out of the ignition, placed them on the console between the two front seats and got out of car to stretch my legs. As I did so, I inadvertently hit the lock button and didn't realize it until I heard that ominous click as I swung the door shut. I knew immediately what I had done—locked my car with the keys inside. My game "uniform"—blazer, slacks, shirt, and tie—were in the trunk . . . also locked.

I was annoyed with myself, but thought it was no big deal because I had done the same thing a couple of other times in my life and had always gotten the door open with a coat hanger. When I went inside the motel and told the bellman about it, he said not to worry and to go have my soup, he could open it with no problem.

When I came out of the coffee shop, I was informed the bellman had gone on an airport run and wouldn't be back for a half hour. It was now about 4:30 in the afternoon, so I borrowed a coat hanger and tried to open the door myself. It didn't work. The Ford Motor Company, in an effort to reduce car thefts, had taken steps to make such entries next to impossible—with special emphasis on

(continued)

the Thunderbird models. There was no space for the coat hanger to slide down and release the lock. By that time, the bellman had returned. He said that he had a special tool for the purpose, but that didn't work either. He then told me that a police car patrolled the area and that the officers surely could get the door open. It was now 5:00 o'clock and I was due at the Spectrum for pregame preparation in a half hour. I tried to call the Sixers' office, but it being late on a Saturday afternoon, I got only recorded messages.

When the police car arrived about 20 minutes later, the officers had no better luck opening the door with their tools and techniques, so I finally broke a window to get in the car.

By the time I dashed into the Spectrum carrying my clothing, it was 15 minutes before airtime, and play-by-play man, Jim Barniak, was talking with John Nash, the Sixers' general manager, about filling in for me. I dressed hurriedly and we went on air as scheduled. It was not the best way to start a new job.

The Heat was a wonderful organization to work with. Cunningham and Lewis Schaffel were the managing partners of the team, and both were very supportive. Eric Reid, my broadcast partner, and I worked well together and became close friends. The radio broadcasters—Jose Pineda (Spanish), Dave Halberstam and, later, Mike Inglis (English)—along with the television producers (Aaron Silberman, Joe Vencius, and Ted Ballard) traveled with us and we enjoyed each other's company thoroughly. It was a great experience for me and produced lasting friendships.

When Micky Arison, whose family owned Carnival Cruise Line, bought out the financial interests of Cunningham and Shaffel, the conditions remained the same as far as I was concerned. Kevin Loughery was the coach when I started with the Heat; then Alvin Gentry took over briefly before Arison was able to persuade Pat Riley to come onboard in 1995. All those coaches were great to work with. They allowed me access to practices, let me mingle and sometimes give advice to players, and were supportive of my television work. I, in turn, greatly enjoyed the relationship I

Raising the Heat: Kevin Loughery, Alvin Gentry, Pat Riley

Bringing the Miami Heat into contender status proved to be a case study in the importance of personnel to the success of an organization. There were great differences in the personalities of the franchise's first four coaches. Ronnie Rothstein was the Heat's earliest coach. He had been assistant to Chuck Daly at Detroit and was a highly intense person. Loughery replaced him. Kevin was a let-'em-play type of coach, whose laid-back appearance masked his fierce competitiveness. Gentry relied on close rapport with his players and has been head coach of two other teams (Detroit and the L.A. Clippers) since then. Riley, acknowledged as one of the game's greatest coaches, is extremely hardworking and disciplined, and he demands the same from his players.

At the beginning of Loughery's last season with the Heat (1994–1995), he approved a deal that sent Steve Smith to Atlanta, Rony Seikaly to Golden State, and Bimbo Coles to Sacramento in exchange for Kevin Willis and Billy Owens. Cunningham knew that Arison was going to take over full ownership and told me that he and Schaffel wanted to give Loughery the team he wanted before they left the organization. On paper, it looked like it could work. Loughery was enthusiastic about it. He had never liked either Seikaly or Smith as players and looked forward to adding Willis and Owens. The deal turned out to be a failure. There is an apt saying among NBA coaches, "You never know a player until you get him on the practice floor." Loughery quickly discovered the truth of that adage.

I was sitting on the edge of the scorer's table at courtside, watching practice about a week after the new players were in place. Loughery was walking back and forth in front of me, following the up-and-down action. After a stretch of uneven play in which there were several turnovers by both teams, Kevin walked over to my position, and with his back to me, he turned his head in my direction and said in a matter-of-fact tone, "I fucked up, Jack . . . I fucked

(continued)

up." He then went back to direct the practice. Loughery meant that he now realized that the trade that he had approved wasn't going to work out.

It is always difficult to rearrange team personnel during the season. A coach doesn't have enough practice time to plug new players into his game plan, and the result is often a series of losses before the new players settle in. This is especially true if the new players occupy key positions—as did Willis and Owens. That is what happened with the Heat.

When Arison officially took control of the franchise just before the All-Star break in 1995, he became a hands-on owner. He knew that I had been around the league for about 30 years and asked to have a meeting with me—to which I readily agreed. When I sat down with him in his spacious office in Miami, the first thing he said was: "Tell me about the NBA."

I responded, "First of all, the NBA has become big business . . ." and was going to tell him how much the league had grown economically during my tenure. But Micky smiled and raised his hand to stop me. He pointed to a half-dozen models of his latest and largest cruise ships that were positioned around his office. "That's big business," he said, "the NBA is down here," placing his hand below desk level.

After that, we talked about the team. Arison asked my opinion of the players and coaches. I couldn't give a very optimistic rating of the personnel, but said that I liked Loughery and thought he was doing as good a job as could be done. Arison told me that he was willing to spend whatever it took to bring a contender to Miami, and wanted to make some bold moves right away. He told me that he planned to let Loughery go and replace him with Gentry. When I said I wasn't sure that Alvin was ready for that big a step upward, he replied, "What have we got to lose? Alvin has the rest of the season to show whether he can do the job. If the team plays well, I'll keep him. If it doesn't improve, I'll have time to go after a more experienced coach . . . someone like Pat Riley."

Arison told me all this in confidence, so I was never able to forewarn Kevin that the axe was about to fall on him, nor that

Gentry's position was so fragile. Of course, the Heat didn't jump forward for Gentry, and Arison was able to attract Riley to Miami. The new owner opened his purse to get Riley and gave him freedom to make whatever deals he could, regardless of cost, to raise the Heat to contender status. Within a year, Riley had cleared his roster of all former players but one (utility man Keith Askins) and had acquired a solid core of players led by Alonzo Mourning, P. J. Brown, Tim Hardaway, and Jamal Mashburn. In his second full season, the Heat won 61 games—a remarkable turnaround.

had with each of them. I stayed with Miami for eight seasons. And I was still with Miami when my next opportunity came knocking.

During the 1991 NBA Finals between the Lakers and Bulls, Mike Bogad, a producer at ESPN asked me if I'd be interested in providing studio commentary for the series. When I said I was, ESPN invited me to come to their main studios in Bristol, Connecticut, to talk about the upcoming series. I arrived around noon, Mike met me, we had lunch, and then he ushered me into a conference room filled with producers, directors, and on-air personnel. Mike introduced me to the group, and said, "Tell us about the Finals." Thanks to my experience doing television broadcasts for the Miami Heat, I had seen both teams play on many occasions, so I had a pretty good handle on the coaches and players of both teams, including what the principal issues were and who I thought would win and why. (I picked the Bulls to win a hard-played series.)

I spoke for about 20 minutes without interruption, while the group listened attentively. When I was finished, Mike asked for questions. There were none. Then Mike said that he thought ESPN viewers would like that kind of information and approach, and added, "If you can pare that down some, I think we'll be fine." I asked how much time I would have. Mike said, "You'll have two hits [appearances]. In the first one, you'll have about two minutes, twenty seconds, and about a buck and a half [a minute and a half] in the second." I laughed and said, "You want me to give the information I just gave you in that amount of time?" Everyone in the room smiled back, and someone said, "That's television."

Thus, I learned another important lesson: how to get ideas down to the bare bones of expression and to say them concisely, quickly, clearly, and with enthusiasm. It also marked the beginning of another long-term (12 years) successful relationship with an organization.

Riding the Radio Wave

When ESPN Radio got underway in 1992, it operated only on weekends at first. Then it increased to daily programming from 6:00 A.M. to 6:00 P.M., before it became a 24/7 operation. ESPN Radio got the contract to broadcast the NBA Game of the Week for the 1995–1996 season and made me the lead game analyst. I hadn't done game broadcasts on radio before, but the station manager, Mark Mason, and John Martin, producer of sports for ESPN radio, had seen and heard me doing television broadcasts for the Heat, as well as my appearances as an NBA analyst on ESPN television. They thought I could make the adjustment to radio.

I did a trial broadcast of a game at San Antonio with long-time play-by-play man, Jim Durham. I had never done a full radio game broadcast before, and I asked JD before we went on the air how to signal him when I had something to contribute. He told me to jump in whenever I wanted; but radio game broadcasts are carried play-by-play, and I told him I didn't want to run the risk of stepping on his words in midsentence. So he said, "All right, let's do it this way. I'll call the play until a team scores; then I'll pause. If you have something to say, jump in there, and give it back to me when the ball is in the front court." That made sense to me. We followed that procedure in the game, and the broadcast seemed to flow quite well. After the game, radio producer John Martin indicated that he was satisfied, and we've been doing it like that ever since.

The radio experience, though enjoyable, is obviously different from television; hence it presents new challenges. In contrast to television, where the fans see the action and the analyst tells why and how things are happening, on radio, the analyst has to be the listeners' eyes and ears. I had to learn to paint a mental picture for the fans in addition to

Time on the Clock: Jack Ramsay

Every job has its particular demands. When I had the opportunity to get into television and radio work, I struggled with some aspects of both jobs. My first radio gig was in the mid-1950s to take over for Jim Leaming for a week in the summer at WIP in Philadelphia. Jim did a five-minute sports wrap-up at drive-time in the morning and evening news segments.

It sounded easy enough, and I was at the station around 5:00 A.M. to get ready to go on air at 6:05. I gathered the items that I wanted to use off the wire machines, arranged them in order of priority, and timed them out to fit into the five-minute slot. Because the traffic report by helicopter came on automatically at exactly 6:05, I had to take the program to that time, then get off so that the traffic report could be heard. I started on schedule and was taking my items one by one, putting the used ones in a separate pile.

At one point, however, I inadvertently picked up two items instead of one, so that when I got to the end of my reports, I was an item shy of what I had planned—with about 20 seconds of airtime to fill. I was shocked to see the bottom of the pile with time still left because I had timed it out so carefully. Nevertheless, I signed off. There were still about 12 seconds on the clock before the traffic reporter came on, so I signed off again! Then, in a save-play, Joe McCauley, the morning disc jockey, rushed back from his coffee break to rescue me. By the end of the week, with six broadcasts a day under my belt, I felt like an old pro—but I still get the sweats thinking back on that first morning.

just identifying the plays; and I had to be able to provide the information quickly, without disrupting the play-by-play man's flow of the game. I found it fascinating, and working with Durham was pure pleasure.

I also got a lot of help (again, testimony to the importance of having the right people on your team). The production people—Martin, Beth Faber, Ivan Sokalsky, Jon Madani, and Bob Sagendorf—were on top of every broadcast and provided insight that helped me do my job the best way possible. They are top-quality people and fun to be around.

The 2002–2003 NBA season marked the eighth for ESPN's radio broadcasts, and in those years, I've worked with some great broadcasters They include the all-sports guru, Brent Musburger, with whom I do the NBA Conference Finals and NBA Finals each year; the lively and likable Kevin Harlan; the crystal-clear-voiced Kevin Calabro, who does Sonics games regularly; Toronto's Dan Shulman, now known more for his broadcasts of Major League baseball; Glenn Ordway, one-time Celtics broadcaster; and various ESPN personalities like Dan Patrick, Mike Tirico, Charley Steiner, Chris Moore, and Doug Brown. I also did some games with Beth Mowins, who pinch-hit on some NBA broadcasts one season and did a nice job with it. I have enjoyed working with all of them, but it's still a special treat to do games with Durham.

I have met a lot of quality people since I joined ESPN, many of whom are still with the company. They have been cordial and receptive to my perspective of NBA basketball, and have given me plenty of work. I have analyzed everything that has happened in the NBA—upcoming games and those just played, trades made, coaching changes, who was hot and who was not. I worked out of ESPN headquarter studios in Bristol, Connecticut; game sites around the league; network and private studios all over the country; in lobbies, special-events rooms, and guestrooms of hotels; and in my homes in Ocean City, New Jersey, and Naples, Florida. I have talked about and interviewed the NBA's greatest stars and coaches. Opportunities don't knock much louder than that.

Leadership Playbook

Accepting Responsibility

HISTORY HAS RECORDED THE achievements of countless leaders in all branches of human endeavor: politics, the military, education, religion, society, the arts, and sports. They include renowned rulers of countries and empires; brilliant strategists of war; those who spearheaded social, religious, and educational reform; others who forged creative paths of self-expression; and some who developed dynasties in sports.

Leaders come in both genders and in all sizes, shapes, and ages. They get the job done in diverse ways; generally, the only characteristic they have in common is that they lead in a unique manner. That is, they are who they are; no leader succeeds by assuming the personality, mannerisms, and style of another. Great leaders also know where they want to go and how they plan to get there; they are well organized, are comfortable delegating authority, know how to communicate pertinent information appropriately and effectively, and are able to prepare their personnel thoroughly. They are fiercely motivated to attain success, are firm and

Enduring Leadership: Ernest Shackleton

A historical figure that I find particularly inspiring is Sir Ernest Shackleton, who, in 1914, led a small (28-person) expeditionary force that was stranded in the Antarctic for almost two years. Shackleton and his men had sailed from England to Antarctica, where they planned an 1,800-mile crossing of ice-covered terrain on foot. But tragedy struck just one day short of their destination on the Arctic coast: Their ship, the *Endurance* became ensnared in the ice and was finally crushed by it. Thereafter, the expeditionary force lived under unimaginably extreme conditions before being rescued. Each of the survivors later credited their survival entirely to Shackleton's leadership.

Sir Ernest accomplished that feat by never losing his poise; maintaining his confidence that they would all survive; organizing the group's activities in a meaningful manner; establishing excellent rapport with every member of the group, which brought them closer together as individuals; and adjusting his game plan to meet changing conditions.

Shackleton's Way, by Margot Morrell and Stephanie Capparell (New York: Viking Penguin Books, 2001), details Shackleton's heroic dedication to the arduous task of survival for his men and himself. When I read about the principles he used in his life-or-death struggle, I was struck by how well one could apply the same leadership tenets to the coaching profession (as I've said, good leadership principles apply universally). Except for the life-threatening conditions that Shackleton experienced with his expedition team, every successful NBA coach goes through the same process with his team of players in the long 82-game season. *Shackleton's Way* should be on the summer reading list of every leader or aspiring leader.

consistent in their demands, and are poised to make decisions in times of stress.

To Lead or Not to Lead

Leadership roles are thrust on most of us at one time or other in our lives, but perhaps from an early age those destined to be leaders fill those roles more willingly than others. Before I reached my teens, I took it on myself to stake out a baseball field in a vacant lot across from our house in Milford. I measured the distances from home plate (a barrel bottom sawed to measure) to the pitcher's mound (a wooden slat) and to the bases (dirt-filled chicken feed bags), and built an improvised backstop of discarded pieces of flooring. I telephoned the 18 players to make sure they would show up; and thereafter, every Saturday morning in the spring we played games there. That was a kind of leadership, but I filled that role because I wanted to play baseball, not because I wanted to be the leader of the group.

At Upper Darby High School, I was captain of the baseball team; and I captained the basketball team at St. Joe's. As a Navy ensign, I led the first platoon of UDT 30 and became the captain of YP 643. I did not seek these positions of leadership, but once I was either elected or appointed to them, I wanted to do the best job I could.

Many—maybe most—people are satisfied with safe, secure lives. They take jobs with limited authority, but with longevity and modest pay increments built into them, and stay there for their entire working lives. Generally, these jobs are structured around 9-to-5 workdays, with little or no weekend duty requirements or travel demands. The lives of such people become as regular as clockwork, and they are content with that. If they are fortunate enough to have an adequate pension, they retire at age 65 and "live happily ever after." For others like me, however, being safe and secure is not enough to bring happiness. We seek greater challenges—the opportunity to create something of our own and to lead others. And we're willing to take risks to achieve those rewards.

Most of the teachers I worked with at Mount Pleasant fell into the first group. They had an excellent teaching situation: The students were capable and wanted to learn; there were few disciplinary problems, and the pay scale was among the highest in the state of Delaware. So they couldn't understand why I would leave to take a one-year contract for about half the pay to coach at St. Joseph's. But, to me it was a no-brainer. I wanted to coach at the college level, and this was a wonderful opportunity that I wasn't going to let slip by. I was confident I could do a good coaching job and could find a way to make enough money to provide for my family. (I took teaching jobs in the Philadelphia School District and at St. Joseph's Evening Division that first year of coaching, and we managed to get by financially.) At the end of that first year, I received an offer to coach at Yale, and my salary at St. Joe's was significantly increased and extended. I was off and running.

Competitive sports afford wonderful leadership opportunities to players and coaches alike, but a coach must assume overall command—his players expect it and the success of his team depends on it.

Textbook Leadership

Classroom teachers are in wonderful positions of leadership. It is my perception that every person who has gone through an educational system has had teachers who have had a profound effect on their lives. Too often, this kind of leadership goes unappreciated. I remember with gratitude all the teachers who were part of my educational life, though certain ones occupy a special niche in my memory bank: Miss Platt, the grade-school teacher in Milford who demonstrated her love of children and teaching every day; Miss Kerr, our class advisor at Upper Darby High School (whom everybody adored); my professor of philosophy at St. Joseph's, Father Edward Gannon, SJ; and the esteemed Dr. McMullin, my professor at the University of Pennsylvania. Each helped me to achieve whatever success I've had in life.

Just as leaders in other fields bring their personalities to bear on their particular style of leadership, there have been all kinds of personalities among notable coaches. They range from domineering types, like Vince Lombardi and Bob Knight, to quiet, orderly directors like John Wooden. Those three represent vastly different personalities, but they all achieved high levels of success. The vital factor was that all three of them were who they were; they didn't try to be someone else. This brings to mind again Bruce Ogilvie, the sports psychologist mentioned in Chapter 2. In his study on the principles of leadership, Ogilvie found that those in authority who achieved high levels of success shared three characteristics: an intense intellectual curiosity about their jobs, a burning desire for success, and "transparent personalities"—what you see is what you get.

That is not to say that leaders are not influenced by other leaders; many aspiring leaders have mentors who are more experienced. It is no different in coaching. Most people who enter the coaching profession have been influenced by coaches they played for or assisted. They may want to emulate those coaches, or they may want to follow a different path. Some attend colleges that offer courses in coaching methods; many enter the profession directly from the playing field. The ultimate goal is to have a team of their own, to be a head coach. That position lets them create their own philosophy and style of playing, allows for developing individualized methods of teaching, affords great motivational circumstances, and gives them freedom to determine how they conduct their game. And after a lot of trial and error, the survivors become the kind of coach they really want to be. I use the term "survivors" deliberately, because each level of coaching demands adjustments that not everyone can make.

The first is going from player to coach. I have recounted how unprepared I was for my first job. But I learned from it and then was better prepared for college coaching. The jump from college to professional coaching involved the most severe adjustment because the rules of the game, the style of play, and the number of games are all different from those of college basketball. College coaches who come directly into the NBA get a rude awakening. No matter how successful they've been at the collegiate level, they find the NBA is a tough nut to crack.

I had coached 6 years in high school, 11 at the college level, and had been general manager at Philadelphia for 2 years before taking the coaching job there. I had followed the NBA game very closely as a GM and felt comfortable at training camp with the general coaching duties: forming my game plan, organizing and conducting practices, and developing teamwork. We had been having good scrimmages, too, but we hadn't played a full practice game, and in my first preseason game I became confused by its time segments. In pro basketball, the game is played in four 12-minute periods, whereas the college game is played in two 20-minute halves. The Sixers and Knicks got into a high-scoring game at Camden, New Jersey—both scoring in the mid-30s in the first period—and at halftime Philly held a slight lead, with more than 60 points on the board. When the buzzer sounded to end the half, I reacted as if I were coaching a college game—my team had played two periods, we were ahead at the end of the second, so we must have won the game. I leaped off the bench, both fists clenched in the air, and started toward the locker room. I took one step, and it hit me: "This is the half, dummy, not the end of the game." I looked around at my players. Nobody said anything; their amused expressions said it all. I knew that they knew that I had made a rookie coach's mistake.

Years later, I watched others suffer even more intense growing pains. I was doing Miami TV analysis in 1992 when I interviewed Jerry Tarkanian before a Spurs-Heat game soon after he took the San Antonio job. Tark had had a tremendous career at UNLV (University of Nevada, Las Vegas) and expected to adjust easily to coaching in the NBA. While we waited for the camera crew to set up, Tark and I chatted. I asked how he liked coaching in the NBA. He looked at me with a kind of wide-eyed bewilderment and said, "Jack, this is a tough, fuckin' job. I had no idea that coaching here was so different."

He went on to say how fortunate he was to have retained veteran assistant coach Rex Hughes from the previous season. He had expected to bring his entire college staff with him, but kept Hughes on as last-minute decision. "Rex knows the rules and the players. I'd have been really lost without him."

On camera, we talked about the transition from college to pro coaching, and I ended the interview by asking, in jest, whether Tark thought he would finish the season. He answered, "I don't know. The end of the season seems like a long way away right now." About two weeks later, Tark resigned. The Spurs were 9–11 at that point.

Paul Silas, too, struggled. He had finished a fine 16-year NBA playing career at Seattle and immediately took a head-coaching job with the San Diego Clippers in 1980. I was coaching Portland at the time, and the Blazers were playing in a preseason doubleheader in Los Angeles that also involved the Clippers. After a morning team practice on game day, I went to the fitness center of the hotel where we were staying to get a workout before lunch. When I entered the locker room, I saw Silas, bathed in sweat, sitting on a stool in a slouched position with a towel draped over his head. He was staring at the floor. He looked up, saw me, and fixed me with a prolonged gaze. After several seconds, he said, "Why didn't you tell me that it was like this?" I knew that he was talking about coaching.

For about a half hour, we discussed the difficulties he was having with all the detail work that went into coaching, which he had never encountered as a player. I offered some suggestions—mostly about how he might organize better—but when he showered and left the room, he was still shaking his head, deep in thought. Paul stayed with the Clippers for three years without much success. He didn't have players good enough to be a playoff team, and he wasn't prepared to start his coaching career as the headman. He worked 16 years as an assistant before he got another chance as a head coach. He was assisting Dave Cowens at Charlotte and took over for him at mid-season when Dave left over a disagreement with management. Silas was successful this time and stayed with that franchise when it moved to New Orleans, but was not rehired when his contract ran out after the 2002–2003 season. Cleveland quickly signed Paul as its coach, to teach the NBA game to prodigy LeBron James.

In a League of His Own

No one in sports exemplifies the qualities of leadership better than the NBA's own David Stern, who is widely regarded as the most successful sports commissioner of all time. Born and raised in Chelsea, New York, he graduated from high school at age 16, from Rutgers University at 20, and earned a law degree from Columbia University when he was only 23. He was immediately hired by a prestigious law firm in New York City, Proksauer Rose, one of whose clients was the National Basketball Association. Stern soon found himself immersed in legal work involving the NBA and some of its players, management personnel, and even Maurice Podoloff, the league's first commissioner, who held office from 1946 to 1963. After a 12-year period with that firm, in 1978, he was hired by the NBA as its legal counsel. Two years later, he became executive vice president, and in 1984, was named commissioner of the NBA. His accomplishments since then have been truly remarkable.

He took over a league that was plagued with financial problems (several teams were on the brink of bankruptcy), that was rife with labor unrest, and whose image had been damaged by player connections to the drug culture. Stern wasted no time in cleaning things up. Then he established a salary cap that would allow franchises from smaller markets to compete on more even terms with their big-city brethren, and more recently he instituted a luxury tax to heavily penalize teams that exceed the cap. NBA Entertainment became part of the league structure and got greater viewing exposure for its burgeoning stars, which at the time included Larry Bird, Julius Erving, Moses Malone, Magic Johnson, Kareem Abdul-Jabbar, and the new kid on the court, Michael Jordan. Stern also negotiated lucrative television contracts with the networks and cable companies.

The league has expanded from 23 to 29 teams during his tenure, and soon will add another franchise in Charlotte, North Carolina. He opened international offices in major cities around the world. In 1997, he created a professional basketball league for women, the WNBA, and then formed the National Development League for players who didn't quite make it to the NBA level.

In 1999, Stern set up a 24-hour digital network, NBA.com TV, as well as computer web sites. Just as important, he instituted a viable plan to help players who came forward to overcome drug and alcohol problems, while taking a firm stance against those who continued to be users.

On the financial front, despite the salary cap, player salaries continued to escalate, until in 2003, the average pay reached about $4.6 million. It is estimated that NBA revenues have increased by as much as 500 percent during his term as commissioner.

How did he do all this? Great leadership.

But when I asked him about his qualities as a leader, he hedged a bit: "I'm not one for introspection," he said, "but I always had the ability to set a tone. I've always been compulsively interested in acquiring facts, forming an opinion, then pursuing that opinion with conviction. I did that in grade school, in camp, in high school—and I still like to debate issues."

When Stern began as commissioner, he had 24 employees to help him launch his turnaround of the league. Now, by his estimation, about 1,100 personnel are spread all over the world. He has a great facility for knowing each person on his staff, what each person's job is, and what's happening with it at the moment. He seems to be on top of every situation. (I recently asked him if he still knew all his staff members by name. "Not any more," he said. "That stopped when we had 500 or 550." But I'm certain that he still knows who's doing what and how well.)

Stern hires only the highly competent, who are willing to work hard. Long hours are a given. Staffers know they are expected to invest whatever time is necessary to complete a task. They also know that no one works harder than the commissioner. Stern told me, "We established the motto 'The relentless pursuit of perfection' before Lexus [the car manufacturer], knowing that true perfection is never reached. Our first concern, after we've done what we consider to be a great job is, 'How can we do it better?' I want the NBA to be judged by the finest standards of the business world, not just as a sports entity."

Stern also serves as a mentor for all who work for the NBA, although he minimizes his role in that regard, saying, "I only expand their opportunities and responsibilities. I give them a chance. The rest is up to them."

But you can be certain that those who have succeeded have followed Stern's example of meticulous preparation and hard work. Gary Bettman was a vice president and general counsel for the NBA under Stern until he left to become commissioner of the National Hockey League in 1993. Bettman observed firsthand how Stern imbued his leadership characteristics into the culture of the NBA. Regarding his association with Stern and the NBA, Bettman told me, "The characteristics for high-level accomplishment start with the CEO. All the traits that are associated with success in any endeavor start at the top—things like hard work, loyalty, integrity, determination, careful preparation, ethical conduct, establishing

Tough Opponents: Drug and Alcohol Abuse

Often, a coach's toughest opponents are not the most competitive teams on the schedule, but outside influences and personal forces, which can be much more difficult to conquer. In the early years of the NBA, before the implementation of Stern's plan to help players with drug and alcohol problems, unmonitored alcoholic consumption was a common practice. Each home team was required to have an ample supply of beer available to both teams in the locker rooms after every game. Players would often drink a couple of beers immediately after the game, and some took a few more with them in their gym bags when they left the arenas. In my first year of coaching at Philadelphia, I had made no provision for limiting the consumption of alcohol, but I discovered early in the season that it was necessary to do so. In the days of commercial travel, alcoholic beverages were provided freely in the first-class section, where the players sat. On a trip to Chicago, one of my players drank so much that he could hardly make it off the plane and later needed help to get to his hotel room. I fined him $500 for not being physically fit to perform. Thereafter, I prohibited drinking alcohol on all future trips to game sites. I kept that regulation in force at my other coaching stops and, with some exceptions, found that it worked effectively. Two other players that I coached struggled with drugs and alcohol, one with a positive outcome, the other, sadly, with the opposite.

When I was coach/general manager of the Sixers, I worked out a trade for Bob Rule in the 1971–1972 season. Rule, a 6–9 left-handed center, was drafted by Seattle in 1967 and became an All-Star player for them. He had an unorthodox shot that no one could block—including Bill Russell, the premier shot-blocker of all time. I was intrigued by Rule's ability to score, so when the opportunity came along to acquire him from the Sonics for a couple of second-round draft choices, I jumped at the chance.

The Sixers were thin at the center position since losing both Wilt Chamberlain and Luke Jackson (Jackson, Chamberlain's intended replacement, had snapped an Achilles tendon and never fully regained his ability to run and jump). The trade for Rule was finalized early in the season, and he immediately stepped into the starting lineup. In his first games, he showed he could still score (he averaged 17.3 points a game that season), but his rebounding was marginal and his defense was ineffective. I talked to him several times about increasing his overall performance, and he made the effort in practice, but it didn't carry over into the games.

One night, after a road game, I returned to the hotel and looked into the lobby bar in time to see Rule tossing down a straight shot of what I later learned was vodka. I wasn't surprised to see Rule in the bar, but drinking straight shots is sometimes a red flag, so I thought I'd better check it out. Bob had ordered another one by the time I got to his side, and he greeted me affably. He was a bit glassy-eyed, and I suggested that he ease off. He said he was going to have just one more and then turn in. We chatted a bit longer; I left the bar but waited in the lobby to see how long he would stay. Another half hour went by before he left and went to his room.

Sensing that alcohol might be a problem with Rule, I talked with him a couple of times about limiting his consumption, explaining that I believed it was affecting his playing ability. He responded that he was only a social drinker and needed it to help him unwind from games, and he swore that he'd never let it affect his game. But he clearly was not the same player he had been in Seattle.

I left the Sixers after that season to go to Buffalo, and Rule was traded to Cleveland early the next year. He had two unimpressive years there and played one game at Milwaukee the following season, then was gone from the league. I didn't hear anything about him for several years; then, when I was coaching the Blazers, he called to me as I was catching a plane in Chicago. He came over and, as we shook hands, said that he wanted me to know that he had cleaned himself up, was no longer drinking, and had a steady job. He looked good, and I told him how pleased I was that he was doing well.

The second player, Billy Ray Bates, was a talented 2-guard, who was undrafted from Kentucky State in 1978 and was acquired by Portland as a free agent in 1980. Stu Inman had seen him play for the Maine Lumberjacks of the CBA and thought he might give the team a backcourt boost in the stretch drive of an injury-plagued

(continued)

season. Inman arranged for Bates to come to New York where the
Blazers were scheduled to play the Knicks so that I could work him
out and decide whether to sign him.

After the team shootaround on the day of the game, I put
Bates through a number of drills, to which he responded quite well.
He was very raw, but had obvious offensive skills—he could shoot
from a distance, drive and slam at the hoop, and was adequate with
his ball-handling. I knew he'd have trouble defending, but the
team was struggling on its way to a 38–44 finish, so I elected to
sign him.

The players, who watched the drillwork while waiting for the
bus to take them back to the hotel, were impressed. Kermit Washington asked me if we were going to sign him. When I told him we
were, Kermit's face lit up. "He can play, Coach, that boy can play."

By the time we finished the six-game road trip, Bates was coming off the bench and injecting some life into the team offense. He
had trouble remembering the plays, so we ran simple screen-and-roll
plays for him when he came into the game. But he knocked down
shots, rebounded, and played with a lot of enthusiasm—and the
Portland fans loved him. Billy Ray became something of a folk hero.
The Blazers signed him to a new contract, and before the following
season, Billy's face loomed large on billboards around town promoting milk for the area dairy association.

But we were soon to discover that, despite his boyish charm and
his ability to put points on the board, he had problems off the court.
It turned out he had learning disabilities. The coaches noticed that
on road trips, when most of the players were reading books or maga-
zines, Billy was gazing absently out the window or listening to music
on his headset. We found that, on testing, his reading level was only
that of a third grader. He agreed to begin a remedial reading program that the team arranged for him, but didn't stay with it.

We also found that Billy Ray couldn't say no to his new admir-
ers, who regularly offered to buy him beers after a game, and sometimes he became belligerent when he'd had too many. Once when
he had overconsumed while on the road, he put his fist through a
stained-glass panel in a door leading from the barroom in the hotel
and was refused further drinks. As time went on, he began using illegal drugs and once didn't arrive at a home game until half-time,

despite attempts by trainer Ron Culp to call him by phone and those of a Portland police officer who tried to rouse him by banging on the door of his apartment.

All the Blazers—management, coaches, players—and his agent, Steve Kauffman, were concerned about Billy. No one wanted to see him lose out on a great opportunity to make a career in the NBA, but his off-court habits began to affect the quality of his play. We had many meetings with him, to try to get him to accept help for his dependence on alcohol and drugs. He went twice to rehabilitation facilities in the Portland area, but walked away before making any progress. In two years, he was out of the league.

He later played in a league in the Philippines, where he put up big numbers; and I saw him last in Philadelphia in the mid-1990s after a Heat-Sixers game I had helped telecast. He told me he was living in Camden, New Jersey, and was fine, though he didn't say what he was doing.

As it turned out, Billy wasn't fine at all. Kauffman told me that Bates kept coming to him for money, which Kauffman provided for a while. But, finally, Kauffman decided that he couldn't keep doing that indefinitely and cut him off. He told me later he felt remorse about doing that, but realized that he wasn't helping Bates by being a source of funds when Bates wasn't finding a way to make ends meet himself.

Sadly, Bates was later convicted of armed robbery and served time in prison. It was a tragic waste of talent, but not really surprising. Billy Ray was blessed with abundant athletic skill, but much less mental acumen. He was a simple, engaging guy whose athletic talents got him to college and ultimately into the NBA. He had been allowed to play four years of basketball at Kentucky State although he had only elementary school level reading skills. He had that brief, shining moment in Portland, where he basked in the adulation of the fans. But he wasn't able to take responsibility for his own behavior and got caught up in the drug and alcohol scene. He reveled in the attention of casual acquaintances who used his notoriety and money to feed their own addictions, while resisting the efforts of those who wanted to help him straighten out his life. When his basketball skills deserted him and he ran out of enablers, he turned to crime.

an effective plan, and the desire to succeed. David exhibits all of those traits and demands them from everyone who works for him."

Bettman has applied the same formula for success in the NHL, and has gotten outstanding results. In comparing those organizations, Bettman says, "The culture of the NHL is not the same as that of the NBA; hockey is a different sport from basketball, so some of the things we do are different. But those internal qualities I just mentioned are effective anywhere. That's why David Stern could step into an executive position with any Fortune 500 company and have the same success that he's had in the NBA."

Make Active Choices

There is truth in the old bromide that when the team wins, the players get the credit; if it loses, the coach gets the blame. Coaches—all leaders—are certain to be criticized; it comes with the territory. But, as Harry Truman said, "If you can't stand the heat, stay out of the kitchen."

Michael Useem and Warren G. Bennis, in their excellent book on leadership, *The Leadership Moment* (New York: Times Books, 1999), write that leadership is the "act of making a difference. [It] entails changing a failed strategy or revamping a languishing organization. It requires us to make an active choice among plausible alternatives, and it depends on bringing others along, on mobilizing them to get the job done. Leadership is at its best when the vision is strategic, the voice persuasive, the results tangible." It struck me that all those characteristics apply to a coach who takes on the challenge of a struggling franchise. Three of the four teams that I coached fit that description perfectly. Consequently, I was afforded great opportunities of leadership.

One of my primary objectives as a coach was to let my players know from the beginning what I expected of them and what they could expect from me in return. (I never forgot my disheartening experience as a freshman at St. Joe's, when I expected to start a game, then never got off the bench.) I wanted each player to know his role on the team—even if it wasn't what he wanted to hear. All players want to start and play at least 40 of the 48 game minutes. But the fact is that only five players can start, meaning that very few are going to play as many minutes as they'd like.

The number of players a coach uses depends on the quality of his players and the number of games on the schedule. In high school and college, where teams usually play once or twice a week, and the length of the games is 32 and 40 minutes, respectively, a coach may play only his best five or six players. Most NBA teams use an eight- or nine-man rotation. That means that five start, three or four come off the bench, and three or four don't get in the game at all—barring blowout wins or losses. So, after training camp and the preseason games ended, I told my team collectively which starters I thought would best enable us to win and how long I expected each to play; who would come off the bench and at what point in the game; how long they would play; and, at times, which players wouldn't figure in the rotation at all. I also made it clear that those

Alternate Approach

I was surprised to learn that Chuck Daly, a Hall of Fame coach, whose Detroit Pistons won back-to-back championships in 1989 and 1990, never told his team about his plans for rotating players off the bench. Ron Rothstein, as assistant to Daly, told me that Chuck seldom spoke to individuals. Rick Mahorn, who played on the 1989 championship team, said that players knew from practices who was in the starting lineup; reserves learned from preseason games who would come off the bench; and those not called on for either—and Chuck only played eight—knew they were destined for a season as observers.

When I asked Chuck about his approach, he said, "I don't like confrontations, so I only talk to the whole team." I asked if that procedure caused any dissension among the bench group. He admitted that there might be some grumbling, but added, "I've lost some of my hearing, so if they're bitching about not playing, I don't even hear it. And I prefer it that way." Chuck, like all successful leaders, was being himself—and it worked for him, too.

decisions depended on performance, and were not carved in stone. In this system, every player had to *do* his job to *keep* his job. That meant there was always opportunity for someone to move up.

I didn't expect everyone to be happy with my decisions and invited private meetings to further explain my position as well as to listen to op-posing opinions. But I felt sure that letting players know in advance what they could expect from me was far superior to their not knowing. And, as long as the opportunity to advance was there, there was a good spirit of competition for playing time, which most players accepted.

Prioritize Personnel

In Chapter 5, I talked about the value of people optimizing opportunities that come their way. As a leader, personnel is of paramount importance. For a coach planning for the season, personnel is his first concern.

When I went to Portland, the Blazers had just finished an unsatisfac-tory season (37–45), were last in the Pacific Division, and had fired a fu-ture Hall of Fame coach, Lenny Wilkens. The team had several big-name players—Bill Walton, Geoff Petrie, and Sidney Wicks, the team's leading scorers—and other quality personnel including Lionel Hollins, Bobby Gross, Larry Steele, and Lloyd Neal. The team finished the season with a starting lineup of Wicks, Gross, and Walton up front, and Petrie and Steele in the backcourt.

When I told Director of Player Personnel Stu Inman that the team was too slow, he seemed surprised. But I knew what I wanted to do. I saw the potential for a fast-breaking team, but not with the existing person-nel. Wicks and Petrie (who needed knee surgery) were both playing out their contracts. I met with both players. Petrie wanted a new contract be-fore he had surgery and the Blazers wouldn't do that. Neither side budged. Wicks told me that he'd play out his contract year with the Blazers and would play well. However, he then added that the money the club was paying Lenny Wilkens for the year left on his contract after he was fired should be going to him, Wicks, and that the issue about extending his contract could have been avoided. Wicks had just demonstrated his "me first" attitude. When he left the room, I knew I had spoken with him for the last time as a Trail Blazer.

The Blazers traded both players—Petrie (along with Steve Hawes) to Atlanta for the fifth pick in the ABA Dispersal Draft; Wicks to Boston for cash. When the Blazers went to training camp, there were many new faces: guards Johnny Davis, Dave Twardzik, and Herm Gilliam; big men Maurice Lucas and Moses Malone; small forward Wally Walker; and center Robin Jones. Free agent Corky Calhoun was signed before the season began. Along with holdovers—Walton, Gross, Hollins, Neal, and Steele—the new personnel enabled me to shift gears, to change the Blazers from a plodding team into one that could fly. In that process, I had input with Blazer management to acquire not only outstanding personnel, but the quality that I needed to play the game style that I wanted. I knew that it was then up to me to take charge and develop that personnel to its fullest. It was an example of productive thinking and effective planning—team play at the management level.

Take Charge

"Being the boss," which is essential to good leadership, requires that you observe the basic tenets: Take care of the details of the job, be determined to succeed, organize properly, teach the game, motivate players, and delegate authority. In fact, everybody likes the person in charge to *be* in charge. There is nothing worse than an administrator who won't exercise authority. That applies to all walks of life. It is certainly true in sports.

I had a chance meeting with Yankees manager Joe Torre one day at a restaurant in Chicago. We talked about the Bulls game that I had just helped broadcast and that he had watched on television in the clubhouse before his team took the field against the White Sox. Then we started talking about coaching/managing. I commented that he had a tough boss in George Steinbrenner. Joe surprised me by saying, "He's a pussycat. You just have to show him that you're running the team."

He went on to say that shortly after he had been hired, the Yankees got off to a slow start and he got a call from "the Boss," who told Joe that he was unhappy with the way the team was playing and that he wanted different players in the lineup. Joe told him that he had been hired to make those decisions and if that Steinbrenner wanted to make them himself, he should get another manager. Torre said that they have never had a similar conversation since.

I had heard similar words early in my coaching career, when I took on my first NBA coaching job at Philadelphia. Eddie Donovan, the Knicks' general manager and former St. Bonaventure coach, called to wish me luck and offer some advice. Eddie had had great success as a college coach, but he hadn't had the same results with the Knicks, so I was interested in what he had to say. We talked for a while about the differences between coaching in college and the NBA, then he ended our chat with a simple statement, "Be the boss."

Donovan was implying that, to survive, someone coming from college coaching without previous NBA experience needed to assert himself, take charge, and lead the group of high-profile, established pro players. He said that it took a firm, confident approach. It was meaningful advice.

Extending the Lead: Phil Jackson

Phil Jackson, who has coached the Chicago Bulls and the LA Lakers to a combined nine championships, is a man in charge. And he seems to strengthen his leadership role by extending the opportunity to lead to others.

Speaking of the makeup of his 2002–2003 Lakers team, he said, "We have different kinds of leaders on this team. Shaq leads by his dominance on the court more than with the spoken word—although when he talks they all listen up. Kobe is a more inspirational leader. He takes over in games and sometimes just wills us to victory. It's fascinating for me to watch him. And a player like Rick [Fox], who has a great heart, shows and tells about the value of staying in the [team] offense. Those are the kinds of leadership by the players that I encourage; it helps my own [leadership] within the team."

I learned the wisdom of those words at Buffalo, when I had an experience much like Joe Torre's. Paul Snyder, the team owner, was in the habit of coming into the locker room after team losses—and there were many in the first expansion years—and ranting on the players and coaches. He fired Coach Dolph Schayes after an opening night blowout in the team's second year. I was his third coach after two seasons. To assert myself from the get-go, before I signed my contract to coach the team, I told Paul that I didn't want him in the locker room after losses, that I wanted full control in running the team. He replied, "I'm glad you said that. I want a coach to take charge." Our relationship was not always satin-smooth and got quite stormy at the end, but he never again came in the locker room to display his displeasure with the team.

Be a Rule Maker

Players want the team to be well organized. They want practice and other team activities to begin on time; they want to spend their time meaningfully; they like to know their roles; they want everyone to receive fair treatment; and most of all, they want to win. The coach sets the tone for all those things. His authority may be tested—perhaps daily—but players expect the coach to handle those occurrences and to be the boss.

The rules I felt called on most often to enforce with my teams mainly had to do with time, place, physical condition, and equipment. I required players (and coaches) to be punctual and at the designated site for all team activities, to be physically prepared to do their jobs, and to have the necessary equipment to carry them out.

That meant, if practice began at 10:00 A.M., players had to be at the practice site early enough to receive whatever physical therapy they might need from the trainer, to get their ankles taped (a requirement for all players), and to be dressed in the team practice uniform and on the floor ready to begin workouts at precisely 10 o'clock. The fine for lateness at that time (1970s) was $5 per minute. A missed therapy session or failure to have the necessary equipment cost the player $50; a missed practice, $500; a missed game due to his own negligence, $\frac{1}{82}$ of his salary. A player committing an offense serious enough to be suspended was fined at the rate for missing practices or games. Though I never had to suspend a player, invariably, one or two players on the squad were chronically late for practice or missed bus transportation to airports. Fines for those infractions were deducted from their paychecks and put in a separate fund. At the end of the season, the players and coaches decided what to do with the fund. (I was with some teams that used the fine money for an end-of-season outing for the team, and with others that donated the fund to an agreed-on charity.)

Players recognize the need for discipline, because they all know it's the only way for a team to succeed. But they want the same rules to apply to everyone—they don't want double standards. The rules must apply equally to the stars of the team as to the role players and the benchwarmers.

That is not to say that everyone was expected to follow the same practice routine. Players who log big game minutes are not going to practice as long as those with limited playing time or those who don't play at all. Big-minute players practice long enough to maintain their conditioning at performance levels and to keep teamwork smooth and individual skills sharp. The low-minute players get extra practice time to make sure they're ready to perform well when called on. But everyone must attend, unless excused for a validated illness, injury, or serious family situation. An injured or ill player must have verification from the team doctor to be excused from practice.

Other circumstances demanded implementation of additional rules, as described in the sidebar on drugs and alcohol. Less serious, but still demanding attention was an issue that I believed was having a detrimental impact on player pride: dress code. When I was coaching the Buffalo Braves, pro basketball had no dress code (whereas professional baseball and hockey had compulsory jacket, shirt, and tie dress requirements for players appearing in public). Although many players dressed in the latest fashion, others dressed more "comfortably"; and, occasionally, entire teams adopted a decidedly casual look. One of those teams was my Buffalo Braves.

The Braves I inherited were in their third year of existence in the NBA. Made up mostly of expansion-pool castoffs and draft picks, they were a young and carefree lot who achieved little and from whom little was expected. They dressed in sweatsuits and sneakers to travel, wore floppy caps, and carried their boom boxes with them in airports and on flights—with the volume at near-peak levels. You could hear the Braves coming before you saw them.

The team had meager success in its first two seasons, and even those numbers were skewed because the three expansion teams played each other more often than they played the rest of the teams in the league. Because of their poor record and the fact that they had come from other teams or straight out of college, there was little evidence of team allegiance or pride. On one occasion, I heard a player identify his team as simply "New York" when asked the inevitable airport question, "Which basketball team are you with?" He was hoping the fan would assume he meant the New York Knicks—at the time one of the league's best teams.

Going on a road trip also meant the opportunity to party with friends in the various cities around the league. No curfew hour had been set and some players would come from a night on the town directly to a 10:00 A.M. practice.

That wasn't the attitude or the image that I wanted for a team I was coaching. I believe that, deep down, everyone wants to be proud of the organization with which they're associated. Members may gripe about their superiors or working conditions but innately they want success for their group; and when it comes, they are quick to identify themselves as members, and do so with great pride. Therefore, I instituted some rules for travel including mandatory travel attire.

Suit jackets, dress slacks (no jeans), collared shirts and dress shoes became mandatory for my Braves. Hats, if worn, had to be removed on planes and in dining areas. I established a curfew hour, based on arrival time at a game site and the time the game ended, and placed a prohibition against visitors in a team member's hotel room. I also required players to wear a headset when listening to their personal music.

Light Traveler: Kiki Vandeweghe

The most interesting player I ever observed when traveling was Kiki Vandeweghe, who was with Portland in the mid-1980s. Kiki never checked any luggage, no matter how long the trip. He carried all his gear in a small duffel bag that he stored in the overhead compartment at his seat. In it he had a couple of paperback books, toilet articles, his practice gear (including sneakers), and, I presumed, one change of clothes. He wore corduroy slacks and a white, open-necked polo shirt under a blue blazer. Once on the plane, he rolled up the blazer, squeezed it into his duffel, and settled in to read one of his book selections until the plane arrived at its destination. Everyone connected with the team took great delight in watching Kiki come onboard. Somehow he was always neat and presentable. (He's now the general manager of the Denver Nuggets and has upgraded his wardrobe to conform to a more upscale image demanded by his executive status.)

There was grousing at first, but gradually the players began to take pride in their appearance and team morale perked up, even though the Braves continued to struggle through their third season. I implemented the same rules, with no objection, on teams I coached later.

Lead and Learn

Just as an athlete must exercise his body to be a winner, a leader must exercise his position of authority. If he doesn't, he loses that authority. I first realized this when I was a junior at Upper Darby High School and was studying the works of William Shakespeare. Many passages from his plays seemed to speak directly to me, but one in particular, from *Hamlet*, stood out: "To thine own self be true; And it must follow, as the night the day, Thou canst not then be false to any man." In everyday speech, Shakespeare was saying that if you are straight with yourself, you will be straight with everyone else. That made immediate sense to me, and I decided way back then to try to live my life that way.

That premise influenced my dealings with other people. I wanted them to know that when I said I would do something, they could count on it getting done. I determined to work as hard as possible to complete any task put before me. If I gave my word to someone on a matter of confidence, that person could be assured that the matter would remain between us. Those qualities all seemed to come out of that one quotation from Shakespeare.

I also expected the same treatment in return. In almost every instance, in my personal life and throughout my years of schooling, military service, and professional life in sports and in the field of communications, I felt satisfied that my associates and I had established mutual trust in whatever project was at hand.

One exception occurred after I joined the Portland Trail Blazers. I had decided to leave the Buffalo Braves after a confrontation I had with owner Paul Snyder during the 1976 season (details in Chapter 9), and the word had gotten out that trouble had been brewing between Snyder and me. While my assistant at that time, Tates Locke, was on scouting trips, several teams asked him what he thought my status was for the coming year. Tates told those who inquired the truth: I wasn't going back to Buffalo.

Stu Inman, the player personnel director of the Blazers called to tell me that they might be seeking a new coach (Lenny Wilkens was coaching there at the time) and asked if I would be interested. I responded that if Lenny was not going to coach there, I would indeed be interested, so we set up a meeting.

I met Stu after a Braves-Celtics playoff game in Buffalo, and we discussed the Portland personnel and the kind of game I felt the team could play. The meeting seemed to go well and he told me he'd get back to me.

When he called later, he told me that the team had decided to make the coaching change and that I'd be hired after meeting with the team owner, Larry Weinberg. At the end of that meeting, after Larry and I had talked further about the team and the job, he offered me the position starting at $75,000 plus a number of bonuses that depended on how the team performed. I had been making $100,000 at Buffalo—which Weinberg knew—and wasn't pleased at the proposed cut. I asked for $80,000 and agreed to defer $30,000 of that. We settled on that. The bonuses—$10,000 for each round of the playoffs that the Blazers reached and $25,000 for winning the championship—made me confident that, in the long run, the deal would work to my advantage. I felt the team could make the playoffs—something it had never done in the history of the franchise—and maybe advance to the next round. At the time, I had no thoughts of winning the title, and neither did Weinberg, which was clear when he chuckled as he offered the final bonus for winning the championship.

Perhaps it was a sign of things to come that the change of command was handled awkwardly. The Blazers told Wilkens and his assistant, Tom Meschery, they were fired only one day before they called a press conference to announce my hiring. That left a bad taste in my mouth, in particular because Lenny is one of the class guys in the coaching profession.

The first snag in my own relations with Blazer management came soon after, regarding the car that I was to receive as part of my contract, which stated that the Blazers would provide a car for my use during the time of my employment. At my previous coaching stops, Philadelphia and Buffalo, team management worked out an arrangement with a car rental agency or dealership to provide cars for staff members' use in exchange for advertising or complimentary tickets. I assumed the same would happen at Portland. When I came to Portland for the draft and rookie camp that followed, Harry Glickman said that they had a Ford sports model that Meschery had used when he was with the team and asked if that would be satisfactory. I said yes and used the car for the three weeks I was there for the draft and camp. When I prepared to leave, to return to Ocean City, New Jersey, for the rest of the summer, Inman asked if his daughter might use the car while I was away. I had no objection to that and Stu took the car when I left Portland.

When I received my first paycheck from the Blazers, there was an amount deducted for the car. I thought there was some mistake and called Glickman. He told me that the Blazer policy regarding cars for their personnel was to give a car allowance, and that the person using the car was responsible for whatever amount was above the allowance. I told Harry that my contract called for a car, not a car allowance. He responded that the allowance was team policy and advised me not to "rock the boat." I was not happy with that interpretation but decided to make my own arrangement for a car as soon as I got back to Portland. I worked out a deal with a car rental company and told Glickman that he could have his car back. He appeared pleased with the new arrangement. I was not.

Then, about a week after that glorious first season ended and the Blazers had won the NBA Championship, Glickman called me into his office. He said that as he recalled our contract negotiations (in which he had no part whatsoever) my bonuses from Portland would be reduced by the bonus that the NBA provided. (At that time, an NBA head coach received a full player share of playoff money.) I was flabbergasted. Nothing of the kind had entered into the negotiations I'd had with Weinberg. I could only assume that he and Glickman were trying to avoid paying me the bonus money we'd agreed on. I was steaming, but calmly told Harry that the matter had never been discussed and quickly left his office. Nothing more was said, and I later received the bonus amount called for in my contract.

Shortly thereafter, I made a new contract with the Blazers for more money and fewer bonuses. My last contract with Portland was for $350,000 for each of three years (1985 through 1987). It included an offset provision stipulating that if I left the Blazers before the end of the contract and took another coaching job in the NBA, the money Portland owed would be offset by the salary the new team paid.

In the second year of the contract, the Blazers season didn't go especially well, and I could sense growing dissatisfaction among management concerning my coaching. Also disturbing to me was that the Blazers organization was no longer the "mom and pop" operation it had been when I first came to Portland. They had hired Jon Spoelstra, a marketing wizard, who increased income from radio and television rights fees and got involved in basketball issues as well. One of those issues was his authority to design the team uniforms. Apparently, he had made a deal with a new sports shoe manufacturer, to produce a red basketball shoe, which he assumed the players would wear. But NBA players choose their own brand of shoe, and no one wore Spoeistra's shoes at that time. He called me into his office one day in the summer and had a red basketball shoe sitting on his desk. He was beaming as he asked, "What do you think?" I assumed he wanted my opinion of the shoe and said that it looked all right—not realizing that he took that to mean that I accepted the shoe as a part of the team uniform.

Later in the fall, Spoelstra advertised that the team would unveil its new, red road uniforms at a preseason home game, as if it were a big fashion event. He also made it clear that he expected the players to wear the new, red shoes that he had stocked. Of course, those players with shoe contracts with other manufacturers wouldn't wear the new shoes, and most of them objected to the red color. Now there was a dilemma. Although players were allowed to wear different name brands of shoes, they all had to be the same color. So, at the last minute, Spoelstra sent out for red paint and had trainer Ron Culp and his aides paint over the white shoes that most of the players wore. On game night, the young players with no endorsement wore the new red shoes; the rest wore their regular shoes, painted a red color that didn't match the new ones. It was a distraction that I didn't need at that time of the year when I was getting the team ready for the season.

Spoelstra also expanded the office staff by adding "account executives" who promoted the team avidly while selling advertising. They were talking championship, while I knew the Blazers would struggle to make the playoffs. There was not a good atmosphere around the office, and I began to spend less and less time there.

Weinberg, the owner, was a highly successful land developer in southern California. He lived in Beverly Hills and visited Portland infrequently, but he kept in close touch with Glickman and Inman by telephone. Weinberg also had an assistant in his Beverly Hills office, Harley Frankel, who was a real "Basketball Benny" (a fanatical follower of the game). Frankel liked to dabble with computerized player statistics of minutes played in a game, comparing the team's point production with various combinations of players. He had taken a liking to a young Blazer point guard, Steve Colter, who as a rookie got in the game late or with a pressing team when the team needed a different defensive look. I liked Steve, too. He was a free spirit who hustled on defense and had long-range shooting ability. I put him in some games when the Blazers were trailing, and he knocked down some three-pointers; and sometimes he scored pretty well with the pressing group. But Colter lacked the play-making and defensive skills of the starting point guard, Darnell Valentine. Frankel had compiled numbers that showed that the team was more productive with Colter in the game than with Valentine, and sent me dispatches by mail and called on the phone to talk with me about the matter. I didn't have the time to explain to him that the numbers were deceptive. Colter played a lot of minutes in "garbage time," when games were already decided and opposing defenses loosened up, and he also benefited from playing with the pressing team, whose job it was to force the action for short segments of the game. When I turned Frankel off, he pursued the matter with Rick Adelman, my assistant. I assumed that all of this was done with Weinberg's approval.

Another indication of Weinberg's discontent was the forced resignation of Stu Inman, the team's director of personnel since its inception. Stu had an outstanding record of drafting players who stayed in the league—if not with Portland, on the rosters of other teams. But he was often abrupt in his dealings with Weinberg and rubbed Spoelstra and Frankel the wrong way as well. In contrast, Bucky Buckwalter, a long-time scout for Inman, and a one-year assistant coach, was friendly and cooperative with all three, and was elevated to Inman's vacated post.

The winds of change were blowing, and I sensed that my name was next on the list. Another indicator came when Dave Twardzik, a former player on the championship team (who was then doing color on the radio game broadcasts with Bill Schonley), told me about a conversation he'd had on a crowded office elevator with Marshall Glickman, Harry's son, who had joined the Blazers' management team. According to Dave, the younger Glickman said that the team's problems began with me and that "the coach has to go." I wasn't surprised by Glickman's assessment, but I thought it was in poor taste for him to have made that observation where others, not associated with the team, were within hearing distance. So I called Glickman in and told him what I'd heard. He denied saying it. I called him a liar and told him to leave. I sat back and waited for the fallout. When a team doesn't do well, the coach always takes the brunt of the criticism. That's a given; everyone who enters the coaching profession accepts it. But it is especially discouraging when it comes from your own organization.

Later that day, Harry Glickman apologized for the incident; and the next day, I received a written note from Marshall saying that he had indeed made the remarks but was wrong to have done so and that he regarded me as a "great coach." I didn't respond to either of the Glickmans. The event further distanced me from the management group. More was yet to come.

Blazers fans—the best in the league—had been calling in to a local radio talk show hosted by Steve Jones (who was also the color commentator on Blazers televised games) to find out why the team wasn't doing better. Jones, who had played in the ABA and had had a brief and unproductive career in the NBA—and no coaching experience—had become the Blazers' unofficial spokesperson about the team. He put forth various opinions to answer fans' questions. He never criticized any players, instead implying that different coaching tactics would turn the team around. He made vague references to such changes as extending the defense and using an up-tempo offense. Though I didn't listen to the broadcasts, Rick Adelman did, and he would come to practice steaming about some of the things that Jones had said.

Adelman suggested that we have a face-to-face with Jones, which we did. In defending his position, Jones said that he wasn't being critical, but was only trying to give a player's view of the game. I pointed out that Adelman (in the NBA) and I (in the Eastern League) had as much playing experience as Jones had and discussed other issues with him. He softened his stance somewhat; and although the meeting didn't bring any tangible results, at least Jones knew how we felt.

I also took the opportunity to comment further on Jones's lack of qualification for criticism in my own public forum: a column that I wrote for The Oregonian. After the column appeared, Harry Glickman called me in to say that I'd been pretty tough on Jones. When I rebutted by reminding Glickman of the criticism Jones had been giving me, Harry defended it as being all part of talk radio. I said that I didn't agree with his point of view.

To say that the situation was uncomfortable is an understatement. I felt isolated, counting only on Adelman as an ally. It felt like a me-against-the-world kind of situation. I determined that all I could do was to get the team to play its best basketball, win as many games as we could, then let the chips fall where they may. As in the situation with Buffalo, I sensed that management didn't want me as coach any longer, and I really didn't want to coach under conditions as they were. But with a year left on my contract, I wasn't going to make the first move and resign. If I did that, the team would have no obligation to pay the last year of the contract. If they fired me, they were responsible for paying me the final year.

The Blazers muddled through that season (1985–1986), finishing 40–42, scoring 115 points a game (third best in the league), but allowing 114 points (fourth from the bottom). I was not happy with the results, my coaching, the team, or the organization. We made the playoffs, but lost to Denver in the first round—3 games to 1. After the final game, Weinberg came into the trainer's room, where I was standing alone.

"I think I may want to change coaches," he said. I responded that it was all right with me, adding that I wasn't sure I wanted to coach in Portland another year anyway. He said not to say anything publicly about it and that he would get back to me in a week or so. About a month later, Weinberg called to tell me that he had hired Mike Schuler as coach. Then he said that as he recalled the chronology of events, I had stated that I didn't want to return as coach before he had indicated that there was to be a coaching change. There it was again, another apparent effort to avoid payment called for in my contract. If I had indeed made that statement first, then in effect, I would have resigned, and the Blazers would have had no obligation to pay me the last year of my contract. When I reminded Weinberg exactly how the conversation had gone that day after the Denver loss, he quickly dropped the issue.

Owners have the right to hire and fire. I had no quarrel with that. But I resented a lot of things the Blazers had done over the years, especially their attempts to evade contract obligations and the efforts of Weinberg, Frankel, and Spoelstra in recent years to insinuate themselves into my coaching responsibilities.

So, in that state of mind, when I agreed late in the summer to coach Indiana, I resorted to some subterfuge of my own. I specified to Indiana that I would take only $100,000 of the $400,000 due me in the first year and defer the balance until after I had finished coaching in the NBA. With the offset stipulation of the Portland contract, the Blazers were still responsible for $250,000 of the final year of my contract with them. Weinberg was irate and accused me of "double-dipping"—which of course I was, but in a legal manner. He refused to pay anything, including deferred money that was due me after I retired. We were at a stalemate for several months.

Finally, I called him and suggested that we split the monetary difference. He continued to object, saying that taking a salary of only $100,000 was unrealistic. "You're Jack Ramsay," he exclaimed. I reminded him that I had been Jack Ramsay when he offered me $75,000 to take the job in Portland, even though I had made $100,000 the year before in Buffalo. He paused, agreed to the settlement, then added, "I guess we were both wrong."

I had won a small victory, but I didn't feel good about any of it. I had always fulfilled my obligations in every job I'd ever had in a straightforward manner and I didn't like the revenge motives that had prompted my actions in this matter. That wasn't how I had lived my life. In my disgruntlement, I had forgotten that line from Shakespeare: "to thine own self be true . . ." I vowed I'd never do that kind of thing again. And I never have.

Though my experience with Blazers management clouded my recollections of the organization for some time, I always kept fond memories of the players and fans, as well as an appreciation for living in the great Northwest, Portland in particular. To this day, I think of those years as the best period of my professional experience in basketball. And I've found the old adage "time heals all wounds" to be true. I now accept that, to Blazer management, the practices I found objectionable were just a matter of "doing business"; nothing personal was intended.

Many years ago, Weinberg began sending a family greeting card at the Christmas season, which was nice to receive; and he was very cordial when I saw him at a couple of Lakers games that I helped broadcast for ESPN radio. Then, late in 1992, I received a phone call from Glickman, who stayed with the Blazers as president after Weinberg sold his interest in the team to Paul Allen in 1988. Harry told me that the Blazers were

Getting Technical: Jack Ramsay

In one other instance, I failed to follow my "be true to self" motto, and with similar results.

With few exceptions, I got along well with officials. When I started coaching in the NBA, there was a widely held belief that the coach who got the first technical called on him got the breaks from the referees, and his team usually won the game. I wasn't sure I believed it, but I wasn't going to take the chance that it wasn't true—even though in 17 years of high school and college basketball coaching, I had never been given a technical foul, preferring to concentrate on coaching my teams rather than worry about the officiating.

So, for a few years, I became a sideline tyrant, frequently badgering officials, becoming one of the league "leaders" in technical fouls received. It wasn't really who I was, but I thought it was necessary for my team to win.

When I went to Portland to coach the Trail Blazers, I started with the same approach until one particular game when I went out to half-court to berate an official instead of going to the bench to talk to my team at a timeout. Bill Walton intercepted me before I got within shouting range of the official and said, "Coach, don't you know that we don't play well when you do that?" That stopped me dead in my tracks and changed my bench behavior for as long as I coached after that.

going to retire my number (77)—the year of the championship season—at a home game in mid-January 1993. I was pleasantly surprised and greatly appreciative of this gracious gesture by the Blazers management. It turned out to be a most enjoyable event and gave me a chance to properly thank the Portland fans for their generous and loyal support during my tenure as coach. In more recent years, I've met with all those involved in that difficult period of my time with the Blazers, and would like to feel that I have friendships with them all.

Lead On

A leader must exercise his position of authority. If he doesn't, he loses that authority. I felt that I'd let the intrusion of others erode my authority as coach at Portland and hadn't taken the necessary steps to correct it. Perhaps it wouldn't have worked out there anyway; I may have stayed too long with the Blazers—10 years is a long time to coach at any NBA location. Although the player rosters change over the years, team management and the fans are more permanent; and sometimes they tire of the same message from the coach. But even if it was time to move on anyway, I nevertheless regret that I didn't make more of an effort to hold onto the authority that comes with the position of coach.

At Indiana, the setting was right for me to reclaim that position. And, initially, it looked as though things might come together as I hoped. As it turned out, the experience would lead me down another path altogether.

After a highly successful period, which included three championships in the ABA, the team had struggled the 10 years it was in the NBA. The Pacers had made the NBA playoffs only once, and that under my former assistant Jack McKinney. They had won only 22 and 26 games in the two previous seasons.

The Pacers were owned by Herb and Mel Simon, civic-minded international real estate developers; Donnie Walsh was the team president. I brought in Dick Harter as my assistant. We inherited a roster of good, not great players (by NBA standards)—Herb Williams, Wayman Tisdale, Vern Fleming, Steve Stipanovich, Ron Anderson, and Clint Richardson. Clark Kellogg was a solid player with All-Star capabilities, but he had a serious knee injury and would play in only four games for me before retiring. Walsh had drafted Chuck Person, a high-scoring small forward from Auburn, and had traded for John Long, a tough-minded 2-guard, and Kyle Macy, a long-range shooter. That was the team we went to war with. Making the playoffs was my objective, but I knew it would be difficult to accomplish.

The Pacers scratched and clawed their way to a 41–41 finish that season (1986–1987) and a place in the playoffs. Although we lost to

Atlanta in the first round (3–1), we all felt a sense of accomplishment. Six players scored in double figures, led by Person's 18.8. Chuck also led the team in rebounds and was voted the Rookie of the Year. The team played hard, there was a good response from the players to the things Harter and I were emphasizing, and team morale appeared good.

In the following season (1987–1988), we had added Reggie Miller to the roster, and we appeared to be headed for the playoffs again, but then faltered down the stretch drive. I sensed that the level of team play was eroding and connected it in part with Person's apparent first priority of scoring 20 points a game. I had addressed that issue with him on several occasions, but didn't see improvement in his play. Then, at a practice session, I stopped a scrimmage after Person's matchup, Ron Anderson, beat him several times going to the basket. I told Chuck emphatically that his play was unacceptable. He tried to pass it off lightly, and I cut him off. We had heated words, and I told him to leave the practice: "Chuck, just go home."

We exchanged expletives and he left the court, but not the gym. He sat in the stands at the end of the court, and when practice ended, I went to him and we talked it out. I told him that we needed a better all-round effort from him if we were going to finish the season the way we both wanted. He said that he understood, apologized for his behavior, and offered to reiterate the apology in front of the team. I told him that it wasn't necessary and thought the incident was over.

It wasn't. The rest of the squad regarded my action as backing down in a face-to-face confrontation. Team morale wasn't the same after that, and I had no one to blame but myself. I should have taken a stronger stand. When Person didn't leave the gym, I should have told him he would be suspended if he didn't. If he had left then, I would probably have retained my position of authority. If he had still refused to leave, I would have had to make certain that he was suspended.

The team limped through the conclusion of the schedule, made a belated charge at the final playoff spot by winning consecutive road games at Detroit and Atlanta, but lost a season-ending showdown to the Knicks at home, when Stipanovich's layup attempt to tie the game rimmed out at the buzzer.

That loss caused Indiana to finish with the same record, 38–44, as New York and Washington, and in a three-way tie for the final two play-off spots in the Eastern Conference. But since the Knicks and Bullets (now Wizards) had a better winning percentage in games played among the three teams, they both went to the playoffs and the Pacers didn't. It was a frustrating way to finish the season.

Postseason, I talked with Walsh about making personnel changes. I liked Stipanovich, Fleming, and Miller, but was willing to deal anybody else. I wasn't happy with the contributions of Williams and Tisdale and wasn't sure if Person was ever going to be a solid team player. Walsh said he'd pursue opportunities. It didn't happen.

The Pacers had the second pick in the 1998 draft and chose 7–3 foot center Rik Smits. I supported the selection, although I knew that Rik needed a lot of experience before he could make a positive contribution. I expected him to play behind Stipanovich until he adjusted to the NBA game. But then Stipanovich, the glue to the Pacers' interior game, was diagnosed with a career-ending knee condition. That left the rookie Smits to handle the center position.

The Pacers got off to a terrible start that season (1988–1989). Training camp, the time when a coach gets his team organized, did not go well. Smits, who needed a crash course in NBA basketball, wasn't able to play at all for several sessions because Reebok, the shoe company with which he made a late deal, hadn't finished production of the special shoes he required for his unusual foot structure. The season was on us before we were ready and I wasn't happy with either the personnel or the direction the season was taking.

In an early season game at Phoenix, the Pacers came from behind to take the lead, then gave the game away in the closing minutes with careless misplays. The loss put our record at 0 and 7. On the bus ride back to the hotel, several of the players were laughing it up as if we had won. In my earlier years of coaching, I would have stopped the bus and told the players that if they wanted to laugh about the game we had just lost, they could do it while walking back to the hotel. This time I sat and listened, and came to realize I didn't want to coach anymore. I didn't want to agonize through a losing season with players who didn't seem to care, and feel unable to change that attitude.

When the bus arrived back at the hotel, I told Walsh how I felt and resigned as coach. (The Pacers went through three other coaches that year—Mel Daniels, George Irvine, and Dick Versace—and ended with a 28–54 record. Midway through the season, both Williams and Tisdale were traded. The Pacers received Detlef Schrempf, La Salle Thompson, and Randy Wittman in exchange.) I felt good about my decision. I always believed that a person should enjoy his work life, and if the time came when the enjoyment was no longer there, it was time to do something else. I had completed a long (20 years) coaching career in the NBA and, until the end, had enjoyed it thoroughly. Coaching is an extremely challenging job, and I had achieved a measure of success at every level. But the events at Portland and Indiana indicated to me that it was time to put active coaching aside and do something else with my life. Opportunities for a life outside the NBA came quickly.

Lead by Example

I agree with David Stern: Those in leadership positions don't often analyze themselves while in that role. Looking back at myself now, I think my players would say that I led by example and by doing. I was a hands-on coach. I tried to stay in top physical condition, ate a proper diet, abstained from drugs, and consumed only modest amounts of alcohol, to show that what I was demanding of them, I was also demanding of myself. While I didn't have NBA-level basketball skills, I was able to demonstrate adequately what I wanted done on the floor. I worked hard at developing an effective team game, spent long hours analyzing opponents, and never gave up on an opportunity—no matter how slight—to win a game.

Leaders do the things they do without introspection because they are just being themselves. Occasionally a coach gets feedback from his players that helps him know if he's on the right track. I once heard Bill Walton say in an interview, "If our team was behind by 8 points with a few seconds left to play in the game, Jack Ramsay would design a 9-point play at the last timeout." That was an exaggeration, but it emphasized Walton's belief that, for me, the game was never over until the final horn sounded.

At the 20th reunion of that championship team, another player, Bob Gross, paid me this compliment: "You were the best I ever played for at making key decisions in close games." At a later meeting of that team, I said that it was the unselfishness of the players that made that team great, but Lloyd Neal shook his head and said, "You were the one; we just followed you."

I realize that memories improve with the years, but I must admit to being proud to hear comments like those from my players. What they said indicated that I had been the kind of coach that I wanted to be.

The Inside Man

Internal Leadership

THE BEST DISCIPLINE IS that which comes from within. Self-disciplined people know what they must do to meet their responsibilities. They set priorities in their lives and faithfully observe daily routines that equip them to reach their goals. They have a high level of determination—nothing stands in the way of accomplishing their appointed tasks.

Many athletes have this kind of self-discipline. Their coach needs only to point them in the right direction and they'll do the rest. They're punctual, reliable, and responsible self-starters. Not surprisingly, often they also become internal team leaders.

Internal leadership is vital to establishing a strong core of discipline and rapport among team members. It is created when one or more members of a group set positive standards, in addition to those that the leader espouses. This internal example has the potential to forge goals or modes of conduct and behavior that the group leader cannot achieve alone.

Internal leadership can be as simple as an unspoken—and momentary—demonstration of purpose from a single team member. The following incident took place prior to a game when I was coaching the Portland Trail Blazers. John Davis and a couple of other players were standing in front of a bulletin board on which were posted the current stats of the Blazers, alongside those of the rest of the NBA teams. This was standard practice each week so that players could see their individual and team stats (which I used occasionally to compare how the Blazers stood with other teams in the league and to show where a player had to upgrade his numbers to help the team be more successful).

Maurice Lucas strode into the room that night, looked over the heads of those standing in front of the bulletin board, saw what they were reading, and with one swoop of his big hand, ripped the stats from the board and threw them in the trash can, before heading to his locker and starting to dress. Davis (who reminded me of this incident at the August 2002 reunion of the champion Trail Blazers) said Luke didn't say a word, but the serious look on his face carried a strong message. Davis interpreted it to mean that the Blazers wouldn't win games by looking at stat sheets but instead by playing successfully on the floor. "Luke's attitude told us it was time to lace 'em up. We went back to our lockers, sat down, and got ourselves mentally ready to play." To this day, Davis remembers that spontaneous show of leadership by Lucas as having been "very powerful." Moreover, it is invaluable to a leader as a wonderful dynamic that can only enhance a team's focus and success.

Powerful Insiders

Internal leadership is even more powerfully demonstrated on a continuous or regular basis by standout players on a team—often marquee names, but sometimes the role-players, too. One of the foremost attributes of great "inside men" is their ability to improve other players. Four outstanding examples of this characteristic are "greats" Larry Bird, Michael Jordan, Joe Dumars, and "role-player" Avery Johnson.

The Legend: Larry Bird

Almost from his first season (1979–1980), the Boston Celtics were Bird's team; he was clearly their leader, but he did it more by example than by word. During warm-ups, he was intensely focused on his preparation—all business, a look of cold concentration on his face. In stark contrast was his teammate Kevin McHale. He chatted with teammates and opposing players, exchanging quips with both groups, as if getting ready for a night of fun. Only Robert Parish was stoical like Bird; most of the other Celts behaved more like McHale.

When I asked Bird how he handled the differences in demeanor of those players, he said, "I always had a sense of what people needed, and tried to give it to them. Each of those guys was different. You should have seen our locker room. It was wild. I remember when [Danny] Ainge, before a big playoff game, went around the locker room with a stethoscope, listening to everybody's heartbeat, pronouncing this guy ready and another guy needing to pump it up some. It was a circus. But when he came to me, he passed right by. He knew better than to come to me with that thing.

"Sometimes I'd have to say, 'Hey, that's enough!' and things would quiet down. If it really got out of hand, I'd turn my chair around to face my locker with my back to the room. They got the message then."

Bird was a fierce competitor, another leadership characteristic. Celtics coach Bill Fitch (1979–1983) had always regarded Bob Gibson, the great St. Louis Cardinals pitcher, as the toughest competitor he had come across—until Bird came on the scene. (Fitch had been head coach of baseball at Creighton University and assisted in basketball, where Gibson played both.) Fitch remembers, "After baseball practice, Gibson and I played one-on-one basketball back in the gym. We had some knockdown, drag-out battles—sometimes lasting well into the evening. I never thought I'd again see the likes of him as a competitor. But Larry made Bob look like a Boy Scout by comparison."

Fitch said it was no accident that so many of the Celtics improved on their performances of the previous season after Bird joined the team. Bird led the team in scoring and was second in assists. Seven other players averaged double figures in points. Veterans Nate Archibald and Dave

In-flight Collision: Jack Ramsay and Larry Bird

I experienced Bird's unbridled will to win firsthand during a game I coached at Boston Garden. I was crouched at the sideline in front of the Blazers bench when a ball was knocked loose in my direction. As I waited, I caught a glimpse of Bird coming at me full bore, trying to save the ball. I half rose to try to break his fall as the ball reached me. But Bird—in midair—crashed into me and carried both of us through the bench chairs into the second row of seats. (I had heard people say that they "saw stars" after taking a hard blow. I discovered that it actually happens—I saw stars.) Then I heard his voice, with that Indiana twang: "You all right, coach?" I was a bit stunned, but I wasn't going to admit it. I told him that I was fine, and play resumed.

Jim Lynam, my assistant at the time, said to me after the game, "I think the Birdman did it on purpose. He was looking right at you when he came after the ball . . . like you were his target." Years later, I asked Larry about that incident. He remembered it, but said that the collision hadn't been intentional. "I wouldn't do that," he said. But he had just the slightest trace of a smile on his face when he said it, and that keeps me wondering to this day.

Cowens had significantly better seasons as the Celts turned around the team's direction, from 29–53 to 61–21. It all started with Bird's confidence, competitiveness, and his team attitude.

Another leadership role Bird took on was as reenforcer for Fitch. If Fitch "got on" a player, Bird would prod the player to work on the same things that Fitch carped about. Fitch recalls specifically when the Celtics acquired Robert Parish: "Right from the beginning I rode him like Gene Autry rode Champion. Robert must have wanted to kill me on some of those days. Then Larry would get on him to do the same things I wanted from him, and Robert seemed to take it better from him."

Fitch also recalled that Bird was just as focused in practice as in games. "Larry wouldn't let anybody play less than all-out. He made practice scrimmages like the seventh game of a playoff series—every day."

Don Casey, an assistant to Chris Ford (who coached the Celtics between 1990 and 1995), confirms what Fitch had to say about Bird's intensity during practice. (The Celts' practices at that time consisted mostly of seven field goal scrimmages, and Ford gave Casey the task of organizing drills to supplement the scrimmage segments.) Except for some individual shooting, practices ended after a series of such scrimmages. Casey recalls, "Birdie didn't say a lot, but when he talked, everybody listened. Mostly, he just played and everybody took their cue from that. He played all-out all the time, and expected the other players to do the same."

One of Casey's drills was aimed at establishing a secondary fast break. The purpose was to get the team into a flow of action that would allow good shots if the first fast-break wave didn't produce a score. In it, any player might end up with an open shot from any position on the court. Casey said that at one particular practice, after running through the drill several times, Bird drew Casey aside and asked, "How long is your contract here?" Casey responded that he had a two-year deal. Bird paused as if mulling over a serious proposition, then said, "Two years, huh? I guess I can get you a ring [a championship] in two years—but I've got to get to that box. See that box down there [pointing to the square at the low post on the right side of the floor]: that's my box. We can do all that other shit, as long as I get the ball in that box. If you can do that often enough, I may be able to get you that ring."

Casey revised the drill so that Bird got to his favorite box in the secondary break, and the Celts finished first in the Atlantic Division with 56 wins. But, by then, Bird had developed serious back problems that severely hampered his play. He missed 22 games that season, and 37 more the next, and retired after the latter season. The Celts lost to Detroit then Cleveland, in the Conference Semifinals in those two years, and Casey never did get his championship ring.

Air of Greatness: Michael Jordan

Who knew Michael Jordan would become the greatest ever to play the game? Not Jack Ramsay or Stu Inman, who could have drafted him for Portland but opted for center Sam Bowie when Michael was available as

Tunnel of Love: Don Casey and Larry Bird

In his last playing season, Bird's back bothered him so much that not only was he unable to play, he often couldn't sit for any length of time and didn't even attend the home games. But for a late-season big game, he felt well enough to attend the game in the old Boston Garden. As the players lined up to go out for warm-ups, Casey took his usual position at the end of the player line. But this time Bird was behind him, dressed in street clothes.

Casey still recalls being in the tunnel that led to the court when the crowd caught a glimpse of Bird. A roar started, crescendoing into an earsplitting din as Bird emerged into full view. As they walked toward the bench, Bird leaned forward and shouted into Casey's ear, "Don't think for even one second that any of that is for you."

Casey loved the Birdman, who never missed a chance to needle him.

the second pick in the 1984 College Draft. Not Kevin Loughery, coach of the Chicago Bulls, who drafted Jordan as a third pick, after Hakeem Olajuwon (to Houston) and Bowie. Not James Worthy, a teammate of Jordan's at North Carolina when the Tarheels won the NCAA tournament in 1982. Not even Michael—until he found out what the NBA was all about and Loughery isolated him in one-on-one situations.

Who knew?

But the first time Loughery saw Michael on the practice floor, he *did* know. Loughery's Bulls had a poor record—27 and 55 in 1983–1984. As soon as he saw how good Michael was, Kevin built the offense around Jordan's ability to beat his man—which MJ found that he could do at will. Jordan led the league in total points that season, and the Bulls record improved to 38 and 44 and a spot in the playoffs.

I asked James Worthy several years ago about Michael's development into a great player. Worthy said, "Michael was a freshman during my last season at UNC. He was good (MJ averaged 13.5 points a game that season), but he wasn't the dominating player he became. Every so often in practice he'd put on a special move or fly in the air for a huge dunk, and we'd say 'Hey, Michael, that's pretty good,' but it wasn't like he was killing people every day or anything like that.

"But there was one thing about Michael even then: He had to be first in everything. Coach [Dean] Smith made us make a certain number of consecutive free throws at the end of practice before we could leave the floor. MJ ran to be the first to shoot his free throws, so he could be first off the court, so he could be first in the shower room, so he could be first dressed, so he could be first back at the dining hall, so he could pick out the best steak for his dinner. That was Michael even back in those days. But it never entered my mind that he would be as great a player as he's become."

But the man who would become the best (Jordan led the league in scoring a record 10 times in a row; held the highest career average points per game, 30.12, after the 2002–2003 season; played for a team that won six NBA titles; and was named the NBA Finals Most Valuable Player on all six occasions) was cut from his high school team in Wilmington, North Carolina, as a sophomore. It was then he became determined to prove to basketball people that he was good enough—good enough to play on the high school team, good enough to play at UNC, good enough to play on its NCAA collegiate championship team (1982) and later on two U.S. Olympic gold medal basketball teams (1984 and 1992).

In addition to his athletic talent, which he elevated by his work ethic and competitive nature, Michael possessed many natural leadership skills. Like Bird, he was a leader by example; he also had good speech habits and wasn't reluctant to speak out to improve or correct a situation that pertained to team performance. But he took his time in asserting himself as the Bulls' internal leader. When he first came into the NBA, the Bulls already had many veteran players such as Orlando Woolridge, Dave Corzine, and Steve Johnson; and Michael felt it would have been "disastrous" to be the vocal leader at that time. "So I had to work my game into a situation where *it* became the leadership. Then, when they turned the team [personnel] over a couple of times, I became more of a veteran. That's when I started to speak out a little bit more. From that point, my game, as well as

my voice, became the leader, because of the winning attitude that I have
and the competitive nature that I have."

Jordan's development both as a player and as a leader expanded still
further under Phil Jackson, who took over the Bulls' coaching reins from
Doug Collins (Kevin Loughery's successor) in 1989. John Bach, an assistant to Jackson at Chicago, said that Phil helped to develop Michael's
leadership skills by getting MJ to be more aware of improving the play of
his teammates. According to Bach, Jackson told Michael that he'd just be
known as a high scorer who never won a championship unless he made
his teammates better and the team won. The winning started the second
season that Jackson and Jordan were together with the Bulls.

Michael agreed with Bach's assessment: "I think initially I had that
strong individual talent that could demolish a defense; but Detroit made
me change that. Their defense [the so-called Jordan Rules] made me involve other players to where they became threats; then if they focused on
[my teammates], I could attack. That was the whole idea of the Triangle
[offense]. I resisted it initially because I didn't see how it utilized my talent. But Phil made me figure out things about my game and how to continue to progress as a player. Instead of just relentlessly utilizing my talent,
I had to think about how to get other players involved. He challenged me
and I think he made me a much better player—even today. Now I'm trying to pass that along to other players."

By "passing it along," MJ was referring to the leadership role he had
taken with the Washington Wizards. When Jordan retired from basketball after the final Bulls' championship (1998), he bought into ownership of the Washington Wizards in January 2000, becoming president of
basketball operations. Dissatisfied with the progress of his team, Jordan
revamped the coaching staff, hired Doug Collins, a former mentor with
the Bulls, and returned as a player in 2001. The Wizards were at a playoff
pace that season until Jordan's knee problems forced him out of the
lineup after he had played in only 60 games.

After knee surgery and strenuous rehabilitation during the summer,
Jordan came back for the 2002–2003 season—during which he turned
40—to try one last time to make the Wizards a playoff team. He competed fiercely despite chronic back problems and an aching knee, scoring

in the 40s when his team needed it, but also defending, rebounding, setting screens, assisting for scores, diving for loose balls—whatever it took. Michael took responsibility not only for his own game, but for the Wizards' total team performance, as well as the development of the team's young talent. It was an awesome task.

I watched Jordan closely during games: He worked his defender to get his own shot; gave up open shots to pass inside to Kwame Brown or Brendan Haywood; set up Jerry Stackhouse for an open look; or screened away from the ball to involve rookie Juan Dixon in the offense. Michael talked and directed—sometimes pushing a slow reactor to the proper spot on defense. He gave instruction during dead balls and vocally encouraged those who made the proper plays.

I asked MJ during that season if this was the greatest challenge he had ever faced as a player. He answered, "By far . . . the greatest. I'm 40 years old, trying to exert these types of energies, as well as mentally trying to help these kids understand. It's by far the toughest [challenge] because they don't really understand and they think they do. That's the biggest issue."

Great Expectations: Michael Jordan

Jordan has always been as demanding of himself as he is of his teammates. If he doesn't think a player is expending enough energy, or doesn't have the mental toughness to withstand pressure situations, he rides him hard. His theory is that if a player can't handle that stress, what can the team expect from him in big games?

Prior to the 1992–1993 season, the Bulls acquired Rodney McCray from Dallas. MJ had doubts about McCray's toughness and rode him relentlessly at practices. John Bach watched this and spoke to Michael about being too hard on McCray. MJ responded, "If he can't take it here, how's he going to help us when we need him?"

McCray, a marginal contributor to that championship Bulls team, was gone after one season. Many years later, when I asked him about McCray, Jordan said simply, "He couldn't play, coach."

(continued)

The flipside of Jordan's take-no-prisoners expectations of others is his loyalty to those who have earned his respect and trust. The 2002–2003 Wizards staff was dotted with MJ's "guys." Head coach Doug Collins and assistant John Bach are former Bulls; assistant general manager Rod Higgins, director of player personnel Fred Whitfield, assistant coaches Larry Drew and Patrick Ewing; scouts Walter Davis, Darrell Walker, and Scott Howard; and conditioning coach Jim Hughes, who worked with Tim Grover in Chicago, all have connections with Jordan that go back many years.

On a more personal note, when Jordan arrived in Chicago for the first time after being drafted in 1984, no one met him at O'Hare Airport. George Koehler, who had a small limousine service in Chicago, was there to pick up a passenger who didn't show up. Koehler, a big hoops fan, recognized MJ as he came from the airport. He said to himself, "That's Michael Jordan!" He went quickly to Jordan and, in his excitement said, "You're *Larry* Jordan"—the name of a teammate of Koehler's from high school and, coincidentally, Michael's brother's name. Before he had time to recover from his faux pas, Michael said, "No, Larry's my brother. I'm Michael."

Koehler broke the ice by explaining his mistake, drove Jordan to his hotel, and gave him his business card, telling him to call if he ever needed anything. Two weeks later, he got a call from Michael asking him to pick up MJ's parents at the airport, and then to be at their disposal during their visit to Chicago.

That was 19 years ago. Since then, Koehler has become MJ's reliable associate, at home and on the road, serving as a kind of security guard/personal friend. "I love it," he told me. "You couldn't find a better guy to work for."

MJ also has great people skills. I've never seen anyone as good with people as Michael. He appears to have time for everybody. I've watched him before games, mingling with 40 or 50 friends and fans—unhurried, shaking hands, exchanging hugs, posing for pictures—then going into the locker room, putting on his uniform, and dropping 40 or 50 points on some unfortunate opponent.

Jordan hung up the Nikes after the 2002–2003 season—he swears for the last time—after the Wizards failed to make the playoffs again. MJ put up admirable numbers: 37 minutes, 20 points, 6 rebounds, and just under 4 assists a game, not up to vintage Jordan standards, but remarkable for a player in his 40th year.

Jordan's intention was to devote his full attention to getting the Wizards on the playoff track. He was keenly disappointed that his efforts on the court didn't bring that about, but was determined to find a way to get it done from the front office.

Owner Abe Pollin had a different plan. Shortly after the season ended, Pollin severed Jordan's position with the Wizards. Coach Doug Collins and others on Michael's hand-picked staff—including assistant general manager, Rod Higgins, and personnel director, Fred Whitfield—were later eased out of the organization. Michael and the basketball world were stunned. Pollin cited his wish to go in another direction and that was that.

Jordan deserved better treatment than that. He had breathed life and energy into a franchise gasping for survival and was dismissed without so much as a proper explanation. MJ issued this statement, which summed up his feelings: "Without prior discussion with me, ownership informed me that it had unilaterally decided to change our mutual long-term understanding. I am shocked by this decision and by the callous refusal to offer me any justification to it." (The Wizards later hired Eddie Johnson, a long-time assistant at New Jersey, as coach, and Ernie Grunfeld, former general manager of Milwaukee, as president of basketball operations.)

Immediately following his sudden departure from the Wizards, speculation surfaced that Jordan would join Bob Johnson, new owner of the Charlotte Bobcats, due to enter the league for the 2004–2005 season, as its head of basketball operations and perhaps as an investor. Nothing happened.

Then, around the time of the NBA Draft, there was a report that Jordan was heading up a group to purchase the Milwaukee Bucks, which owner Herb Kohl had put on the market during the just-completed season. Kohl acknowledged that he was negotiating with Jordan's group, but at the last moment—although graciously acknowledging Jordan's interest, time, and efforts—he decided not to sell.

I hope Jordan will find an activity in the NBA that suits his considerable talents, fuels his competitive fires, and enables him to continue an association with the game he loves.

Too Good to Be Bad: Joe Dumars

Joe Dumars, from McNeese State (Louisiana), was Detroit's first-round pick—the 18th selection overall—in the 1985 NBA Draft. Although he had good stats as a collegiate player, few in the NBA expected him to develop into such an outstanding player for the Pistons.

Stan Novak, a scout for the Pistons at the time, recalls that Dumars dominated the Southwest Conference when he played at McNeese. "The more I saw him, the more impressed I became. I knew he'd be the perfect complement to Isiah [Thomas]. But we never thought we'd get him with the eighteenth pick. We thought he'd be long gone by then."

Dumars was a 6–3, 195-pound 2-guard; he averaged 16 points a game in 14 seasons for the Pistons and remains the team's career leader in games played and three-point field goals attempted and made. He ranks second in total points, assists, and steals.

Maurice Cheeks, a guard on Philadelphia teams of the same era and now the coach of the Portland Trail Blazers, remembers him as a great team player—a quiet, tough-minded defender who also could score. "He was one of the 'Bad Boys' [as the Pistons of that era were known], but he didn't play like that. He just played hard. He was a great player; you'll never hear a bad word from anybody about Joe D." Novak goes so far as to say, "Joe Dumars is the nicest human being among all the players that I ever met."

Even coaching against him, he came across to me as a selfless, steady, high-energy player who gave his best effort in every game he played. He and Thomas formed a dynamic backcourt. Thomas initiated the team offense, while Dumars took on the opposition's top perimeter scorer, backed up Thomas at the point, and seemed to knock down every open shot that came his way. Dumars was the NBA Finals MVP when the Pistons won the title in 1989 and was a key player when they won again in 1990.

Dumars always had the respect of those in the league for his intensity and integrity. He was the inaugural recipient of the NBA Sportsmanship Award (1996), an award now named in his honor. When he retired after the 1998–1999 season, the Pistons retired his number, 4. But Dumars' influence on the team was to continue. The next season, he joined the Pistons front office as vice president of player personnel; then, in 2000, he was elevated to president of basketball operations. He set about orchestrating the Pistons return to power. Although he appeared to be somewhat reserved and reticent as a player, Dumars says that he has "always been vocal enough to convey my vision" and has never had a problem saying what needed to be said. But, he adds, "I don't pontificate beyond that. I'm not a soapbox kind of guy."

Detroit was 42–40 in Joe D's first season in personnel work and made the playoffs, but was swept by Miami in the opening round. Then, in 2001, the Pistons lost free agent Grant Hill to Orlando, an event seen by many as a devastating blow to the franchise. But Dumars worked out a sign-and-trade deal with the Magic that brought Ben Wallace and Chucky Atkins to his team. He also signed free agent Joe Smith—for just one year as it turned out—and worked out a deal to bring Corliss Williamson to the Motor City. Although the Pistons' record dipped to 32–50, the makings of a good team were starting to fall in place.

Before the 2002 season began, Dumars had put the pieces together. He hired Rick Carlisle as head coach, after talking with some more experienced candidates (Rick had never been a head coach, but had been a valued assistant to Larry Bird at Indiana). He said of his decision, "Rick was very well organized; he knew the game and knew the league; said what he wanted to say in an easy-to-understand, efficient manner; and got to the point quickly. Rick is very disciplined, very poised. I thought he'd be able to transmit those qualities to our players—and he did." Carlisle was named Coach of the Year for 2002.

In that same year, Dumars traded John Wallace and Jud Buechler to Phoenix for Cliff Robinson, traded Mateen Cleaves to Sacramento for Jon Barry, acquired rookie Zeljko Rebraca from Toronto for a second-round draft pick, and signed free agent Damon Jones. The Pistons went 50–32, reversing their record from the year before, and won the Central Division.

In the playoffs, Detroit nipped Toronto, three games to two, but was eliminated by Boston, 4–1, in the Conference Semifinals.

Before the 2003 season, Dumars went to work again: He traded Jerry Stackhouse to Washington for Richard Hamilton and Hubert Davis; signed free agent point guard Chauncey Billups; drafted versatile Tayshaun Prince late in the first round; and signed Mehmet Okur of Turkey, the team's second-round pick in 2001. All the new acquisitions made significant contributions as the Pistons won the Central Division, again with a 50–32 record, the best in the Eastern Conference.

In the playoffs, the Pistons fell behind Orlando, one game to three, but battled back to win that series. Then they beat Philadelphia in six hard-played games, but were swept, 4–0, by New Jersey in the Conference Finals.

During the playoffs, there had been some rumblings of player discontent with Carlisle's player rotations and aloof manner. Although Rick was finishing the second year of a three-year contract, there had been no talks of extending the deal, despite the team's success. Shortly after the playoffs were over, Dumars announced that Carlisle would not be retained; and soon after that, Larry Brown, who had permission to leave an unfulfilled contract at Philadelphia, was appointed the Pistons' new head coach.

Dumars was never specific about why he felt a coaching change was in order, and Carlisle dismissed his ouster as typical of the uncertainties of the coaching profession. But the feeling around Detroit was that the decision to make the coaching changes was made by Bill Davidson, owner of the Detroit franchise, who disliked Carlisle's sometimes abrupt manner—especially when dealing with staff members. Dumars, ever the team man, simply said, "I'll take the arrows [criticism]."

But Dumars had to feel uncomfortable with those events. He had told me earlier in the season that he took pride in his ability to deal with his players and coaches with complete honesty. "They know me. They know I'm going to be straight with them. I can't be something I'm not, and that makes the relationships easier to flow."

Going into the 2003–2004 season, Joe D had a new highly successful coach, Brown, and one of the prizes of the 2003 draft, 7-foot Darko

Early Lead: Joe Dumars and Chuck Daly

Chuck Daly, Dumars' coach during the championship years, recalled Joe's early days with the Pistons. "We had some strong personalities with that team—Isiah Thomas and Bill Laimbeer—who were very vocal; Joe was just a rookie, but stayed above it, quietly watching, with a kind of knowing smile on his face. He was quiet, but he was never afraid to express himself.

"I already had good guards on that team—Thomas, Vinnie Johnson, John Long—and Joe came to training camp overweight. The team struggled early that year until I put Joe in the starting lineup, then we took off. He never came out of it [the starting lineup] after that. Joe played both ends [of the court] and did everything well—defended, handled, shot the ball—and I never had to worry about him. He was always there. Joe probably never got the recognition he deserved."

Daly also remembers that Dumars led by the way he played— hard and for the team—all the time. "But I noticed that he became involved in business opportunities early on and appeared to do well with them. I knew that Joe D was going to do all right in life."

Milicic, to complement an already strong Pistons team. His goal remains the same: Get the Pistons back at the championship level.

Don't bet against it.

Best Leader in a Supporting Role: Avery Johnson

Though his playing skills were never at the caliber of Bird, Jordan, and Dumars, Avery Johnson's leadership skills most assuredly are. These leadership traits appeared early, he says. "I've always been a leader, from the time I played kids' basketball. I wasn't always the best player, but I was always a leader on the court."

Johnson attended St. Augustine High School, in New Orleans, and began his college career at New Mexico Junior College, which he attended for a year, before enrolling at Cameron University (Oklahoma). His stats at either school didn't attract serious attention, but he hooked on at Southern University, where his game took off. Just as notable, he formed a great relationship there with Coach Ben Jobe, and after sitting out a year as a transfer student, Avery became Jobe's dynamic point guard, leading the NCAA in assists in both his junior (10.7) and senior (13.3) years. He was named the Southwestern Conference Player of the Year and MVP of the conference playoffs both of those years, 1987 and 1988. "Coach [Jobe] would let me come in and watch film with him, and then we'd sit and just talk basketball. I learned a lot from him. He was a great man."

But despite his collegiate success at Southern, Johnson went un- drafted by NBA teams. He played for the Palm Beach Stingrays of the United States Basketball League in the summer after graduation, and Seattle brought him to training camp as a free agent that fall (1988). Johnson made the Sonics squad, but played sparingly there for two years. He was then traded to Denver, waived by the Nuggets on Christmas Eve, 1990, and picked up by San Antonio the following January. When the Spurs waived him the next December, he signed on with Houston and stayed with them the rest of the 1992 season.

In November of that year, Johnson signed again with the Spurs, the year Jerry Tarkanian (Tark) was their coach. While doing a television game there early in the season, Tark bemoaned to me that he didn't have a good point guard. "I want to get Gary Grant from the Clippers—he was a great player at Michigan. But it doesn't look like it'll happen." I told Tark that I liked Avery Johnson, who was already on his squad. Tark thought Avery was too small.

But then Tarkanian left the team in December with a 9–11 record, and John Lucas took over the coaching duties. He put Avery in the start- ing lineup. Avery scored just under 9 points a game and led the team in assists with 561 (7.5 a game) against only 145 turnovers (1.9 a game). The Spurs finished the season with a 49–33 record, then beat Portland in the first round of the playoffs before being eliminated by Phoenix in the Conference Semifinals.

It was a breakout year for Johnson, who became a free agent at the end of the season and signed with Golden State. After a solid season there, the Spurs brought him back again. This time he stayed. For the next seven seasons, AJ was the Spurs point guard—getting the team into offense, scoring when the team needed, and assuming a leadership role on the court. When the Spurs won the NBA title in 1999 by defeating New York 4–1, Johnson made the clinching field goal in the final game.

Johnson became a free agent again in 2001, and signed on with the Denver Nuggets. In February 2002, Johnson was part of a seven-player trade that sent him to Dallas. He played sparingly for the Mavericks, who then had Steve Nash and Nick Van Exel ahead of him at the point. During the 2002–2003 season, Coach Don Nelson ("Nellie"), who saw that Avery had the respect of his players and made good observations at team meetings, turned team practices over to him on several occasions. The players liked it. When I asked Steve Nash at the All-Star break that year who was the Mavs team leader, he thought for several seconds and then said, "I'd have to say that Avery Johnson is."

That is most unusual. An NBA team leader is almost always a prominent, full-time player—Johnson was playing less than 10 minutes a game at the time. When I asked Nash to elaborate on his statement, he said, "We respect Avery. He's been on a championship team and knows what it takes for us to be one. He has good things to say. When he talks, we listen."

When Nellie turned practices over to AJ, he was well organized and conducted the workouts in a crisp, businesslike manner. "I always start out with defensive drills and put a lot of stress on fundamentals," he said.

When the Mavs faced a critical Game 7 in their first-round matchup with Portland in the 2003 playoffs, Nelson elected to have Johnson give the pregame talk to the team. The result was a rousing victory for Dallas.

When I asked Malik Rose how the Spurs could pump up another stellar performance like they had in Game 5 in the NBA Finals against New Jersey, he said with a smile, "Maybe we should get Avery Johnson back to give us our pregame talk. Avery would get us going."

Gregg Popovich, Avery's coach at San Antonio, says that Avery will make a great head coach. Coach Nellie agrees. Johnson, who had a year remaining on his player contract with the Mavs going into the 2003–2004 season, says he's in no hurry. "I'm enjoying the moment. I've got no timetable to be a head coach. If it happens, I'll do my best to make it work out."

Avery has all the tools: He knows the game, teaches it well, has great charisma to motivate others to play the team game, and has shown poise under pressure. I agree with Nellie and Pop: AJ will make a great coach. In the meantime, he remains an exemplar of the power and potential of the "inside man."

The Game Plan

Making Decisions

BEING SUCCESSFUL IN LIFE takes careful planning. You have to make decisions on a continuous basis; and as often as possible, you want them to be the right ones. Ideally, you should have time to study a situation or condition and reach a sound, rational conclusion; but often, you must make the decision "on the fly."

Coaches face both circumstances on a regular basis: They must plan ahead for the next season, which requires making decisions over days, weeks, or sometimes even months; and for "game time," which requires making highly time-sensitive decisions, typically on the spur of the moment. Yet even those decisions require long-term preparation, in order to anticipate any and every possible situation that might arise.

Draw up the Game Plan

In business, long-range planning is often referred to as the "mission statement"; in sports it's called the "game plan." This is a unified plan for the group; it helps all members understand how their individual roles influence the end result and defines for those involved in a specific activity the purpose and direction of their actions. For the game plan to succeed, everyone in the group must understand it, believe that they can accomplish it, and that the result will meet the goals of the group.

The game plan defines how a team plays its game. Even though individual players may excel in their skills, unless those skills are blended into a team game plan, the results will be unsatisfactory. That is why a team of good players following a well-designed game plan will beat a collection of superstars who are playing for themselves.

We see illustrations of that principle every year in every sport. The teams that win championships demonstrate the highest level of team play. That is not to understate the value of highly skilled players—in the history of the NBA, teams that won back-to-back championships also had great players on them. Here's a brief look at those teams chronologically, starting with the Minneapolis Lakers.

The Minneapolis Lakers

The Minneapolis Lakers won four titles in five years from 1948–1949 through 1953–1954. The Lakers had two great players: George Mikan, the game's first dominating big man, and versatile Jim Pollard, the first of the "Kangaroo Kids" (players with the ability to elevate quickly). The rest of the big-minute players—Slater Martin, Vern Mikkelsen, Clyde Lovellette, Whitey Skoog, and Pep Saul (amazingly, the Lakers had only nine players on their roster for the 1953–1954 season)—were highly skilled and played wonderful team basketball under Coach John Kundla's direction. I watched that team close out the New York Knicks in the NBA Finals in 1953, a game played at the 69th Regiment Armory because a circus was performing at the old Madison Square Garden. The Lakers won four straight after losing the series opener in Minneapolis. They dominated the Knicks in the final game with a great display of team basketball.

The Boston Celtics

The Celtics, winners of eight championships in a row from 1958–1959 under the shrewd coaching of Red Auerbach, were led by the defensive wizardry of Bill Russell, whose shot-blocking and rebounding keyed the fast break. There were other great players over those eight years—Bob Cousy, Bill Sharman, Tom Heinsohn, Sam and K. C. Jones, Satch Sanders, and John Havlicek—but Russell's defense, the high level of team play at both ends of the floor, and the unified togetherness of the players set that group of Celtics apart from all others. Auerbach retired as coach after the 1966 championship and Russell became the team's player-coach.

The Celtics lost in 1966–1967 to a great Philadelphia team coached by Alex Hannum. But the Sixers suffered a critical injury to Billy Cunningham in the playoffs of 1968, and weren't able to repeat. The Celtics won again, then repeated the following year, for an incredible run of 10 championships in 11 years.

And, digging deeper, the Celtics also won in 1956–1957 (Russell's first year in the NBA), then lost to St. Louis in 1958, before their eight-straight titles. Russell was there for all of them. No other player or team in professional sports has enjoyed that level of success for as long a time.

The Celtics bread and butter on offense was the fast break, but they also had six plays that they used for half-court offense. Every team in the league knew those plays, but the Celtics executed them so well that they always worked, and they never added to that basic game.

The Los Angeles Lakers

Coach Pat Riley's Lakers were the next back-to-back winners, with championships in 1986–1987 and again in 1987–1988. Riley had three great players to execute an up-tempo game he called "Showtime": Kareem Abdul-Jabbar, Earvin "Magic" Johnson, and James Worthy. But when Riley reminisces about those teams, he never fails to cite the value of Michael Cooper, Byron Scott, Kurt Rambis, and Mychal Thompson as an underlying reason for their success. With Johnson at the throttle, Riley's team set a blistering game pace, and, because there was uniformity in size among his main players, they employed a switching defense with effectiveness. Magic kept everybody involved in the flow of their "team-first" game.

The Detroit Pistons

Detroit won the next consecutive championships in 1988–1989 and 1989–1990 with only one special player, Isiah Thomas, but with a fistful of tough role players that Coach Chuck Daly relied on: Joe Dumars, Bill Laimbeer, Vinny Johnson, Dennis Rodman, John Salley, and Mark Aguirre. Chuck also had the intimidating Rick Mahorn the first championship year, and gave his minutes to James Edwards in the second. The Pistons played a rock-ribbed, physical, defensive game, and scored just enough points to win.

The Chicago Bulls

Chicago won its first championship in 1991, led by the incredible Michael Jordan—then in his seventh NBA season—and blended by Coach Phil Jackson. The fiercely competitive Jordan and talented Scottie Pippen were the catalysts of a team that dominated the league for six of the next eight years. Both were unrelenting, aggressive defenders, who fit seamlessly into the Triangle Offense of assistant coach Tex Winter. That attack created open shots for everyone, and allowed Jordan to go one-on-one when the Bulls needed a crucial score. The result was three straight championships.

The Houston Rockets

Then, while Jordan was off playing baseball, Houston won championships in 1994 and 1995, using a game plan built around the ballet-like inside moves of Hakeem Olajuwon and a corps of three-point shooters—

Vernon Maxwell, Kenny Smith, Robert Horry, Sam Cassell, Mario Elie, and Matt Bullard. (Coach Rudy Tomjanovich would not take a perimeter player on his team that couldn't shoot the three-ball.) Olajuwon was unstoppable from the post and developed into a good enough passer to find open teammates when double-teamed. The Rockets made maximum use of that inside-outside threat. In their championship seasons, they took more 3-point shots and made more of them than any other team. On defense, Olajuwon was the team's stopper at the hoop; that enabled perimeter defenders to pressure their match-ups, knowing Hakeem was there to back them up. Clyde Drexler added his athleticism to the Rockets overall game in the second championship season.

The Bulls Three-Peat . . . Again

With Jordan back in form for the 1995–1996 season, Chicago was further strengthened by the addition of outstanding rebounder and defender, Dennis Rodman, and established an NBA record with 72 wins. The impressive Bulls led the league in scoring that season (105.18 points per game) and allowed 92.93 for an outstanding point differential of +12.25—a mark bettered only by the 1972 championship Lakers' 12.3. The Bulls won two more titles and then were dismantled in 1998 by owner Jerry Reinsdorf and general manager Jerry Krause—who was quoted as saying that organizations, not players, win championships. (Unfortunately for Krause, the Bulls, with the same management, had the worst record in the league from time of the team's breakup through the 2002–2003 season.)

Although the Bulls have seen their last championship for the foreseeable future, Jackson is still tallying them up. After a year's break from the game to reenergize himself and wait for an attractive opportunity, Jackson became coach of the LA Lakers in 1999. He took the same approach with his star players there, Shaquille O'Neal and Kobe Bryant, as he had done with Jordan and Pippen in Chicago: He got them to accept the team concept of the Triangle Offense and combine it with tough half-court defense.

The Los Angeles Lakers Redux

Jackson quickly organized the Lakers into an effective force that won three straight titles from 2000 to 2002. Those teams manifested the best qualities of Jackson's coaching: excellent team unity, outstanding poise, and the maximum use of player skills. Jackson got the most from Shaq's power game; and managed to blend Kobe's open-court artistry and half-court creativity with steady performances from veterans like Ron Harper, Robert Horry, Rick Fox, Derek Fisher, and Brian Shaw. The Lakers were also tough defensively, with the capability of reaching back for increased tenacity when it was necessary.

The Lakers winning streak ended in the 2003 season. A number of factors contributed to their demise. O'Neal, who had surgery on his arthritic right toe and missed the first nine games of the season, never seemed to be in peak physical condition. Jackson himself missed games for the first time in his coaching career, first with kidney stones, then with a heart blockage that necessitated an angioplasty procedure. There were injuries to other players as well. Fox and his backup, Devean George, both suffered ankle injuries at nearly the same time. The result was that, even though Bryant was brilliant, the Lakers never really found their best rhythm at any time in the season and were eliminated by San Antonio in the Conference Semi-finals.

Gain Key Support

A solid, well-formulated game plan is essential for success in anything. It is also imperative that the leader of the group gains endorsement for that plan from his key personnel. On all of those championship teams, the coach had the support of his best players. Kundla had Mikan and Pollard; Auerbach had Russell and Cousy; Riley had Magic; and Daly had Thomas and Laimbeer. Rudy T. had Olajuwon, and Jackson, of course, had Jordan and Pippen in Chicago, and Bryant and O'Neal in Los Angeles.

When Jackson took over the coaching reins from Doug Collins at Chicago in 1989, he got MJ to buy into the concept of the Triangle

Offense by convincing him that it was the best way for the team to win, and that he could still score heavily, yet suffer less wear and tear on his body because defenses wouldn't concentrate on him as much. Once Michael signed on, Pippen and the rest of the Bulls fell in step behind him.

The Triangle is an intricate offense that requires a lot of passing and screening by all players. Jackson liked the team aspects of it and demanded that his players carry it out. Phil, who was a good defender as a player, took charge of that aspect of the team game, with help initially from a second assistant, John Bach. Jordan and Pippen were also key players there. The result was a team game that was highly entertaining and successful.

When Jackson signed on at LA with six championship rings to back up his theories of the game, O'Neal and Bryant, the memory of the previous season's first-round sweep by San Antonio still fresh in their minds, also went along—although Kobe showed some reluctance. Knowing he had the league's most dominant center, Jackson wanted to get the ball to O'Neal as often as possible. He challenged Shaq to play the kind of team game that Wilt Chamberlain played when his teams at Philadelphia and Los Angeles won championships. That required Shaq to be in great shape (in 1961–1962, Chamberlain averaged over 48 minutes a game for the season) to improve his passing skills (Chamberlain led the league in assists in 1968), and to become a stronger rebounder (Wilt's career average for rebounds was just under 23 a game) and shot-blocker (blocks were not kept as an official statistic when Wilt played, but Sixers stats guru, Harvey Pollock, remembers games when he tallied up 25 blocks for the big guy). Jackson assured Shaq that he'd have plenty of opportunities to score, but his priority must be on those other qualities that helped his team win. Shaq agreed.

Convincing Kobe was a different matter. He had no problem with taking defensive responsibility, but knew that he was at his best in an up-tempo, drive-it-to-the-hoop, open offensive game where he could create scoring opportunities for himself or his teammates. He worked hard at his game and felt he could score at will. Kobe was not unwilling to pass to Shaq; but slowing the game to feed the post constantly meant a controlled pace with few fast-break opportunities, and that deprived him from showing the best part of his game. There seemed at times to be an unbridgeable gap between the game that Jackson wanted from Kobe and the one that Kobe felt was in him.

But, despite gaps in communication and occasional public bickering among the coach and his two stars, the Lakers won three straight titles. Jackson eased the reins on Bryant somewhat and Kobe became more patient within the structure of the Triangle. In his third championship season, he often started games looking only to get his teammates involved early, before going after his own shots. He told me, "I can get my shots any time. I like to get the team going first." It was a sign of maturity that didn't go unnoticed by Jackson.

During the run of championships, Shaq, plagued by nagging injuries, didn't put up Chamberlain-like numbers, but was a devastating force in the paint, an excellent passer from the post, a double-digit rebounder, and among the leaders in blocked shots. Role players like Fisher, Fox, Horry, George, and Shaw were excellent defenders and chipped in with their particular offensive skills. The result was a team that didn't beat itself and had unbounded confidence in its ability to win. That Lakers team also gave Phil Jackson his ninth NBA championship—a distinction that tied him with the legendary Auerbach for most titles by an NBA coach.

The team play that these great teams demonstrated didn't just happen. It had to be taught. The coach had to decide on the most effective game plan for his personnel, transmit that plan to his players, and have them accept and absorb it. Then he had to break down that game and drill it with his players until it took on a style of its own. It became who they were—like a collective team signature.

Execute the Game Plan

Championships await teams with a sound plan and players who are good enough and mentally tough enough to carry it out with maximum efficiency. Fats Waller, the great old piano man, popularized a tune, "It Ain't What You Do, It's the Way That You Do It" that has always stuck in my mind. This philosophy fits nicely when talking about working out a game plan: The very best game plans work only if they're carried out properly.

At Buffalo, the year before I went to Portland, I used a game plan that I called the "Turn-Out." Its built-in, multiple-pass, screen-and-cut system took a fair amount of discipline to make it work. The Braves were able to score well enough to rank second in the league in that category, but the points came mostly on fast breaks. If opposing teams limited those opportunities, my players were impatient with the half-court execution of the Turn-Out. Center Bob McAdoo, who won his third straight scoring title that year, played a key role in our attack. If no fast break was available, Mac's job was to set a baseline back-pick for the wing man on his side of the floor. If that cutter wasn't open, Mac stepped out, got the ball, and was supposed to look for a second cutter coming from the weak side. On most occasions, rather than wait for the cutter, Mac shot the ball or drove to the basket. And most of the time, he scored.

Periodically, I pointed out to him the need for patience—if only to keep his teammates involved in the game. He agreed, would then wait for the cutter, and would make the appropriate pass. But if that player missed the shot, Mac would look over at me as if to say, "I did what you wanted, but we didn't score. We'd do better if I shot it." McAdoo was a great scorer at Buffalo and a dynamite clutch shooter; I admired his competitive spirit, but he didn't record a lot of assists. (He later played in Europe, then returned, looking to sign on with an NBA team. I wanted him at Portland, but he declined, saying that he was no longer the scorer he was at Buffalo and preferred to go with a contending team for whom he could play a lesser role. McAdoo signed on with the Lakers and helped Pat Riley win a championship.)

In contrast, at Portland, using the same Turn-Out system, Bill Walton was the player setting the baseline back-pick. He was a good shooter, but an incredible passer, and loved to give assists. Walton was patience personified. If a player was open, Walton always delivered the ball. His attitude became contagious and kept everybody running their cuts and making the extra pass. As a result, we were able to add more options to the Turn-Out that made it very difficult to defend. Same basic offense, different results.

Patient execution of the Turn-Out, however, wasn't all that separated the Buffalo and Portland teams. The Blazers were also strong defensively, which Buffalo was not. Walton and Maurice Lucas were the
best pair of rebounders in the league and had help off the bench from
Lloyd Neal. The perimeter defenders—Dave Twardzik, Lionel Hollins,
John Davis, Bobby Gross, Larry Steele, and Herm Gilliam—were quick
and tenacious. It was a dynamite combination. In all my years of coaching, I never had a team as quick and eager to learn and as dedicated to
carrying out the game plan as that group of Trail Blazers.

And Walton was the consummate team player. At timeouts, he sat
on the edge of the scorer's table because the bench seats were too low. I
could see him out of the corner of my eye nodding in assent to what I was
saying to the team. When I finished, he would often exhort his teammates with an impassioned, "Now let's go out and do it, goddamn it!"
McKinney would look at me and smile. We both knew that the game
plan was going to be carried out the way we wanted.

The Real Deal: Bill Walton

Bill Walton was the most skilled player I ever coached. He was also
the most coachable, most critical, and most caring. He loved playing
in big games. "Anybody can play well at home," he often said. "The
real players play their best games on the road." Bill was a real player.

After my pregame talks, the Blazers gathered by the locker room
door waiting for some last word from Bill before going on the floor to
warm up. Bill waited until the whole squad was around him. Then he
would shout, "Let's go get those fuckers," and away they'd go.

At a playoff game at the old Chicago Stadium, the loudest
venue that I've ever experienced, Bill had his eyebrows furrowed
and was doing his little boxer's shuffle following introductions.
The noise level was so intense that one had to shout just to have a
chance to be heard. Bill leaned over and yelled in my ear, "This is
the greatest, isn't it Coach?"

To ensure success, any leader's game plan has to include preparation for making time- and pressure-sensitive decisions. That's why it is so important to simulate end-of-the-game situations on the practice floor. Both the coach and players learn what works best under the most intense pressure. Every team designs plays for last-second scoring opportunities, which they work out on the practice floor.

In a Portland-Sixers game in the 1980–1981 season that went down to the wire, Dr. J (Julius Erving) made two free throws to give Philly the lead with two seconds left on the clock. I set up a play we had practiced, whereby Billy Ray Bates, a great leaper, circled to the basket from the top of the circle without any screen. Kermit Washington made the pass from sideline out of bounds, threw it high—just short of the rim—and Billy went up, and in one fluid motion caught the ball with two hands and stuffed it. The timing of the cut, the movement of other players to clear the basket area for Bates, and the accuracy of Washington's pass all had to be perfect.

Such split-second attention to detail won't happen unless the team has practiced the play. All close games don't end up the way you want them to, but you multiply your chances of success when you make the proper preparations.

Trust Your Gut

Long-range, logical game-planning is ideal, but there are times when you must trust your intuition, or gut feelings. Sometimes an idea pops into your mind that makes very good sense at the moment. On those occasions, I say "go for it." Needless to say, this is not a good idea if the stakes are higher—say, if your life depends on the outcome—but on lesser matters, I like to play the hunch.

There are plenty of chances to do that in sports. Many gut-based decisions succeed simply because the action is bold and unexpected. I recall games that I played in at the high school, college, and pro levels where my team needed a possession in the closing seconds of a game. In each case, I played off my man, inviting a pass to be made, then came through the passing lane when the ball was in the air to get the necessary possession—hunches or gut feelings that paid off.

The zone press that I discussed earlier in the book is predicated on the same principle of luring the opponent to make passes that can be intercepted or deflected. Deciding when to apply the press and when to take it off is, at least in part, directed by gut feelings. I can't count the number of games my teams won using that tactic, but one early instance was a game at St. Joe's. After we had rallied from a huge deficit to tie in a game against Gettysburg, I put a very good shot-maker into the game in the closing seconds. The player I took out had been largely responsible for our comeback with his terrific defense, and he was clearly unhappy that I took him from the game. But the shooter made the shot to win the game.

That is not to say the strategy always worked. I did the same thing later in an NCAA tournament game, and the same shooter missed the front end of a one-and-one, and we lost a key game to Wake Forest. Although going with your gut feelings won't always yield the outcome you desire, I still believe you've got to go with them.

Trust Others

In Chapter 2, I talked about learning from others, essential to success in any job. Leaders also need to trust in the knowledge of staff and, sometimes, outsiders to help them reach the goals of the group. I came to this understanding only with time and experience.

In my field, the person who immediately comes to mind is the assistant coach. In my first high school coaching experience at St. James, I had no assistant. I was it—the varsity and the jayvee coach. At Mount Pleasant, I did have an assistant, a nice fellow who had been the varsity coach before me. But he had no playing experience, and I didn't feel that he understood the game, so at both places, I made all the decisions, right or wrong, and tried to learn from the results.

When I got to St. Joseph's College, Dan Kenney was my assistant. He was a great guy who had played for the Hawks in the late 1930s. Everybody liked Dan, including me, but I was accustomed to doing things by myself and seldom involved him in planning or decision making.

It was when I hired Jack McKinney, shortly after he graduated from St. Joe's, that I began to understand the value of another's input to help me do my job better. Jack's role was to coach the freshman team, help me with the varsity, and share the load in the athletic director's office. He was terrific. He had played for me at both St. James and St. Joseph's and knew the kind of game I wanted. He helped me to plan the offense and defense, and was excellent on the practice floor with drillwork.

During games, it was my practice to kneel or squat in front of the players' bench and concentrate on the game action. A constant stream of variables would run through my mind, and I made decisions based on which ones I thought would positively affect the game in my team's favor at any given moment. As an aid to that process, I told McKinney that I wanted him to pass along any pertinent observations he had as he watched games. I also told him I might not acknowledge his verbal notes, but that I wanted to hear them. So, from time to time during a game, McKinney would come up, say something in my ear, and then sit down again. His comments were always concise and meaningful, such as, "Do you want Lynch [the back man on the zone press] that deep?" Or, "I think Bobby can beat his man." Or, "The middle of their zone opens when we reverse the ball."

I always processed the information and considered it. Sometimes I acted on it, sometimes I didn't—but I always wanted the information. By doing that, McKinney became an excellent resource, and he helped me to be a better leader of teams at St. Joseph's and, later, at Portland.

As a leader, I also discovered the importance of knowing when to go outside my organization to get the help I needed. Toward the end of Sam Bowie's rookie season in 1985, I asked him to come to the Blazers' summer league site—that season in Sacramento—for some individual attention. When he agreed, I got in touch with Bill Russell to ask him if he would be willing to come and spend a couple of days with Sam to help improve his overall game, and his team defense in particular. Russ quickly agreed to do it, and we set the dates for that to happen.

I was elated, and so was Sam. I regarded Russell as the best big man defender ever to play the game then—and still do—and felt sure that he'd have a positive impact on Bowie's game. Stu Inman, director of player personnel was also impressed that Russell was going to spend some time with Sam. But it wasn't until shortly before the workouts were to begin that the subject of money came up. Harry Glickman called me to ask how much I had agreed to pay Russell. I said that I hadn't discussed money with him at all. Harry was concerned. "Suppose he wants $50,000?" Team finance was Harry's responsibility, so I understood his concern. Russ hadn't mentioned a fee, but I felt that whatever it was it wouldn't be out of line.

When the time came, Russ worked on the floor with Bowie for two days. He demonstrated the positioning and footwork needed to keep his man from receiving the ball in a strong scoring position; how and when to play off his man to be a basket intimidator; the techniques of shot-blocking, with emphasis on using the hand nearer the shooter, keeping the ball in play rather than swatting the blocked shots into the seats; and countless other tidbits of advice for playing the center position effectively.

By the end of the sessions, Sam's reaction time had improved and his confidence had grown noticeably. Russ even gave Bowie his phone number and told him to call him any time during the season if he needed his help, and added that it was easy to come to Portland from Seattle, where Russell lived. He had done a terrific job, and we all felt good about it.

After the final workout, I thanked him and asked how much we owed him. He said, "Nothing. I really enjoyed doing it." When I objected, he thought for a minute, then said to have the team make a donation to some charity in his name.

Eighteen years later, Bowie still remembered the workouts very well. He told me, "Bill was an intimidating guy for me. He had those penetrating eyes that looked right through you. But he taught me an awful lot—footwork and positioning—and maybe more about my mental approach to the game. He also gave me a different approach to offense: he told me to make contact with my defender. I was more inclined to take the ball away from my man to shoot a fade-away jumper. Bill said, 'Take it to him; be the aggressor.'"

Then Bowie told me something that I didn't know. He said, "After that session in Sacramento, I played in the summer league in Seattle on my own. I was surprised to see him [Russell] there. He was like my personal tutor. He met me for breakfast, we went to the workouts together in his black Jaguar, and had lunch afterward. He talked about my game, but more on the mental approach to it. It seemed like he really took a personal interest in me. I was impressed."

Bowie was an improved player as he began his second NBA year, but 38 games into the season, he broke his leg in a game at Milwaukee. While he was still in the hospital there, he got a call from Russell. "He didn't offer me any sympathy. He said, 'Now that you're down, what are you going to do to get back up?' He wanted me to start planning to play again rather than to feel sorry for myself that I broke my leg."

Bowie rehabbed the leg and returned to play the final five games of the following season (1986–1987); then in a preseason game the next fall, he broke his other leg. Bowie missed the entire season in 1987–1988 and played only 20 games the next year. He was traded to New Jersey before the 1989–1990 season and had his best season (15 points, 8 rebounds) in 1991–1992. He finished his career with the Los Angeles Lakers.

Sam Bowie, the player Portland selected rather than Michael Jordan, never had a chance to show how good he could be with the Blazers. Reminiscing in the summer of 2003 about that period of his life, Sam said, "You know, I don't mind being ridiculed about the mistake Portland made taking me instead Michael; what bothers me the most is not having done more to justify your and the franchise's faith in me." I told Sam to let it go. "You win some and lose some in life. Some things are beyond your control. The main thing is to make your choices for the right reason. We [Portland] made ours about you for the right reason," I told him.

One choice that's always for the right reason is to tap the talent of others when it means the difference between achieving your goal and failing to do so.

Do the Unexpected

Gut feelings and hunches are often positive additions to a basic plan of action. Another trait that also pays dividends is doing the unexpected. The element of surprise is an aggressive tactic that has proven effective in every human endeavor from war maneuvers to birthday celebrations.

Doing the unexpected is a bit different from a hunch because it's already in your overall game plan. Once again, there are ample opportunities to use this tactic in sports. The unexpected aspect of the action helps to assure its success.

A St. Joseph's-Temple game in the early 1960s was a defensive battle that had gone to the wire—tie score, about two minutes to go, and St. Joe's in possession. The game was played before the shot-clock era, and we had held the ball for over a minute without trying to score. I noticed that Temple's defense was losing its focus a bit, expecting us to continue to hold the ball until the final seconds. So the next time our high-scoring guard, Steve Courtin, got the ball on the wing, I signaled him to drive the ball to the hoop. Courtin burst to the hoop and scored before Temple's defense reacted. The Owls, now trailing by two points, were unable to get off a good shot, and we held on to win a big game.

Two of my best coaching friends, Don Casey (Temple) and Paul Westhead (La Salle), met in a game that epitomized the unexpected. Westhead's style of play, with its heavy emphasis on scoring, was always different from the norm, and opposing teams could never be sure what to expect. In this game, Casey's heavily favored ball-control Temple team, held a comfortable 8-point lead late in the first half and had possession of the ball. On a signal from Westhead, one of his defenders went to the basket area at the other end of the floor, leaving La Salle in a four-man zone (which Westhead called "box and none"), and Temple with a 5-on-4 advantage. When Casey ordered his team to continue to hold the ball out, Westhead sent a second defender to the offensive end, leaving Casey with a 5-on-3 advantage. He still held the ball out.

The fans were in an uproar. Even the Temple rooters urged Casey to take some action, and some started to boo, when he continued to hold the ball. Finally, one of his players took a shot against La Salle's three-man zone defense, missed, and La Salle got a quick score on a long pass down-court. When La Salle scored, it went into a full-court trapping defense to accelerate the pace of the game. Temple players, thinking more about getting back to defend than concentrating on their shots, missed from both the field and free-throw line a couple of more times allowing La Salle to narrow their deficit to a few points by half-time.

Temple eventually held on to win the game, but the Owls and Coach Casey had to sweat it out. Though, doing the unexpected didn't win the game for Westhead, it raised havoc in a game that his opponent apparently had under control.

One of the best opportunities to do the unexpected is in the closing seconds of a tight game after a timeout, when the opposing team has had a chance to draw up a last-shot play. That is when the defending team should use a different defense or vary its defense in a way that upsets the plan of the opponent. There are a lot of close games in an NBA season. As the saying goes, "You can't win 'em all," but to stay in coaching, you must win more of those games than you lose.

Symbol of Greatness: Jerry West

Jerry West raised his level of play even higher when he joined the LA Lakers in 1960. In his playing days, the future Hall of Famer was about 6–3 and 185 pounds, but he seemed gaunt, almost emaciated, by the end of an NBA season, so intense was he. In the final minutes of a close game, at a break in the action, he would stand bent over at the waist, hands on knees, apparently at the point of exhaustion. Then, when the ball was put in play, he'd come alive and make a steal or block a shot if defending, or on offense, back his man down and fire an unerring jumper over him when his Lakers needed a hoop to win. And during an illustrious career, he did that over and over again—more than once to teams I coached—to earn the nickname, Mr. Clutch.

West was the glue that held the Lakers together in 1972 when they set a league record of 33 consecutive wins and won the NBA championship. Jerry averaged just under 26 points a game and handed out a league-leading 9.7 assists. West was a 10-time All-NBA First Team selection and was named the NBA Finals MVP in 1969—a season the Lakers *didn't* win the championship. It's no wonder that it's the silhouette of West's body that serves as the NBA's logo.

I was on the receiving end of this principle in a St. Joseph's-West Virginia NCAA tournament game. The great Jerry West was the Mountaineers' leader and I knew that we had to somehow keep him in check if we wanted to win.

I assigned Joe Spratt, my best defender, to cover West. Spratt—6–2, lean, tenacious, and quick-footed—did a great job, and the Hawks held a double-digit lead midway through the second half. But Spratt fouled out with about eight minutes to play and West took over the game—scoring 19 of his total 36 points. He was everywhere—scoring, rebounding, passing, defending, and stealing balls—as West Virginia came from behind and, with 26 seconds to play, took the lead 91–90. I called for a timeout and set up a last-shot play. At the end of the timeout, as my team took their positions on the floor, I watched where Coach Fred Schaus positioned his players, then called another timeout. From the positions of the opposing players, I felt confident that we could yet execute our originally planned play, and sent my team out to get the winning shot. But West Virginia's point guard, Ron Retton, sensed where the inbounds pass was going, burst through the passing lane, stole the ball, and scored the decisive layup. It was a crushing loss for St. Joseph's, but a great win for West Virginia.

On Second Thought

In my professional life in basketball, I have made countless decisions, mostly successful; but there are some I would like to make again if I had the chance. Three in particular that I wish I had made differently involve three basketball giants: Michael Jordan, Wilt Chamberlain, and Moses Malone.

Michael Jordan

The one decision that NBA fans remember and want to talk about most is Portland's decision to pass on Michael Jordan in the 1984 NBA Draft and instead to select Sam Bowie. Even now, Michael brings it up every year at his Senior Flight School on which I serve as a staff member. In August 2002, after signing a picture of himself with my son Christopher and me, MJ said with a smile, "In the next life, you'd pick me, wouldn't you?" I told him that I should have done that when I had the chance the first time.

But at that time Portland had good players—Jim Paxson and Clyde Drexler—at Jordan's 2-guard position. Paxson was the team's leading scorer and had played on the West All-Star Team that season; Drexler had just finished his rookie year and showed promise of developing into a superstar. The Blazers had won 48 games and had the second-best record in the West. Mychal Thompson was the starting center, backed up by Wayne Cooper. We felt that if we moved the 6–9 Thompson to big forward and acquired a true center, we'd be in a better position to challenge the Conference-leading Lakers. Two centers were available in that year's draft—Hakeem Olajuwon and Sam Bowie, and possibly a third, Patrick Ewing—and the Blazers were in the coin flip, resulting from an earlier trade with Indiana, to determine the team that picked first in the draft.

Shortly before the draft, Ewing elected to return to school (George-town) for his senior year. Portland's management group, which included owner Larry Weinberg, team President Harry Glickman, Director of Player Personnel Stu Inman, head scout Bucky Buckwalter, and the coaching staff agreed to take Olajuwon if we won the flip and to take Bowie if we lost it. We felt good about our guard situation, needed a center, and knew one would be there. To us, it was a no-brainer.

As it turned out, Houston won the flip and took Olajuwon; the Blazers took Bowie, and the Bulls selected Jordan. The choice turned out to be a bad one for Portland. Bowie was not a dominating center and had an injury-plagued career. In retrospect, Portland should have selected Jordan, then used either Paxson or Drexler to package some sort of deal to obtain a center.

Had I known how good Jordan was, I would have lobbied hard to select him. But coaches don't have a chance to see enough college and international competition to form solid opinions on player talent. They rely on the team's personnel director and scouts to apprise them of the ability of those in the draft. While NBA scouts all agreed that Jordan was a good player, I hadn't heard anyone say that he was going to be as great as he became. During our predraft meetings, none of the Blazers' scouting personnel recommended that we select him.

Kevin Loughery, Jordan's first NBA coach, told me later that the Bulls would have done the same thing as Portland had the positions been reversed. Loughery said he was stunned to see how good Jordan was in the first workouts his team had that season. The basketball world was soon to discover the same thing. I often think about the pleasure it would have been to coach Michael and the impact he would have had on the Portland teams.

Wilt Chamberlain

Another "do-over" decision I still think about was more of a delayed decision, but nonetheless had a negative result. It centered on the man I regard as the most talented, intelligent, complex, and interesting of all the players I've known—Wilt Chamberlain. Prior to the 1966–1967 season, in Philadelphia, Wilt had set all kinds of scoring records (he had been the league's perennial leader in scoring and rebounding, at one time averaging over 50 points a game for a season), but he had won no championships.

The Boston Celtics ruled then, having won eight titles in a row. Wilt seemed to sense that this Sixers team had the player personnel, in addition to new coach, Alex Hannum, that together could reach that goal. Under Hannum's influence, Wilt became a true team player, scoring a modest—for him—24 points a game, grabbing 24 rebounds, and dealing just under 8 assists. The Sixers set a league record at the time for most wins with a 68 and 13 mark, and went on to win the 1967 championship, Wilt's first in his eight seasons in the NBA.

I was general manager of that Sixers team and got to know Wilt quite well. When Alex Hannum left the Sixers to coach Oakland in the ABA, I talked with many candidates to replace him. Among them were Frank Maguire, John Kundla, and Earl Lloyd, each of whom could have had the job but declined it for various reasons. Chamberlain often stopped by the Sixers office to inquire how the coach search was going. When time went by without a selection, he told owner Irv Kosloff and

Local Boy Makes Good: Wilt Chamberlain

Wilt was a native Philadelphian, who played his scholastic basketball at Overbrook High School, before going to Kansas University. When I graduated from St. Joseph's, Wilt was a teenager. The next year, while I taught and coached at St. James, I played for Harrisburg in the Eastern League on weekends, and for an independent team (sponsored by Blocks Department Store) during the week. We played teams in the Philadelphia area, and on one occasion, played at a recreation center near Overbrook. As we were warming up, I noticed a tall (about 6–10), slender kid shooting at a side-court basket. He appeared very agile and surprisingly skilled. I asked one of the rec supervisors who he was, and was told it was Wilt Chamberlain, a ninth grader who lived in the neighborhood.

Wilt noticed that I was watching him, and proceeded to show a repertoire of dunks that I'd never seen before. Following each one, he'd look over and nod in my direction, as if to say, "I'm showing you my game. How do you like it?" I nodded back, indicating that his stuff was pretty good. Wilt smiled, and when our game started, took a seat to watch. I didn't have any direct contact with him again until I coached against him in at St. Joseph's, but I heard plenty about him as a player.

Wilt dominated scholastic basketball during his high school career and was involved in a city championship game that Philadelphians still talk about to this day. The game was against rival West Catholic High School, which was located not far from Overbrook. West had a good but small team that was thought to have no chance against Overbrook, which had other good players to complement Wilt's superior size and skill.

But West played a well-planned, ball-control game led by its hot shooting guard, Billy Lindsay. Lindsay took only 13 shots, made 12 of them, and scored 32 points as West pulled off a remarkable upset.

(Years later, Lindsay contracted a terminal form of cancer, and Wilt, unable to come East for a quickly organized testimonial in Billy's behalf, sent this handwritten letter of good wishes: "Hey, Billy,

(continued)

[I] heard from an old friend things could be a little better, so I wanted you to know that you have, as I am sure you have many, a friend out on the West Coast hoping that all the best will come your way. Our paths have not crossed very much, but it always seemed to me that it was not close to 45 years ago but only a couple of yesterdays that you almost single-handedly, cool as a cucumber, shot that jumper on us to give West Catholic that victory. Did you know that I almost went to West Catholic? We could have been a great pair— that's if you would have given me the ball some. Keep the faith; my prayers go out to you and yours.")

The only time that Wilt played in Philly during his short collegiate career was the St. Joseph's-Kansas game, played at Palestra. There was tremendous interest in the game, and on game night, the Palestra was packed to the rafters. St. Joe's had a young, developing team of mostly sophomores, while Kansas had a powerhouse and was expected to win the NCAA tournament later that spring.

I focused our defense against Wilt, playing him very physically, and swarming him with two and three defenders every time he touched the ball. St. Joe's led by a point at the half, but as the game went on, Wilt got our big men in foul trouble with his power game around the hoop. He also showed his finesse in passing to open teammates, and Kansas pulled away to win.

me that he'd be interested in becoming player/coach if I would help him with the Xs and Os. The suggestion took both of us by surprise and we said that we'd give it some thought. We agreed to meet again in a week, after Wilt had returned from a trip to the West Coast.

I liked the idea. I thought that Wilt would play with added intensity knowing his name was on the line, and I was confident that I could help with the technical aspects of the job. Koz and I talked it over and agreed that we'd make a deal with Chamberlain to be the team's coach. But when Wilt returned, he said that he had changed his mind, that he was not going to play in Philadelphia again, and he demanded a trade to a

West Coast team—to Seattle, Los Angeles, or San Diego. When we indicated that we weren't interested in trading him, he said that he'd jump to the ABA team in Los Angeles. (The ability of NBA players to leave their existing teams began in 1967 when Rick Barry, a free agent at the time, left the San Francisco Warriors of the NBA to join Oakland of the newly formed ABA. Barry was forced by a court order to sit out a year, but then played for Oakland in 1968–1969, and played three more years in the ABA for other teams before returning to the NBA with the Golden State Warriors in 1972. With that precedent established, NBA players who were not under contract looked to enhance their bargaining position by threatening to "jump" to the ABA. Chamberlain knew that he was playing with a strong negotiating chip.)

I could hardly believe what I was hearing. I had come to the meeting brimming with enthusiasm, prepared to fill the coaching void, and suddenly found myself still without a coach and with the prospect of losing the most powerful player in the game. Koz, who was accustomed to Wilt's negotiating ploys (he only did one-year contracts, had no agent, and did all the negotiating himself), tried to push the discussion aside. But Wilt said that he was serious about his decision and that in no way would he play for Philadelphia again. He walked out of the meeting leaving me with my mouth hanging open.

We eventually worked out a deal with the Lakers—the only team Wilt later said he would go to—and moved on. Had Luke Jackson not torn an Achilles tendon, the deal might not have been so detrimental. (Jackson was a powerhouse rebounder, who could score inside and from the perimeter; but he never regained his ability to run and jump like he once had, and the Sixers started on a downward trend.)

Thinking back, I've often wondered what the outcome would have been if I had jumped on Wilt's first offer to coach the team. Might we have finalized a deal *before* he went to the West Coast? Or, when Wilt visited the Sixers office to ask about the progress in hiring a new coach, could I have been the one to suggest becoming player/coach to him? Or, could the Sixers have kept him if we had not caved in when he threatened to jump to the ABA, and told him instead that he was staying in Philly and that the player/coach opportunity was still open?

If we had reached an agreement whereby Wilt was player/coach and I did the X-and-O work, how would it have worked out? I suspect that Wilt was interested mostly in the title, without doing a lot of the work that went along with it. When he was coach of the San Diego Conquistadors in the ABA, he certainly didn't show a dedication to the job. He even missed a game to make a personal appearance and made his pregame talk to the team by telephone! That said, I would have accepted the challenge of working with Wilt in a heartbeat. Now I'm left wondering how it would have all worked out.

Moses Malone

When Portland added Moses Malone to its roster following his selection from the ABA expansion pool, owner Larry Weinberg told me that Moses had been selected only so that the team could make a deal for him. Moses was bringing a salary from the ABA of about $300,000, and Weinberg didn't want to add that amount to his payroll. When I took the job with Portland, the agreement was that I would have control of team personnel *except* for matters that were affected by financial issues. So I went along with management's position that Moses be selected as a source of revenue rather than as a player on the roster.

His first days at training camp didn't make me question that situation. Moses had a hard time getting a feel for the offense that I was trying to establish. The center and big forward positions were both required to screen, handle the ball, and make passes in traffic. That was fine for Walton, Lucas, and Neal, but Malone really struggled with those demands. His overall game looked awkward and uncertain, although he had demonstrated rebounding ability. At that point, I wasn't overly impressed by what he had shown, but was nevertheless intrigued by what he might become.

In the meantime, Blazers management wasn't having any luck in finding a team to take Malone. NBA people didn't know much about him. He was 21 years old at the time, had joined Utah of the ABA right out of high school, and after a solid rookie year (18.8 points, 14.6 rebounds), then was dealt to St. Louis where he became injured and didn't put up comparable numbers. When Harry Glickman called me after several days of camp to ask how Moses was doing, I said not too well. Harry then asked me to sound out coaches in the Eastern Conference to see if I could drum up some interest in Malone. Knowing I was going to lose him anyway, I agreed to do so.

My first call was to old friend, Red Holzman of the Knicks. I told him that I had a player for him, saying that Moses was raw, but that he could really rebound and would probably become a good NBA player. I added that I was unable to keep him because of his salary. Red paused for a long while, then asked, "Is he as good as John Gianelli?" (Gianelli had averaged about 9 points and 7 rebounds the previous season.) There was no question in my mind that Malone was already better than Gianelli, and I gave Red an emphatic yes. Red paused again, then said, "With due respect, I don't think so." So the Knicks kept Gianelli and the Blazers retained Malone for a while longer.

Then Malone began to improve, and I became more interested in keeping him on the roster. In our last preseason game against Seattle, we played at Oakland as part of a doubleheader, Moses dominated the boards and showed ability to score in the basket area as well. After the game, I told the Portland writers that I had to find a way to keep him.

I called Stu Inman the next morning and made my request. He answered that he thought it was too late, that Larry Weinberg had already made a deal to trade Moses to Buffalo for a first-round draft choice. I suggested that the deal be stopped. He said he'd call Larry to see what could be done. As it turned out, nothing was done to stop the deal, and Moses was gone before the next practice. I was very disappointed, and so were the players. But Malone didn't stay at Buffalo either. They traded him to Houston for two first-round picks, and the rest is history. Malone became a Hall of Famer.

The Blazers won the championship that season without Malone and had a great following year going until Walton and several others were hurt near the end of the season. Walton never played again for Portland, and had we kept Moses, Walton's loss would not have been as drastic. How good would the Blazers have become with both Jordan and Malone? I can only speculate.

When a person is in a leadership position, whatever is done is done, and the leader must move ahead assertively. But, without becoming a second-guesser, it's useful for that leader to review decisions made or not made—especially those that have had negative results, to discover whether a different action might have led to a better conclusion. That kind of reflection helps the leader make better decisions in the future.

At the Buzzer

How to Win, How to Lose

RUDYARD KIPLING'S POEM "IF," the epigram for this book, carries an important message. Although it was written almost a century ago (in a 1910 collection of stories *Rewards and Fairies*), the poem represents a present-day challenge for all who are in positions of authority. Character traits such as maintaining poise in the face of criticism, accepting both victory and defeat with equanimity, remembering those who were with you on the road to success, and giving full effort at all times (and demanding the same of others) are all applicable to anyone in authority, especially those in the public eye. And in a sports-conscious society like the United States, coaches are right up there in the front lines.

Treat Triumph and Disaster the Same

I wasn't long into my coaching career when I had to test the courage of my convictions. In 1961, the St. Joseph's team I coached reached the

215

Final Four of the NCAA tournament held at Kansas City, Missouri, where we lost to Ohio State, but then beat Utah in four overtimes in the consolation game. A third-place finish among college basketball's elite was a high level accomplishment for the Hawks, and I felt good about it. I began to feel even better as I walked back to the hotel after the victory with three principal members of the Philadelphia Basketball Writers Association—Herb Good, Bob Vetrone, and Stan Hochman—who told me I was to receive that group's Coach of the Year award. I was elated. But when I returned to the St. Joe's campus, those feelings of elation were smashed to bits just as quickly as they'd risen.

Shortly after I arrived, Father Geib, the Moderator of Athletics, called and asked me to come to his office to talk with representatives from New York City District Attorney Frank Hogan's office. After introductions, one of the DA's group informed me that they had evidence that three of my players had conspired with gamblers to influence the outcome of three games early in the season, and that they were there to take them to New York to face charges. I was stunned. Their words hit me like a hard, physical blow. I actually fell to my knees and cried out. I couldn't believe it. I had read reports about another point-shaving scandal in college basketball. *Sports Illustrated* had even sent one of its writers, Ray Cave, to cover our practices before the Final Four began, but his approach appeared to be about the little college that had made it to the top. I never associated his presence with any implication of gambling involvement by players on my team.

While I regained my composure, the DA's reps assured me that they indeed could prove that my players were implicated. I still wasn't convinced, and they wouldn't tell me what evidence they had. We had lost only four games all season, and one of the players they mentioned was the team's leading scorer who had played very well all year. I expressed my skepticism, and they listened without comment. They said they would get back to me after they had interrogated the players. I left the room to return to my office.

As I stepped out of Father Geib's office, the three players in question were sitting together, waiting to go in. I told them what I had just heard, and they denied they were involved. One of them said, "We would never do anything like that." I believed them.

It so happened that St. Joseph's began its spring break the following day, so the players' absence was not noticed. There was nothing about the charges in the newspapers or on radio or television either, and a week passed without my hearing anything from the District Attorney's office. It was a difficult week. I wanted to believe my players, but the certitude of the detectives from New York nagged in the back of my mind. I told my assistant, Jack McKinney, about it and we went back over films of the early season games. I recalled a loss to Dayton that had made me very angry at the time. Postgame, I had verbally blistered the team for what I perceived as lack of effort; it never entered my mind that anyone was doing it intentionally. I wanted to believe . . . yet uncertainty lingered.

During the same week, the annual writers banquet took place at which I received the Coach of the Year award. My mind was flooded with a turmoil of emotions as I accepted the award with a few halting words. I appreciated the honor, but I felt unworthy of it if some of my players had been involved in the heinous activity as charged.

About a week later, we were informed that Hogan's office was to announce the next day the involvement of many players from colleges across the country and that the three players from St. Joseph's would be among them. All were charged with criminal conspiracy. But the law wasn't interested in placing them in jail; their objective was to nail the ringleaders of the gambling syndicate. Through the testimony of the players, they got their men, hence, the players were given suspended sentences. The players on my team who were involved were allowed to finish their education at St. Joseph's—which they did at the Evening Division—and went on to lead normal lives outside basketball. One went into law enforcement in New York City and had a son who played several years in the NBA; a second became a highly successful land developer in North Carolina.

I had a hard time coming to grips with my failure to prevent these young men from getting involved in an activity so contrary to the aims of sport. I thought seriously about giving up coaching, but Father Geib and others encouraged me to stay in it. I decided that I would continue to coach and vowed to be better at communicating with my players and understanding their needs. Basketball at St. Joseph's continued to be what it was: a small college (now university) program that successfully

Positive Alliance: Jim Thompson

In response to violence in sports at all levels, as well as inappropriate behavior by coaches demonstrating a win-at-all-costs attitude, a coaching group with a different focus has been organized and is now flourishing. Jim Thompson founded the Positive Coaching Alliance at Stanford University in 1998 for the purpose of instituting a "double-goal" objective for coaches—especially those dealing with young athletes. The goal to win is still there, but a second, more important, goal is to use sports to teach life lessons that will endure after the athletes' playing days are over.

competed with larger institutions. The traditions of extra effort and hustling team play that Bill Ferguson started, and that I tried to carry on, have continued under the coaching of Jack McKinney, Harry Booth, Jim Lynam, Jim Boyle (all former players whom I coached) and, currently, Phil Martelli. The Hawk is still flapping.

Learning this lesson was most difficult for me and required a lot of soul-searching. I had allowed myself to get too caught up with coaching success and had lost sight of my main responsibility as a leader: to serve as guide in the development of the athletes in my charge. I made a trip to New York and met with members of the DA's office to find out all I could about how the contacts were made and the manner of contrivance by the players. If I was to stay in coaching, I was determined to do a better job in the future.

Be Poised in the Face of Criticism

As a coach, I never had a problem taking criticism from those who knew the game; on the contrary, I often sought their opinion about my team and the way I was doing my job. Conversely, I wasn't good at taking critiques from those who had scant knowledge about the game into which I put such time and effort. But that's the downside of criticism: You can't choose your critics; they are always there—even when you win. And as Kipling said, that's the time to, "trust yourself when all men doubt you, but make allowance for their doubting too."

I was to learn that lesson before my fourth year at Buffalo (1975–1976), which got off to a tenuous start. My contract with them was up, and owner Paul Snyder and I had conferred a few times without success to work out a new one. The Braves had made the playoffs in the previous two seasons—the only one of the new franchise teams (Buffalo, Cleveland, and Portland) to do so—so I felt I was in a good bargaining position. I had just completed three years at $60,000 (low by league standards) and wanted three more years in the $100,000 range (a bit above average at the time). Snyder offered three years at $80,000. We were almost into the season when we met again. After about an hour of dialogue, Snyder said that he couldn't pay $100,000 for three years; but could pay that much for one year. I said, "I'll take it." My answer seemed to surprise him and he hesitated. But he realized that he'd made an offer, and I had accepted. The deal was struck—but I sensed that he resented it.

Snyder and I also had disagreements about how I was using player personnel—specifically, Ernie DiGregorio, who had had a terrific Rookie of the Year season in 1973–1974. He had led the league in assists and free-throw percentage, but had torn a cartilage in his knee early in his second season and was struggling to get his quickness back. Therefore, I was playing others ahead of him and had cut his playing time. Snyder contended that there was a large Italian population in Buffalo that came to the games just to see Ernie play and wouldn't buy tickets if he wasn't going to play more. Snyder asked me to start him; I told him I couldn't do it, that it would be unfair to the other players. He wasn't pleased and I sensed that a storm was brewing.

The first storm signal came after the Braves won a close game against Houston at home. Snyder was waiting with general manager Bob MacKinnon when I came off the floor. As I walked past them, I said, "Great win." MacKinnon responded, "You should have won by 20." I was a bit surprised by the remark because Bob was no stranger to coaching. He had coached at Canisius College for many years, and was about to be fired there when Braves GM, Eddie Donovan, asked me if I would take him on as an assistant. I agreed to it, more as a favor than a need, and Bob was my assistant for three years. When Donovan left the Braves to rejoin the Knicks, MacKinnon moved into the GM's job. So, while surprised, I chose to ignore his comment and entered the locker room; the two of them remained outside. I knew that a blowup of some kind was not far away, but I didn't want to think about it that night. I was happy with the win and wanted to spend extra time with my players. When I left the locker room, Snyder and MacKinnon were gone.

The big blowup came after we lost to Chicago about a week later. Again Snyder and MacKinnon were waiting, and this time they asked to talk. As soon as I walked in the room, Snyder said angrily, "It's your fault we lost." I wasn't feeling good about the way we had played and was in no mood to listen to Snyder—who didn't know anything about the game— tell me what I was doing to cause the defeat, so I said, "Paul, I don't want to hear it" and started to leave the room. Snyder grabbed my arm and said, "You're going to listen to me!" I wrenched his hand from my arm and replied, "Like hell I am," and stormed out and into the team locker room. I was steaming. The players had heard the loud voices and were quietly taking off their uniforms and preparing to shower. Then the door to the locker room was pushed halfway open and Snyder shouted from the hallway, "I want to see you in my office." I responded, "I'm not coming. I won't have you telling me how to coach this team. I told you that when I took this fucking job." The door closed and the locker room got quiet as church at a Sunday Mass.

Soon MacKinnon came in and pleaded with me to go to Snyder's office, which was in another section of the building. I was still angry and reiterated my position. "Bob, I'm not going to listen to that guy tell me how to run this team." He said, "He'll fire you, Jack." I said, "That's okay; let him do it."

When I calmed down, I realized I had to answer one question: Did I want to continue my stubborn reaction to Snyder's tirade or could I find a way to maintain my authority yet show a modicum of appeasement?

MacKinnon wouldn't leave the locker room and kept asking me to reconsider. Finally, by the time the players had dressed and left, I had calmed down enough to agree to go with him to Snyder's office. When we walked into his office, Snyder had calmed down, too, and he spoke about his right as owner to know what was going on with the team and that I should be willing to talk with him about it. I agreed to that, but added that after a loss wasn't the best time to have such a meeting. We had a four-game West Coast trip coming up immediately and agreed to meet again when the team returned from the trip.

We won all four games on the trip and Snyder was jubilant at the meeting on our return home. He attributed the team's success to the confrontation that he and I had, and felt that he had caused the team to come together. And, in a strange way, there might have been an element of truth in that. The fact that I had stood my ground against higher authority may have helped the team to bond with me. A "we against them" attitude seemed to have emerged. I sensed that the disagreement was having a galvanizing effect on the team, that it was strengthening my position. However, whatever was causing us to play better wasn't important to me then. What was important was that the Braves went on an 11-game winning streak and everything in the world was right again. But in my heart, I knew I wasn't going to coach in Buffalo the following year.

Keep Your Cool

Over the years, I've learned never to be satisfied with my work. I invite criticism of my performance, study videotapes of my work, and listen to replays of my radio broadcasts. I've also found it important to have someone you trust provide feedback on what you do. Today, I rely heavily on my son, Chris, who has worked in the communications field since his graduation from Rollins College in 1981. Chris is now a senior editor for ESPN.com, but at one time he was a coordinating producer of Sports-Center. There have been times when he was my boss during the coverage of NBA Finals. Chris was not unwilling to tell me that I needed more energy in my delivery, that we'd have to retape a segment, or that I wasn't sitting up straight enough or looking directly at the camera. I know that

Chris tells me the truth, and I appreciate that. It is a great asset in radio and television broadcasting—and every other endeavor—to have objective critiques of your work.

Triumph (winning) is the coach's lifeblood. And, like Count Dracula, he can't live without it—at least he won't keep his job for long. Yet he can't get so caught up with success that he forgets how fragile it is and that it is achieved not only through his own efforts but through the combined efforts of all those on the team. I found that whenever I started feeling

If at First You Don't Succeed: Jack Ramsay

In my first year of NBA coaching, in a game against New York, I ordered my Sixers team to press the Knicks in the backcourt in a critical moment of a game. The Knicks got a quick hoop that turned the game around. In my postgame comments to the media, I said that I had made a mistake, and the loss was my fault. I didn't mind saying it; that was how I felt. The next day I got a call from Knicks' coach Red Holzman, an excellent coach and one of the all-time great guys in sports. "Jack," he said, "Don't ever say that losing was your fault. There are enough people ready to blame the coach. You know that there are a lot of things that go into winning and losing. I thought your move was a good one. It caught us by surprise. It would have worked for you nine out of ten times. We just lucked out."

Red may have just wanted to make me feel better about the loss. He usually had kind words for the coach of the team that his Knicks had just beaten. The larger his margin of victory, the more praise he had for his coaching adversary. But I thought later that he was correct in his assessment that when a plan doesn't work out the way you'd like, it doesn't necessarily mean that it was a bad choice. And, if the plan is sound, it's worth doing again, even though it may have failed once. I also decided that it's almost always better to generate action than to sit on your hands and do nothing. After that experience and Red Holzman's phone call, I was able to accept failures in much the same way I reacted to successes; by putting neither on a personal basis, I was better able to treat "those two imposters just the same."

good about myself as a coach, some team that I least expected knocked mine on its backside. Success is a seductive temptress. I tried to guard against succumbing to her wiles, but it's not the easiest thing to do when your team is red-hot and rollin'—a frequently expressed description of the champion Blazers team. I got a good lesson in humility when, in my second year at Portland, after a 50–10 start in the season, we had a rash of injuries to key players and won only 8 of the remaining 22 games, and lost to Seattle in our first round of the playoffs.

Disaster (losing) calls more for calm analysis than knee-jerk reactions. It requires the coach to find the cause of defeat and a way to correct it. It's the kind of behavior that players appreciate and respond to. It is not surprising to see a team that has just won a big game, get knocked on its butts by a lesser opponent the next time out. Why? Those teams allowed themselves to become too emotionally high from their triumph. Championship teams that are psychologically sound accept victory and defeat with a certain equanimity that speaks loudly of their confidence. They show satisfaction—not elation—from winning; they demonstrate disappointment—not despair—when they lose. They reserve celebrations for when they reach the ultimate goal. Everything else is a part of the journey to reach that goal.

Keeping your head "when all about you are losing theirs" is the definition of poise. It means extreme concentration on the task to be done, and the quick working out of a solution. It requires a person to think only of the task and to eliminate all that's extraneous to it. Sports provide a continuous setting for testing this human trait.

The free-throw shooter who has two attempts coming, with his team trailing by two points, and no time remaining in the game played on an away-court, must concentrate only on the rim and his shooting stroke. "It's you and the rim," is what I told my players. "Block out the game situation, the crowd, and the noise, and focus on the rim and a good follow-through on your shot."

The coach whose team has just lost a 10-point lead in the closing minutes and now has a chance to yet win the game, must act with poise and retain his composure. In the first round of the 1977 playoffs against Chicago, a deciding Game 3 was played in Portland. It was a wild game in

Never Let 'Em See You Sweat: Jack Ramsay

Able leaders give the appearance of being in total control of stressful situations. They seem to have remedies to every problem, and nothing seems to upset them. They show no signs of panic or even dismay. They are unruffled in the midst of turmoil, and when they give directions to others, they do so directly and simply. They inspire confidence in others by their exterior sense of calm.

Others have said that, although I was active on the sidelines, I appeared relatively calm, confident, and poised while coaching critical game situations. That may have been how I looked, but inside, my engine was running hot. At game's end, my shirt was always soaked with perspiration. The underarm sweats usually started at about 5 o'clock on the afternoon of game days and they didn't stop until the game was over. The armholes of my suit jackets and sport coats were ringed with perspiration stains that were not only embarrassing but ruined the fabric as well. It was not the appearance of a leader that I wanted to display to my players, so I tried anything and everything to "stay dry."

I think back on those efforts with great amusement now, but at the time, it seemed an important concern, and I constantly sought solutions. Deodorants prevented the dreaded underarm odor, but neither they, nor antiperspirants, stopped my sweat glands from functioning at full throttle. To keep the perspiration from showing on my jackets, I first tried folding a sweatsock under each arm, between my shirt and my jacket. But during the course of a game, the socks slipped out of position. During a game I was coaching at St. Joe's, while waving my arm vigorously several times to urge my team to get back on defense, suddenly, a sweatsock appeared at my wrist—bringing a bemused, inquiring look from the team's student manager who was sitting beside me. That was the end of the sweatsock experiment.

I next tapped my family for solutions. My wife, Jean, suggested using women's dress shields. I tried them, but they weren't absorbent enough for my deluge of sweat. Then she suggested putting a Pampers diaper under each armpit (which were conveniently available since we had a young child at that time). I was willing to try anything. The Pampers worked! They absorbed the perspiration and kept my shirts and jackets bone-dry. The only problem was that the Pampers were bulky; a whole one was more than I needed. So I cut one in half, and wedged a half-Pamper under each armpit. That felt better and was less noticeable, yet the padding was large enough to absorb the perspiration flow. I established a procedure whereby, as soon as the game was over, I went to the locker room, talked briefly with the team, went to the coach's room, discarded the Pampers, then met the press with dry underarms. It worked—but not always without mishap.

When I cut a Pamper in half, it left one end open, so that the inside packing material was loose. During a Buffalo Braves game in which I was especially active—giving animated arm gestures—some of the Pamper packing came shooting from my sleeve like artificial snow. Ray Melchiorre, the team trainer, in whom I had confided about using the Pampers, knew immediately what had happened and laughed so hard he almost rolled off the bench. The players on the bench looked bewildered as the "snow" drifted to the floor in front of them. Some looked up to the ceiling of the auditorium, half expecting to see real snow coming through the roof. I sat on the bench for the rest of the game with my arms at my sides. Melchiorre let the story slip out to some of the players and they had great fun with it.

The best solution to the perspiration problem came about after I left the Braves and went to Portland. Washable, wrinkle-free ultra-suede had come into existence, and I bought six or eight unlined jackets in that fabric. The NBA required coaches to wear either dress shirt and tie, or turtlenecks without ties. I chose the latter—short-sleeved, cotton turtleneck shirts, or the long-sleeved variety with the armholes cut out. I combined those with ultra-suede jackets, which didn't show perspiration. It worked out fine, and I stayed with that procedure pretty much after that—and felt better about my appearance during those "sweat-it-out" games.

which Bill Walton, Maurice Lucas, Bobby Gross, and Lloyd Neal had all fouled out. The Blazers had held a comfortable lead, but the Bulls put on a furious drive to narrow our lead to 1 point with about 30 seconds left in the game. (This series took place before the 3-point shot was in the rule book, so Portland needed a hoop or two free throws to prevent the Bulls from scoring the winning field goal on their last possession.) We took a timeout, and I watched the players coming to our bench. Only Lionel Hollins, who was having a bad shooting game (something like 3 for 15), looked me in the eye. The others looked at the floor or toward the baseline. In the huddle, I drew up a screen-and-roll play for Hollins; he knocked down an open jumper, and we advanced to the next round. I selected Hollins to take the shot because he was the only player who showed that he wanted the ball. My confidence in him supported his confidence in himself.

One of the best in basketball at encouraging cool confidence is Phil Jackson. The Lakers play—as did Jackson's championship Bulls teams before them—with a calm assurance that make them very difficult to beat. They expect to win. If they don't, they don't get bent out of shape. They just get ready to win the next one. Jackson's self-assured bench demeanor has a lot to do with that success.

Sports can teach you a lot about dealing with the ups and downs of life. You learn to take the hard knocks—both physical and emotional—and get back in the game without a timeout for self-pity. It is easy to bask in the glory of victory and individual and team accomplishment; the hard part is to learn to accept failure and bounce back, ready for the next challenge. The best approach is to take victory and defeat with a balanced perspective. Enjoy the moment of victory, and don't get too dejected by defeat.

Transition Game

Succeeding on the Court of Life

TODAY, A SCANDAL-HUNGRY public seems to prefer to hear and read about athletes who succeed in their respective sports but fail dramatically in their personal lives or after they retire from playing. That is a shame, because many former athletes (stars and role-players alike) make highly successful transitions to real life when their playing days are over. And as intently as we followed their exciting athletic feats, we'd be wise to pay just as much attention to the skillful way they've maneuvered their leadership capabilities off the playing arena onto the court of life. Here are a few exemplars in the Transition Game from the great sport of basketball.

The Quiet Man: Bob Pettit

The voice on the other end of the phone didn't say "hello" or "good morning," just the name, "Bob Pettit," spoken in a quiet, firm tone that

In the Minority: Problem Players

As the time of this writing, the 2003 NBA season had just reached its conclusion, and the success of the San Antonio Spurs seemed a fitting climax to a year of unusual ups and downs.

The summer of 2003 proved to be one of discontent for the NBA. An alarming number of players faced criminal charges: Chris Webber admitted to perjury about his complicity in accepting money while a student at the University of Michigan. Damon Stoudamire and Rasheed Wallace had more charges of marijuana possession; Darrel Armstrong, Sam Cassell, Jerry Stackhouse, and Glenn Robinson were all charged with criminal offenses. But the most serious charge—criminal assault—which a 19-year-old woman brought against Kobe Bryant, shook the NBA at its foundation. The results of that case are pending.

I have always found NBA players to be generally good citizens. The vast majority of the more than 400 players that fill the rosters of the 29 teams live exemplary lives and take seriously their responsibilities to family, team, and society. The current series of exceptions raises a red flag of warning to Commissioner David Stern, and I'm confident he will take appropriate steps to get the NBA back on track.

gave an immediate mental image of the person. It was a voice that implied, "You placed the call and now that you've got me on the phone, tell me what I can do for you." It was courteous, confident, and businesslike. It was what I expected, but I knew that it represented a great transition in a man who struggled early to attain his goals in life.

When I had asked Bob, one of the 50 Greatest Players in NBA history, who has made a remarkable transition from team leader to business leader, whether the qualities that made for success in basketball applied to professional life, he replied, "Absolutely. The same things apply: The preparation, the hard work, and dedication you bring to basketball produce the same results in the business world.

"I did the same preparation for my life outside of basketball as I did when I played. I think the proper mental approach is very important: Know what you have to do and then work hard at the job—be very dedicated to success." As to his ability as a leader, Bob said, "I never tried to be a team leader in basketball. I wasn't a guy who did a lot of talking. I just wanted everybody to see that I worked hard, that I'd give my full effort all the time. In business, I try to surround myself with the best people and then let them do their thing." And if that doesn't succeed? "Then we all sit down, talk it over, and work things out."

He also learned early to plan for his future: "Players weren't making the money then that they make now. We all knew we'd have to find a way to take care of our families when we finished our careers. I had done some work in the off-season at the American Bank and Trust Company in Baton Rouge, and the president indicated that there'd be a job there when I finished playing."

So after the 1962–1963 season, Pettit told Ben Koerner, the owner of the Hawks, that he was going to play just two more years and then retire. "I had the opportunity to join that bank in Baton Rouge as a vice president and I didn't want to let that opportunity pass by. But I wanted to let Ben know in advance, so that he could take whatever steps he felt necessary with the team."

After leaving Baton Rouge, he became chairman of the board at the Jefferson Bank in New Orleans and served in that capacity for 15 years. He now operates his own consulting business.

Front Man: Jerry West

Jerry West was a great collegiate player at West Virginia, leading his team to NCAA tournaments three times (1958, 1959, 1960), and was the tournament's outstanding player in 1959 (his team, however, never won the national championship). When he entered the NBA in 1960, West teamed with Elgin Baylor on the Lakers and reached the league finals eight times, although they only won once.

Despite West's individual achievements, his teams had so many near misses that he became almost paranoid about his failure to win. Pat Riley, a teammate of West's on the 1972 team that sailed through the playoffs, beating New York in six games in the finals, once told me, "Jerry was a basket case when we reached the finals that year. He had lost so often to Boston he was sure something would happen to keep us from winning that year."

Looking back at the stats of that series, it was the only time in his career that West shot under 40 percent from the field. But the Lakers won the title that season and West breathed a sigh of relief that was heard from coast to coast.

West was never a vocal leader as a player. When he started in the NBA, he stayed to himself, watching the veterans "out of the corner of my eye," learning to be a professional. As he reached veteran status, his actions were his words: the all-out way he played, his selfless devotion to team play, and his ability to deliver in the clutch.

Injuries cut into his career, but he moved quickly from leader on the court to leader off it. Two years after he retired as a player in 1974, he took on the coaching responsibilities of the Lakers. Though he now admits that he "was ill-prepared for coaching," the Lakers reached the playoffs in each of the three years West coached them. However, coaching was not for him. He had a hard time relating to players who couldn't play with his energy and skill, and he often criticized them severely (and now says that he's "embarrassed by some of the things I said"). And the specter of failure continued to loom large for him. The team's failure to advance in the playoffs during his coaching tenure bothered him terribly, so he resigned as coach after the 1979 season.

He then moved to the front office, first as a consultant, two years later as general manager, and two years after that, as executive vice president of basketball operations, a job he held until 2000. In this arena, success came quickly for West, particularly in personnel work. He possessed an uncanny knack for determining who could play in the NBA and who couldn't. He was a tireless worker; there was no game too far or remote to keep West from checking out a prospect. Most of his selections panned out. Among his prize draft picks were Magic Johnson, James Worthy, A. C. Green,

Eddie Jones, Ruben Patterson, Nick Van Exel, Derek Fisher, and Devean George. West also engineered trades or free agent signings that brought Shaquille O'Neal, Kobe Bryant, Robert Horry, and Rick Fox to the team.

The Lakers ran through several coaches during West's administrative tenure. Jerry knew the problems of coaching in the NBA and gave the coaches his support, but owner Jerry Buss had a stronger voice in hiring decisions. West, however, was indirectly responsible for the two most successful coaching picks.

Buss, in his first year of ownership (1979), hired Jack McKinney to succeed West, and McKinney brought Paul Westhead with him as an assistant. When McKinney suffered a traumatic bike accident early in his first season with the team (the Lakers were 10 and 4 at the time), Westhead took over as head coach and the Lakers won the championship. West recommended Pat Riley, who was doing color commentary on Lakers' telecasts, to be Westhead's assistant. When the Lakers staggered out of the gate at the beginning of his second full season (1981–1982), at the urging of Magic Johnson, Buss let Westhead go, and Riley became head coach.

Riley developed the "Showtime" Lakers, an up-tempo, high-scoring team, led by Magic Johnson's spectacular floor generalship, Abdul-Jabbar's majestic presence in the middle, and Worthy's solid all-round game. The Lakers won four championships during Riley's tenure.

However, Riley stepped down in 1990 after some of the players rebelled at his extra-tough conditioning and drillwork. West then hired Mike Dunleavy, who took the Lakers to the NBA Finals in 1991, but left after the following year to become coach/general manager at Milwaukee. West promoted assistant Randy Pfund to the head job. When Pfund struggled late in the 1993–1994 season, West brought Magic Johnson in to coach; but the Lakers floundered down the stretch and Magic resigned at the end of the season. Del Harris was next, and he got immediate positive results, but no championship. Harris gave way to Kurt Rambis at the end of the 1998–1999 season. Phil Jackson came onboard the following year, and he had immediate success with the Lakers, winning three consecutive titles.

West derived little enjoyment from Jackson's success with the team. He continued to anguish so much over the team's performance that he could rarely watch a game in its entirety. The angst became so great that at one point he was hospitalized. He resigned his position after the 2000 season. Looking back, he says, "I was just burned out. It was a very sad day for me. I thought I'd always be a Laker."

But West's mark was clearly on those Lakers. Shaquille O'Neal once said that West was the reason he became a Laker. Kobe Bryant said that West was his confidant. When the two stars were having trouble playing in harmony, it was West who got them straightened out.

After a two-year leave of absence from basketball, West got the urge to be connected with the game again, so when the Grizzlies moved from Vancouver, BC, to Memphis, under new ownership, West took the job of president of basketball operations. It didn't take long for him to get his new team better organized.

Sidney Lowe was the incumbent coach, but when the Grizzlies started the season winless in nine games and appeared to lack direction, West reached back for a retired, veteran coach, Hubie Brown, to step in and establish order. The appointment raised media eyebrows, because many thought Brown was too old (67) to relate to contemporary players. West responded, "I don't give a damn what people say. I'm going to do what I think is best for the team. If I make mistakes, I'm a big boy, I can take it [the criticism]." West knew that Brown would bring the discipline and fundamental instruction that the team needed, and the coach soon made the Grizzlies a competitive team.

Memphis finished the 2003 season with a 28–54 record, its best since coming into the league at Vancouver in 1995–1996. The team has a rising star in 7-foot forward Pau Gasol, and other young talent that should improve under Brown's guidance. With some luck in the draft and West's propensity for making shrewd trades, most NBA people think Memphis will be in the playoff hunt in a year or two.

West sees a strong connection between his playing days and his management acumen. "As a member of a team, you get to be a part of a group that's striving for high goals. You experience the thrill that comes with winning, and that awful feeling of defeat. You have a greater appreciation of those around you—their intestinal fortitude and mental toughness. I learned a lot by watching the professional way my teammates conducted their lives; they were always ready for the game."

West is—always has been—a goal-oriented person. He says simply, "You must have goals; it's the reason you compete and excel. It's good to have dreams, too; there's no limit on what you can achieve." He looks on his job with Memphis as "the ultimate challenge: to start with a team at the bottom and make it competitive. I want this team to be able to compete with the Lakers."

West believes that an individual's personality dictates the kind of leader that person can be. "I think I have a way of relating to people and getting along with them. I don't talk down to people. I don't try to boss or manage people; I work with them. I'm candid and honest. If someone comes to me for advice, I ask them first, 'Do you want me to say what you want to hear or do you want to know what I really think?' If they're all right with hearing the truth, I'll talk to them. I also think that I can develop a level of trust with others. Mutual trust is very important in leadership." (Kobe Bryant said, "It's great to listen to Jerry West—he's been there; I could always trust Jerry.")

West admits that the fear of failure has been a prominent driving force in his life, but he doesn't look on it as a negative. In fact, he sees the opposite effect. "If you don't want to fail, you have to find out what you need to do to avoid it, then work hard to prevent it from happening. If you have goals, and don't want to miss out on them, that fear is a driving force to success."

Man of Steel: Dave Bing

Dave Bing grew up in a solid home environment the second of four children. His dad, Hasker, was a building contractor who went into business for himself, restoring or rebuilding old, broken-down houses and churches in Washington's blighted economic areas. The Bing family was very religiously oriented, and Sunday church attendance was obligatory. The values of church membership, hard work, education, and good citizenship were deeply entrenched in all the children.

When Dave was 14, his father started to teach him the construction business. One of Dave's first projects was to build a brick wall of modest proportions. Dave went at it with zeal and energy, declining suggestions on the building process. His father waited until Dave had completed the job and stood admiring his work. Then the elder Bing leaned gently on the wall, whereupon it fell to the ground. Dave was chagrined and wanted to know why his father had ruined his work. His dad told him that the first premise of all work is to do the job right; and if it isn't right, you start over, and work at it until it is right. His dad showed him where he had erred, and Dave rebuilt the wall. This time he got it right. He never forgot that lesson: "My father taught me that you have to build a solid foundation to make anything good. I applied that principle to almost everything I did in athletics and, later, in business."

The Detroit Pistons paid Bing $15,000 as a first-round draft choice in 1966. He had married his high school sweetheart, Aaris Young, while at Syracuse, and the couple already had two children when he went to Detroit. Instead of taking summers off like most of his teammates, Dave accepted a job at the National Bank of Detroit to learn the rudiments of banking finance. For seven summers, he gained experience in every facet of the business—from teller to manager. After that, he worked two summers in a training program for car dealers, run by Chrysler Corporation. Dave valued those experiences, but discovered that he didn't want either of those careers. He wanted to get actively involved in business for himself, and the steel industry intrigued him.

When his playing days were over in 1978, Dave took a job with Paragon Steel where he started off working in the warehouse and then spent time in the various departments of the company—shipping, accounting, sales, marketing, and purchasing. He learned the company operation thoroughly and from the ground up.

"From time to time, I'd think back to that lesson I learned from my father about starting from a solid base and doing things right. I stuck with the premise that it was best to learn what you want to do from scratch," he said.

He also negotiated his own financial deal with Paragon for $35,000—a severe drop from the $250,000 he made as an NBA player in his final year. But he wasn't concerned about the money at that time; his objective was to acquire job experience. Two years later, Dave formed Bing Steel and began working out of a rented office with a staff of four employees and a rented warehouse. His company determined the steel needs of carmakers, then bought the metal to fill their orders. Soon after, in 1980, he purchased an abandoned factory, acquired the necessary equipment, and became his own steel processor—cutting, shaping, and bending raw steel to various specifications. Dave Bing was in business— big business.

However, his timing was bad. The steel and automotive businesses were in the throes of a depression. Bing lost $90,000 of his initial $150,000 investment. Though it scared him to lose so much of the money he had saved from his basketball career in such a short time, he never thought of quitting. He called on his experience in athletics to carry him past that hurdle.

"I knew how to deal with defeat," he related in *The Name of the Game Is Life,* by Robert L. Shook and Ramon Greenwood (Lincolnwood, IL, NTC/Contemporary Publishing, 1992). "I learned that lesson well as an athlete. When you don't succeed, you don't see it as a failure because you know you'll always come back the next game. You take on the challenge, and it's something you love every time it happens. Coming from that background, I wasn't about to accept a setback simply because my company lost money during its first year."

Bing Steel rebounded in its second year as sales increased to $4.2 million, and the company was able to show a profit. Since then, Bing Steel has had mostly profitable years. When the economy sags, Bing sets new goals and adjusts his game plan just as he did when he played basketball. "In basketball, I always had other options ready to do what I wanted to do on the court. If the first option of a play didn't get me the shot I wanted, I went to the second, or the third if necessary. I never wanted to be stopped just because my opponent shut down my first option. I found it to be the same in business. You have to keep looking for different, more cost-efficient ways of getting your materials, manufacturing them into quality products, and distributing them to your customers. It's the same process."

In time, Bing Steel was absorbed into the multifaceted Bing Group, which is divided into Bing Metals Group and Bing Assembly Systems. Bing Metals provides steel for manufacturers in the automotive, appliance, and office furniture industries, and includes a Steel Processing Division and a Stamp & Assembly Division. Bing Assembly Systems manufactures and assembles various aspects of the interior and exterior components of automobile construction and has divisions in Detroit, Michigan, and Berne, Indiana.

A couple of years ago, Bing considered joining with Lear Corporation to explore the purchase of auto parts companies in Mexico and South America, but decided to pass on that change in his game plan. "As it turned out, it was a good thing I did," he explained later. "It would have ended up costing us a lot of money. Now there's a movement to do business in China . . . but I want to study that very carefully before I do that. You can't afford to make a mistake at that level; it's too costly."

Bing said that the best lesson he learned playing basketball was the necessity of getting along with others. "Being successful in both basketball and business is all about teamwork. I was a pretty good scorer, but I couldn't score unless someone set picks for me to get open and someone else passed me the ball. And the team couldn't win unless we all defended. I learned early on that basketball was a team game. So is business. I rely on a lot of other people to make my business a success."

Dave has received much recognition for his success in the business world. In 1984, he was named the Nation's Outstanding Minority Small-Business Entrepreneur and was honored at the White House by President Ronald Reagan. In 1990, he received the first Schick Achievement Award for prominence following an NBA career. He is also a highly visible and productive member of the Detroit community. In 1987, he made a six-figure contribution to the United Negro College Fund. And in July 1989, when the Detroit public school system was set to eliminate sports from the curriculum due to budget cuts, Bing was asked to head up a committee to raise the necessary $600,000 to continue programs in sports, music, and the arts. In August, he handed over a check for the full amount. He then initiated a concerted appeal to the voters to pass a levy that would provide funds for those activities in the future. The levy passed in September of the same year.

Bing retains a strong commitment to the youth of Detroit's inner city. In *The Name of the Game Is Life*, he said, "I want to encourage black kids to get a good education and prepare themselves for the future. I feel a responsibility to them. And I want to build my business so it can provide jobs for blacks. Eighty percent of my staff is black, and that's part of my plan."

In 2000, Bing joined with Ford Motor Company to open an employee-training center for minorities, which is still flourishing. There, too, he has set high standards. Any trainee is automatically dismissed who, in the first three months, misses one day without calling in or is late to work four times. The turnover rate for employees is 12 to 15 percent a year. For employees who meet Bing's standards, the rewards are great. Managers get equity in the company after as short a period as three years, and Bing has given about 19 percent ownership to them. He retains the rest.

Bing has become a leader not just in business but in the larger Detroit community. He has attained that niche the same way he did as a player: by working hard and setting an example for others to follow. "My father always said, 'Don't just tell people what to do; show them and work with them and respect them.' I want people to understand that nobody is going to outwork me and I'm not going to ask them to do anything I won't do myself."

Dave Bing is living proof that following the same standards that made him a great college and pro basketball player—setting and pursuing goals, working harder than his competitors, rebounding from setbacks, adjusting his game plan, playing as a team, and giving unselfishly—enabled him to transfer that success to business.

Taking the Heat: Billy Cunningham

For Billy Cunningham, the lessons he learned as a basketball player and transitioned to the business world have led to tangible results. "The hard work that it takes to become a good player is the same that it takes to be a success in business. Set high goals, then when you reach those, set some more that are higher. You have to know everything about your business and about your competition. Your plans have to be flexible enough to accommodate changing conditions in the economy," he said. "And never, never allow complacency."

Ironically, he might have missed out playing in the NBA altogether if his father had had his way. "The NBA was not what it is today when I graduated from North Carolina. I didn't even know I was drafted until a newspaper writer called to tell me," Billy recalled. "My father thought it was better for me to play AAU [Amateur Athletic Union] ball for a team like Phillip 66, where they gave you a job that you kept after your playing days were over. I even visited Bartlesville [Oklahoma] and went over their whole program with them. It was a good opportunity. But I wanted to prove myself as a player, so I went with the Sixers. My first contract was for $12,500—and I had to negotiate all summer with [owner] Ike Richman for the extra $500," he added with a laugh.

Cunningham proved to be outstanding as the sixth man on the Philadelphia championship team of 1967; but the following year he broke his wrist in the New York series as the Celtics bounced back to defeat the Sixers, 4 games to 3 in the Eastern Finals.

Cunningham regards his playing and coaching days as a "phenomenal experience." But they were never the be-all and end-all for him. Early on, he became interested in business and investments. At the beginning of their association, his agent, Shelley Bendit, guided him to some investments; then Billy went out on his own. He started his own travel agency in Philadelphia and bought into a Holiday Inn with some other Philadelphia sports personalities; he still owns a pub near Philly and is an investor in the Fleet Bank and other smaller businesses. He is careful where he puts his money. In describing how he selects opportunities, he says, "I've got to think the product is good, but primarily I invest in the people involved in those businesses."

Cunningham says his most productive business experience was in securing an NBA franchise for Miami, which began operating in 1989. During the negotiations, he says he learned a valuable principle: "Lewis [Schaffel, his partner] and I had done all the work in getting the NBA to accept Miami as a franchise. Then at a meeting we had with the majority owner, Ted Arison, he asked how much we were going to invest of our own money." Cunningham says he was upset by the question at first, but then realized that Arison had a good point. The efforts of Billy and Lewis were vital to establishing the franchise, but to make them viable

True to His Word: Billy Cunningham
and Jack Ramsay

I became coach of the Sixers for the 1968–1969 season, and after the Chamberlain trade, I moved big forward Luke Jackson into Wilt's spot at center, and inserted Cunningham into the starting lineup to pair with Chet Walker as forwards. It was a dynamic front line. Jackson owned the boards and Walker and Cunningham were virtually unstoppable from inside or out. Billy upped his points and rebounds averages to 24.8 and 12.6, respectively, that season, and made the All-NBA first team. But Jackson popped an Achilles tendon after 25 games (the Sixers were 18–7 at the time), and the team was never quite the same.

Cunningham played three more seasons with Philadelphia, then jumped to the American Basketball Association, signing with the Carolina Cougars. Before his last contract year with Philadelphia, Billy had hired an agent, Shelley Bendit, to represent him in his contract negotiations. As general manager and coach, I met with Bendit, who told me that Cunningham, who was making $45,000 at the time, was looking for a significant raise at the end of his present deal. Sixers owner, Irv Kosloff, had instructed me to put a limit of $75,000 on any extended contract, and when I told Bendit this, he said that it wasn't enough. Kosloff didn't feel the need to negotiate the matter, since Cunningham still had a year under contract. Midway through that summer (1971), I got a call from Billy saying that he and Bendit would like to meet with me. They drove to my house in Ocean City and told me that they had signed with Carolina, effective for the 1972–1973 season, when Cunningham was a free agent. Billy told me later, "I couldn't turn the money down. I was making $45,000 to $50,000 with Philly; Carolina offered $250,000 to $300,000."

Cunningham promised me that he'd play his heart out in his last season in Philadelphia, and true to his word, he did. He averaged 23 points, 12 rebounds, and handed out just under 6 assists. But the team had gotten old; it struggled through a disappointing season (30–52), and Billy and I both left at the end of the year.

partners, they also needed to show they were willing to invest some of their own money. Billy said that he often asks that same question of others in business deals before becoming personally involved.

"Lewis and I really worked hard to make that franchise a success. We did whatever we had to do. The night before a committee of owners was coming to inspect the game site, we went out and painted over the graffiti that was on buildings around the Miami Arena. We hired limos to pick up the committee members at the airport, and even instructed the drivers to take them along only the most scenic routes and to avoid the less attractive sights in the city."

Later, as the managing partners of the Heat, Lewis took care of the internal operations, while Billy focused on developing the team. They did an outstanding job. The Heat made the playoffs in the third year of its operation; and five years later, when the Arison family offered to buy out their interests, Billy and Lewis left—very handsomely rewarded for their efforts.

Cunningham also learned another important leadership lesson: "If you want to motivate people, show them first how highly motivated you are. I always want people to work with me, not for me." That formula has worked well for Billy Cunningham—the player, the coach, and the business executive. He's been at the top of the heap in everything he's done.

Most Likely to Succeed: Bill Bradley

Growing up in Crystal City, Missouri, Bill Bradley was a teenage phenomenon. He was an excellent student, a school leader, and an outstanding athlete (who specialized in basketball). These powerful characteristics were reinforced by his strong religious convictions, which he displayed openly. Even at that time, Bradley watchers speculated that he was destined for the presidency of the United States.

As a senior, Bradley led Crystal City High School to the Missouri basketball tournament finals, only to have his team lose—a hard fact for him to accept. When it came time to select a college, he first chose Duke, but switched to Princeton at the last minute when he learned that many Rhodes scholars had come from that Ivy League institution.

While at Princeton, Bradley dominated college basketball, flourishing under the unique guidance of Bill Van Breda Kolff, who coached a loosely structured, motion offense. Bradley was the hub about which the Princeton game flowed. He was in constant, purposeful motion, screening for teammates, rebounding missed shots, and seemingly always open to receive the ball. He also made pinpoint passes and shot the ball with amazing accuracy. Perhaps most important, Bradley made his teammates appear to be better than they were—the benchmark of all great players—and the Tigers became a formidable team. In each of the years he played, the team won Ivy League championships and competed in the NCAA playoffs as well.

After an outstanding career at Princeton, Bradley was awarded a Rhodes scholarship and spent two years at Oxford University, where he earned a master of arts degree, before entering the NBA with the New York Knicks in the 1967–1968 season. At the time, Dick McGuire, the Knicks coach, had a veteran team that featured Walt Frazier and Dick Barnett at guards and Cazzie Russell at small forward. McGuire used Bradley mostly as a reserve 2-guard during his rookie season, and Bill struggled with the speed of his matchups on both offense and defense, averaged only 8 points a game, and shot a career-low .416 from the field.

It was a tough initiation into the pros for Bradley. Die-hard Knicks fans had regarded Bradley as the basketball messiah who would lead the team to a championship and had expected nothing less than immediate proof of their faith in him. When they didn't get it, they wasted no time in reacting harshly to Bradley's disappointing first-season performance. He was booed by his followers for the first time in his life, ridiculed in the press, and suffered taunts from people on New York's streets. That kind of treatment could have ruined him—as it has any number of players—but Bradley was made of stronger stuff. The abuse served as greater incentive to improve his game and find a way to help his team.

Bradley worked hard over the summer to upgrade his conditioning and to better adapt his skills to the demands of the NBA game. His dedication, in conjunction with two circumstances that took place during the following season changed his, and his team's, fortunes. First, the Knicks traded Walt Bellamy and Howard Komives to Detroit for Dave DeBusschere. That trade enabled Red Holzman, who had succeeded

Exceeding Expectations: Bill Bradley

I was coaching St. Joseph's in 1962 when Bradley began his varsity career at Princeton, and I had heard a lot of media hype about him. Then I had the opportunity to see him play at Villanova in one of his first collegiate games. The hype was all justified—and then some. Bradley's all-around skill, focus on his craft, and game performance far exceeded what I expected.

On the day of the game, I arrived at the on-campus field house early to watch the teams warm up and got my first look at Bradley's ritual pregame preparation. After the traditional layup lines, Bradley began his shooting routine. He started in the basket area, shooting short jumpers and hook shots. He next moved out to about 15 feet and took shots from floor positions on either side of the basket, then moved farther out to the corners, wings, and top of the circle to shoot stand-still set shots, jumpers, and finally some runners off the dribble. This was followed by a variety of running hook shots, using different foot moves before releasing the ball. Every shot was taken with perfect balance, fluid motion, and clinic-type form. In 15 minutes of shooting, he seldom missed a shot. And though this, in and of itself, was a mesmerizing performance that even staunch Villanova followers watched with awe, it wasn't done for show: it was how Bradley prepared himself to play a game of basketball.

When the game began, Bradley played the same way: full focus, full control, outstanding results. It sometimes appeared that he shot the ball through the hoop without actually seeing the basket, an uncanny capability that John McPhee, a professor of journalism at Princeton, later described in "A Sense of Where You Are," a segment of his book, *The John McPhee Reader* (New York, Farrar, Straus and Giroux, 1965). When the game ended, I knew that I had witnessed the beginning of something special. Recently, I went back to research the game statistics, to freshen my recollection of that game. Bradley's numbers were: field goals, 10–15; free throws, 7–7; points, 27; rebounds 12. The score: Princeton 68, Villanova 55.

My St. Joe's team later faced Bradley and his Princeton teammates in the first round of the NCAA Eastern Regional Tournament in 1963 at the Palestra in Philadelphia. I had a good team (21–4); we used a variety of defenses—a switching man-to-man, a standard 1–2–2 zone, and a 1–3–1 zone trap—and we had all of them ready for Princeton. In fact, we were expected to beat Bradley's Tigers. We started the game with man-to-man coverage, and I recall giving Jim Boyle, my best defensive forward, the assignment to contain Bradley. The game plan was for Boyle to play Bradley close and physical, and to get help from his teammates when Bill used his patented reverse-dribble moves to get to the basket. My goal was to limit Bradley's shot attempts to about 15 and to keep his point total to 20 or fewer.

Our practice sessions had been good and we came to the game feeling confident we could win by carrying out those objectives. Bradley, of course, had a different game plan. No matter how he was defended, he found a way to get the kind of shot he wanted. And, with his excellent balance and agility, he drew contact from defenders, which got him repeatedly to the free-throw line. By half-time, Bradley had 20 points and Princeton was leading 33–31, and I knew that the Hawks were in a dogfight.

With less than four minutes remaining in the game, Princeton held a 7-point lead. Then Bradley fouled out. Without its leader, Princeton turned the ball over against the Hawks' pressing defense, and St. Joe's tied the game in regulation and went on to win in overtime. As for Bradley, he made 12 of 21 field goal attempts and all 16 of his free throws to score 40 points. He also had 16 rebounds, and held Tom Wynne, the Hawks' scoring leader to 9 points. Wynne later scored critical points to help St. Joe's win the overtime battle.

About an hour after the game, I went to the Princeton locker room to congratulate Bradley on a superb game. He was still in his sweat-drenched uniform, sitting somberly in front of his locker. He shook my hand, thanked me for acknowledging his effort, then added, "but it wasn't good enough."

McGuire as coach, to move Willis Reed to center and use DeBusschere in Reed's vacated spot at big forward. The second event occurred when Cazzie Russell broke his ankle, forcing Holzman to insert Bradley into the lineup at small forward. Frazier and Barnett remained at the guard positions. That unit clicked right away. The Knicks went from a 43–39 season in 1967–1968 to a 54–28 record the next, and they reached the Eastern Conference Finals, where they lost to Boston.

In the process, Bradley became an integral part of Holzman's synchronized, "hit the open man" offense, and tough, hard-nosed defense. Bill was in constant motion and the ball never seemed to be in his hands for more than a two-count: He either passed it, shot it, or quick-dribbled to improve his position. He played very aggressively on defense and was not averse to grabbing, holding, or flicking an elbow to make his presence felt; and he accepted the same from his opponents as part of the game.

Reed and DeBusschere were the obvious, vocal leaders of the team, but coaching against them, I came to believe that Bradley's unselfish, team-first attitude was the key element in the Knicks' marvelous teamwork that enabled them to win NBA championships in 1970 and 1973. Bradley demonstrated his own kind of leadership by his work ethic and by the way he adapted to Holzman's game plan—blending his skills seamlessly with Reed, DeBusschere, Frazier, and, later, Earl Monroe. It didn't go unnoticed by his teammates or his coach.

Phil Jackson, a reserve player on those teams, noted in the Foreword to Bradley's book, *Values of the Game* (New York, Artisan/Workman Publishing Co., 1998): "Bill brought with him the right work ethic—coming to practice early and staying late to work on his game. But what we didn't anticipate was his ability to adapt his game to whatever the Knicks needed for the team to succeed. He moved from guard to forward . . . and from a great scorer to a role player. His ego remained undamaged even though he was no longer the star, or 'the man,' because he understood the essence of the Knicks team game—that one guy couldn't carry the load alone" (p. 9).

Bradley was the kind of player coaches dream about. He had the skills to make a positive impact on the game and was first and foremost a team player. He didn't care whether he scored big or small—as long as the team won. He relished making a scoring pass as much as making the score himself. He worked hard to fulfill his defensive responsibilities. He was also passionate about the game; he loved everything about it: the feel of the ball, the sound of the dribble, the squeak of sneakers, the "swish" of the net as the ball sailed through. On recounting his love of basketball in *Values of the Game*, he wrote: "The only thing I had to do was allow the kid in me to feel the pure pleasure in just playing. In plenty of games, I played simply for the joy of it, shooting and passing without thinking about points. I forgot the score, and sometimes I would go through a whole quarter without looking at the scoreboard" (pp. 21, 22).

Bradley also accepted the discipline required to learn to shoot with perfect form; the necessity of hard, physical competition at practice to prepare for games; the feeling of satisfaction that comes with successful team play; and the exultation of the team in the locker room after a big win.

And, in a portent of things to come, Bradley was initiated to the world of politics when he became the Knicks' player representative to the NBA Players Association. The group was officially recognized at the 1964 NBA All-Star Game played in Madison Square Garden when the great players of that year—Wilt Chamberlain, Bill Russell, Oscar Robertson, Jerry West, Elgin Baylor, Tom Heinsohn, Bob Pettit, and others—refused to take the court unless team owners addressed their demands for a pension, health insurance, and other improved conditions during the playing season. The start of the game was delayed until the players received assurance that their group would be recognized and their demands would be met. It was a bold move on the players' part and marked the start of the union that, over the years, has protected player interests in the NBA. Bradley embarked on the task as his team's rep in his typical no-nonsense fashion: He worked with the other reps and made his voice heard, but not in a domineering way. Phil Jackson (again from his Foreword to *Values of the Game*) wrote, "As the team representative to the players' union, which negotiated labor agreements with the league, [Bradley] brought the same adaptability, a sense of how to get things accomplished even if he wasn't at the helm, directing the action, or receiving all the credit" (p. 9).

After Bradley retired from the game following the 1977 season, he wasted no time in becoming a player in a larger arena: national politics. He was elected to the U.S. Senate in 1978 and served three terms. Bradley found that certain qualities he learned in basketball helped him to assimilate to his new, prestigious "team": "I found that the Senate cloak room was a good place to learn about my colleagues and what was going on politically. It was a lot like a basketball locker room. It was an informal atmosphere—a place to relax if you wanted to. Some senators were reading; there was always someone pacing the floor rehearsing a speech; a couple of others would be deep in conversation. I kind of blended in and came to know people from all different backgrounds as they really were. I got to know them and they got to know me" (telephone interview).

Bradley also learned that working together was just as important in politics as on the basketball court. "I found that if you wanted to get things done, you couldn't do it by yourself. Getting a piece of legislation passed required the same teamwork that you needed in basketball. The important thing was to get the law passed, get it done, and be willing to contribute to the cause without necessarily getting any credit. It's like all the little things a player does on the court so that his team could win" (interview).

As on the court, Bradley excelled in public office. He became a member of the Finance Committee and was the author of the proposed Fair Tax Act, which became the Tax Reform Act of 1986. He identified with many of the social issues of the time: He was a strong advocate for control of neighborhood crime and violence, increased racial awareness, improved opportunities for higher education, better health care for all citizens, and more positive reforms in caring for the environment. Bradley's strong voice was influential on all those issues. And, fulfilling those early predictions made when he was a young man, he ran for president in 1999, but was defeated in the 2000 Democratic Party primary elections by then Vice President Al Gore.

Recently, Bradley told me more about his approach to leadership. He said that, in new situations, he waits for an appropriate time to become an active leader. "I was a vocal leader in high school and college; it was needed and I had no problem doing that. When I first came to the

Knicks, I was new on the scene and didn't play a lot, so I deferred to the more established veterans. It was the same way when I went to the Senate. As a junior senator, I waited my turn and did the best work that I could. Gradually, I took advantage of opportunities to lead." Bradley is remembered in both the NBA and the U.S. Senate as a quiet, yet effective leader, a team player who did everything possible to achieve success.

Bradley is currently the managing director of Allen and Company, an investment banking firm with headquarters in New York City. One of his functions with that company is to identify worthwhile investment opportunities for clients. And in this position, his career in basketball continues to inform him. He told me, "We have a very interesting project going right now with a young company that studies the correlation between a person's physical capabilities and his [or her] choice of a sport in which to participate."

Intrigued by the concept, I got in touch with the founder of the company, Steve Spinner. Steve had been an undersized wannabe football player in high school when the cross-country track coach noticed that he never seemed to tire during the demanding workout drills. He took Steve aside and told him that he was unlikely to ever become a player on the football team, but that he had the stamina and running ability to be an outstanding distance runner. The coach challenged Spinner to join his team for an upcoming meet to see if he could finish the 3.1-mile course. Steve not only finished the race, he won it!

The meet turned out to be just the kind of experience Steve needed; it was challenging and made the best use of his physical skills, enabling him to be successful. After that first race, Spinner went on to win many competitions in distance running in high school and later at Wesleyan (Connecticut) College. But Spinner was doing more than running races; he was also doing some long-distance thinking about the value of measuring athletes' capabilities to find out how they could use their skills to best advantage. Eventually the idea grew into a business concept, and he launched a company dedicated to that objective, called Sports Potential, Inc.

How Bradley and Spinner got together gives credence to the theory that there are no coincidences. Bradley had long been Spinner's hero. To Steve, Bradley embodied the ancient Greek maxim of a strong mind in a strong body, and many of Spinner's required student essays were about his idol. He had even wondered on occasion whether Bradley might be interested in his concepts about skill correlation. On Thanksgiving weekend in 2002, Spinner and his wife were boarding a plane to the West Coast after attending a wedding in New Jersey. On their way to the coach section, Steve was stunned to see Bradley sitting in the first-class cabin.

Steve saw his opening and went for it. He spent the first couple of hours of flying time writing up a business proposal about his young company. Approaching courteously, he gave it to Bradley and returned to his seat. An hour passed. Then there was Bradley heading toward Spinner's seat. He told Steve he liked his concepts and set up a subsequent meeting.

Since that in-flight connection, Bradley has been able to interest a number of investors in Spinner's Sports Potential, Inc., and the company is off and running, with an expanded focus. Part of its mission now is to help underprivileged youngsters discover their athletic potential and achieve success. "The vast majority of black, inner-city, young male athletes expect to play basketball in the NBA," said Steve. "At best, only a very small percentage of them will reach that goal. We want them to find other alternatives for their potential that will keep them occupied in sports, rather than have them drop out of basketball and into dangerous activities." Bradley, Steve notes, was instrumental in implementing the company's efforts in that regard.

When I asked Spinner what about Bradley most impressed him, his answer was immediate: "his integrity." "He's the most ethical individual I've ever met. And now the company reflects that same quality." Bradley simply says, "Never doubt who you're dealing with. If there are any questions about a person's character, you don't want him."

The Magic Touch: Earvin Johnson

Though his playing days are over, Magic Johnson remains committed to the sport that he loves. He is a vice president of the Lakers and serves as an analyst of NBA games for Turner Broadcasting. He enjoys his work with TNT thoroughly. "It's so much fun. We have a good group [Charles

Barkley, Kenny Smith, Magic, and host Ernie Johnson]. It keeps me close to the game." But his horizons have expanded far beyond the game as well, into the business world—a transition he prepared for while he was still playing.

"While the other guys were playing Nintendo games, I was reading the business section of newspapers and the *Wall Street Journal.* I was also able to meet people of influence because I was a player. I would invite 20 or 30 people who had great success in business, and pick up the tab for those meetings, to find out how they had become so successful. I humbled myself; I wasn't afraid to say 'I don't know.' It was a great learning experience—kind of like a course in Business 101."

He also learned a lot playing basketball that he carried over into his business ventures. "It takes the same commitment to excellence, the same hard work, and the same focus on preparation. You have to know whom you're dealing with—kind of like scouting the opposition in basketball. And you've got to be ready to change some aspects of your game plan to meet changing conditions. The same rules apply."

Magic—who was a great leader on the basketball court, setting the tone for how his team played, stopping the action when an offensive play wasn't carried out properly, and redirecting the action until the play was done right—applies the same principles in his business practices: "A leader is a leader no matter what. In my company, I'm the one who initiates and solicits new business ideas, gets the plans in motion, represents us at meetings with prospective clients, and stays on top of what we're doing. My associates know that I'm up at 6:00 in the morning, that I get my workout before starting the business day, and stay at it until late in the evening when necessary. They see what I'm doing and know that I expect the same effort from them. That's what a leader does."

In 1993, Johnson formed the Johnson Development Corporation, whose stated business purpose is to foster local economic growth and financial empowerment in long-neglected minority urban and suburban neighborhoods. The corporation set out to accomplish those objectives by developing entertainment complexes, coffeehouses, restaurants, and retail centers in underdeveloped communities, thereby providing jobs within those communities and using local minority contractors and service vendors in the development processes.

Born to Lead: Magic Johnson and Pat Riley

Coach Pat Riley, who remained close to Magic Johnson after Riley left the Lakers, recently acknowledged that he had no inkling that Magic would develop into the business giant that he's become. He does, however, recall that, "Magic always played it close to the vest. As a young player, there was nothing frivolous about his spending; he was smart with his money and he acquired good advisors."

Regarding Johnson's leadership ability, Riley said, "It was the number-one characteristic that enabled Magic to become who he was as a player and to elevate him to his current status in the business world. He drove himself and was very demanding of his teammates. He had such an intense will to win—he never thought his team would lose a practice scrimmage, an individual game, or would fail to win a championship. He has surrounded himself with bright people and has the personality to associate himself and his endeavors with leaders in other successful industries. He's just a born leader."

Johnson Development Corporation (JDC) comprises four entities: Magic Johnson Theatres/Loews's Cineplex Entertainment, Magic Johnson's T.G.I. Friday's/Carlson Restaurants Worldwide, Inc., Urban Coffee Opportunities/Starbucks, and Canyon-Johnson Urban Fund. Magic is the chairman and chief executive officer of the corporation, which establishes 50–50 partnerships with the most successful businesses in their marketing categories. (He is ably assisted in these ventures by Kenneth Lombard, who is president of the corporation.) JDC's first business venture, in partnership with Paul Walter Properties, was a shopping plaza in West Las Vegas, Nevada, in 1983. In 1994, Magic Johnson Theatres opened a 12-screen multiplex theater with Sony Entertainment at the Baldwin Hills Crenshaw Plaza, near Los Angeles. In 1997, the group partnered with Starbucks to open a store in Los Angeles, and in 1998 joined with Carlson Restaurants to open a T.G.I. Friday's in Atlanta, Georgia, then opened another store in Los Angeles in 2000. In 2001, the corporation acquired the 47-store Fatburger Restaurant Chain, with plans to add another 100 stores over the next five years. In addition to the business ventures of JDC, Johnson also heads up Magic Johnson Entertainment, Magic Johnson Productions, and Magic Johnson Music.

But it's not all about making money. The Magic Johnson Foundation, a separate, nonprofit organization is dedicated to improving the health, education, and social needs of inner-city youth, and to supporting related charitable organizations.

The Legend Continues: Larry Bird

Like Joe Dumars, Larry Bird joined his team's front office when his playing days were over. He became a "special assistant" with the Celtics franchise, a role that charged him with evaluating talent for the annual NBA Draft. But after five years of that involvement, and playing golf and fishing in Florida, Bird had the desire to get actively involved in the game again.

So Bird transitioned his leadership skills into coaching in 1997, when he became head coach of the Indiana Pacers. As related in Chapter 2, he quickly made a success of it (during his three-year tenure with the Pacers, the team won 147 and lost 67 [.687], won two Central Division titles, and reached the NBA Finals in 2000. He was voted Coach of the Year in 1998). But Bird never looked on coaching as a career. In his second year as coach, I asked him if he would consider staying on longer than his contract. He replied, "Jack, you know I'm no real coach. I've really learned a lot and it's been a lot of fun, but I'm done after next year." More recently, when I reminded him of those statements, Larry explained, "I meant that I wasn't going to dedicate my life to coaching basketball. It was really selfish of me to take the Pacers job. I had loved being a player and wanted to find out what it was like to coach—and I enjoyed that too, but I never intended to make a career of it."

In fact, Bird has bigger business ambitions. He wants to own an NBA team. He said, "That's what I'd like to do next. I'd like to run the basketball end of a franchise—get a team and work with it from the ground up." Bird is part of a financially sound group, headed by Steve Belkin, that bid for the Charlotte expansion franchise and was bitterly disappointed when the league awarded the franchise to Bob Johnson in 2002. Now they assess teams looking for a change in ownership. "There are teams available now, but they're mostly strapped by the salary cap and luxury tax and wouldn't be good investments." He added, "Charlotte would have been perfect."

He's hoping it will happen for him yet. "If I can do that, then I'll have done it all in basketball: played, coached, and owned a team—all in the NBA."

In the meantime, Bird keeps busy as owner and operator of a highly successful golf course in Naples, Florida, named The Hide Out Golf Club. He and two of his buddies, Larry and Maurice Kent ("they're from Philadelphia—can you believe that?"), built the course because they got tired of five-hour rounds of golf. Bird also does radio and television commercials and makes appearances for major corporations.

He is also focused on family and, to that end, is trying to reduce his travel time so that he can be at home more with his family. Bird lives with his wife, Dinah, and their two children, Conner and Mariah, in a beautifully situated home on the bay in Naples. His back condition, improved by surgically fusing the fourth and fifth vertebrae, allows him to jog a couple of miles with his dog in the morning, ride his bicycle, and play golf pretty much pain-free.

He and Dinah spend a lot of time with their kids, and Larry thinks Conner (age 11) might become a player. "He's really quick and can shoot it. He doesn't handle well right now, but he's young—and you never know." In the summer, the family goes back to its spread in French Lick, Indiana, where they have, essentially, a three-month reunion with family and friends. "We have a big place there, with a swimming pool and all kinds of playground stuff. It's a blast," says Bird.

A greater "blast" will be to see Bird run a basketball operation in the NBA—to put his stamp on a team, pick the right players and coaches, and instill in them the same level of competitiveness, confidence, and sense of teamwork that made him one of the all-time great players. Bird gets his chance to do all that with the Pacers, who hired him in the summer of 2003 as their president of basketball operations. In that capacity, Bird will have control of everything connected with the operation except contract negotiations, which former president, Donnie Walsh—now franchise CEO—will continue to handle. Bird didn't waste any time establishing his authority. Seven weeks after taking over, he fired Coach Isiah Thomas and replaced him with Rick Carlisle.

Nice Guy Finishes First: Joe Dumars

As a player, Joe Dumars was universally respected in the world of basketball, as much for his sportsmanship as for his skills and work ethic. It comes as no surprise to anyone who knows him that he is now a highly regarded businessman and community leader.

In addition to his duties with the Pistons as president of basketball operations, mentioned in Chapter 7, Dumars is majority owner and CEO of Detroit Technologies, Inc., a major supplier of automotive parts, and a partner in the Joe Dumars Fieldhouse, a highly successful indoor multisports and entertainment complex. Both are located in the Detroit area. And with one eye always on the less fortunate, Joe D organizes an annual charity celebrity tennis tournament (he's a competent tennis player himself) that has earned more than $1 million for the Children's Hospital in Detroit.

Dumars manages all those responsibilities by using what he describes as "effective time management" and by hiring "smart people who know what they're doing and then letting them do their jobs."

To Joe D, there's no doubt that what he learned as a basketball player is a major contributor to his success off the court. He cites several basic principles he learned as a player that helped him make the adjustment: "Sports—and basketball in particular—teach you how to get ready to face challenges. You must prepare yourself thoroughly for what's ahead. You learn to accept and display discipline. You learn to take direction and keep your emotions under control. You learn to respond positively in very competitive situations. You learn to be part of a team—that you can't do it all by yourself. You learn how to interact and work with others to reach your goals." He adds, "Those concepts are the same in real life as they are in basketball."

Air Apparent: Michael Jordan

Michael Jordan's off-court success is almost as well documented as his extraordinary achievements as a player. It was estimated that he made $40 million a year in endorsements and auxiliary income when the Bulls were in their championship run. He was able to do that by budgeting his time efficiently and giving the same attention to detail that he did as a player.

Michael moves quickly through his many daily activities, but he never seems to be in a hurry and never fails to give consideration to anyone who has his attention at the moment; he makes everyone feel that he's glad to see them. He has hired good people to take care of minutiae and that allows him to be himself. It is fascinating to watch him.

Now that his playing days are over, Jordan has more time to attend to his impressive business empire. He is associated with the following corporations and products: Electric Arts, Gatorade, Hidden Beach Records, MCI WorldCom, Michael Jordan Automotive Group, Michael Jordan Celebrity Invitational Golf Tournament, Michael Jordan Flight Schools, NBA Videos, Jordan Brand (a clothing line), Jordan Cologne, Oakley Sunglasses, Sara Lee Corporation, SportsLine, The Upper Deck Company, Wilson Sporting Goods, Nike, and four Michael Jordan restaurants.

Michael is a great spokesman. He is articulate, displays an easy sense of humor, and the camera loves him. Whether he's making a commercial pitch on television or talking to a group, he appears completely at ease and delivers his message clearly and succinctly.

Michael also runs the Jordan Senior Flight School, an annual three-day basketball "camp" for men, 35 years and older, held at one of the plush casinos in Las Vegas, Nevada (he runs two sessions of a camp for young players, both boys and girls, at the University of California–Santa Barbara). Typically, there are about 100 participants, most of whom have played at the high school or small-college level, but there are also some who have never played any organized ball. All the activities are conducted in a large conference hall—big enough to accommodate five full-length, portable basketball courts. After being drafted into teams, the players receive two instructional sessions (one by MJ) and play two team games each day. On the final day, playoffs are held and a championship team is determined. Expensive rings, watches, and trophies go to team and individual winners of competitions. Top college and NBA officials referee the games, and the camp staff consists of the best college coaches in the country, plus several—myself among them—with NBA connections. We give teaching sessions each day and coach the teams, so that by the end of camp, every player has contact with every coach, and, of course, with Michael Jordan.

Michael is wonderful. He is at the camp every day, gives a half-hour lecture/demonstration each morning on some phase of the game, then invites "campers" to come on the court to challenge him one-on-one. The players love it, and MJ makes it fun for them—but ever the competitor, he doesn't ease up on anyone.

As Jordan works through his day—whether as a player, at one of his camps, at a media session, or filming a television commercial—he gives the impression that he is doing it because he enjoys it and that the money he earns is a secondary priority. He is generous with his money, too, contributing to the Boys & Girls Clubs of America, UNCF (United Negro College Fund), Special Olympics, and various other private causes. In 1996, the University of North Carolina, MJ's alma mater, opened the Jordan Institute, as part of its School of Social Work, to which Michael contributed $1 million. The purpose of the institute is to strengthen family relationships, something Michael feels strongly about. (He says his own family structure is now solid.) In the same year, the James R. Jordan Boys & Girls Club and Family Life Center (named for Michael's late father) opened on Chicago's West side for inner-city youngsters and their families. The Chicago Bulls contributed $5 million and Michael $2 million to this project, which attracts more than a thousand participants a week.

Jordan's commercial value may have dimmed a bit, but Michael hasn't lost his touch with the soft jumper, and his knack for business success continues unabated.

The Enigma: Charles Barkley

As a player for the Philadelphia 76ers and, later, the Phoenix Suns and Houston Rockets, Charles Barkley was one of the most amazing offensive players that I've ever seen. At somewhere between 6–4 and 6–5, he could rebound with the biggest in the league; he had soft hands that enabled him to catch anything thrown in his direction, and the ability to power the ball to the basket through players much bigger than he was. He also had the skill of a point guard to "thread the needle" with passes, and he learned to shoot accurately from 3-point distance. He battled without respite around the hoop.

But Charles didn't see the importance of defense unless it was required at the very end of a game. When I was working television games for the Sixers, Charles was their main gun. I gave him full credit for his incredible exploits on offense, but I also noted when he was slow getting back on defense, not playing his man, or failing to give needed weak-side help. Before a game one night, I was in the Sixers locker room when Charles came in, and seeing me exclaimed, "Jack, you're killing me on TV about my defense. Why do you have to do that?" His teammates, in various states of readiness for the game, stopped what they were doing to listen. I told him, "Charles, I can only say what I see. When you do good things on offense, I say it, but when you loaf on defense, I say that, too." The other players all grinned at me and nodded in agreement. But Charles dismissed the subject, saying, "I can't play defense and score and rebound too."

Charles had his own mind-set about how he should play, and none of his coaches could ever alter it with any consistency. He seemed to feel that since he gave his full effort to offense—and indeed performed wonderful feats there—he shouldn't be required to work as hard on defense. And it wasn't because he lacked defensive skills. I had seen him force Magic Johnson into a poor percentage shot on a last possession in a Sixers-Lakers game that Philly won. He also had a knack for stealing the ball from high-post players that resulted in open-court layups. But overall, Charles seemed to regard defense as the time during which he could catch his breath, not pressure his man, and nobody could change his mind about that. It was unfortunate because he became a weak spot in his team's defense that opponents didn't hesitate to exploit—and that characteristic prevents Charles from being included among the all-round great players of the game.

But in addition to being strongly opinionated, Charles also happens to be one of the most good-hearted people I've met anywhere. In the days when teams traveled commercially, Charles' appearance at any airport attracted a small parade. People appeared from nowhere to walk along with him, ask him questions, or request him to sign things. I never saw him turn down a request.

And his behind-the-scenes kindness is well known to those close to him, if not well publicized in the media. When Tony Harris was new on the job as the Sixers trainer and doing postop shoulder therapy on Barkley, Charles asked about Tony's background, his family, and where he was living in the Philly area. Tony told Charles he was from Cincinnati, that he was married with a couple of youngsters, but that his family was still in Cincinnati because they hadn't been able to sell their house there. In the meantime, he was staying at a rooming house in the area. Charles told him to get a place for his family and bring them to Philadelphia, promising to take care of the additional costs until they sold their house. Charles kept his word, and kept his peace—he never said anything to anyone about it. I learned about the incident from Harris.

Loyalty is another admirable Barkley trait. After I left the Sixers and became affiliated with the Miami Heat and ESPN, whenever either group requested an interview with Charles and he knew that I was available, he would say he'd only do the interview if I conducted it—and he never turned me down. When Phoenix was in the NBA Finals with Chicago in 1993, I was among a horde of media waiting outside the arena after a shootaround on a game day. ESPN had sent a camera, a producer, and me, in hopes of getting something of interest to air on the early SportsCenter show. The Suns finished their work, came out of the building, and headed for the team bus. Charles was among them, but when he saw me, he stopped, came over, and answered a couple of my questions before joining his teammates.

Since his retirement as a player, Barkley has become something of a media star as a studio analyst of NBA games for TNT. He is witty and articulate, although sometimes self-contradictory and outrageous. There's no subject on which he doesn't have an opinion and he's never shy about expressing it. Working mostly with Kenny Smith, Magic Johnson, and host Ernie Johnson, Charles often sets the tone by making some bizarre statement that the others play off. The result is a casual scene where three former NBA players sit around talking about the game, and the viewer listens in. Host Ernie does a good job of keeping the conversation from straying too far, and it's popular television.

In any arena, Charles is still Charles—gracious one moment and irreverent the next—and is usually good for at least one surprising—if not startling—comment each program. Ironically, I have even heard him criticize a player for not defending!

Into the Future

Former athlete-leaders have a lot to teach us about making major life transitions. Despite too much attention today on those who "have it all" and then "blow it," there will always be those who take full advantage of the opportunity to transition their on-court leadership skills to the court of life. For a look into the future, you need go no further than Minneapolis, Minnesota, where you'll find Kevin Garnett.

In the fall of 1995, I asked Bill Blair, then coach at Minnesota, what he thought of Kevin Garnett, the Timberwolves fifth pick in the first round from Admiral Farragut Academy—the first high school player ever drafted into the NBA. Blair said that it was too early to tell for sure, but that Garnett appeared to have excellent tools for NBA play. While we were talking, the Wolves players finished dressing and left the room—except for Garnett, who was standing off in a corner, dressed in his top coat, his duffel bag at his feet. He was holding his cap in his hands and watching Blair and me in our conversation.

I had come to the locker room primarily to speak with Garnett, but had stopped first to talk with Terry Porter, a former Trail Blazer I had coached, and then with Blair. When I finished my conversation with the coach, I approached the rookie player. As I came near, he extended his hand and said, "I didn't want to interrupt your talk with Coach, but I wanted to meet you, Doc. I loved that Portland team you coached." Garnett was two years old when the Blazers won the championship in

1977, but as I was to learn, he had watched television replays of some of those Blazer games. "That was a great team," he added.

I was also soon to learn that KG was an avid student of NBA history and showed great respect for everyone who had played some part in it. We chatted for about 10 minutes, and I talked with him about his start in the world of professional basketball. I told him that, from what I had seen that night, he had the skills to become an outstanding pro player. He seemed pleased to hear my appraisal and added, "I know I have a lot of work to do, but I'm goin' to make it, Doc, I'm goin' to make it."

And make it he has. Garnett's success comes as no surprise to his coach, Flip Saunders. "I went to see him work out before the draft, and you couldn't tell that he was (then) about 6–9. He played like a 6–3 guard—the way he ran, his agility, his easy execution of fundamentals. I knew that day that he was going to be a great player."

Garnett put up modest numbers that season, which started badly— Saunders replaced Blair as coach in December—and the team ended a woeful 26–56. Garnett averaged 10 points and 6 rebounds and was named to the All-Rookie second team. But the next year, KG's numbers jumped to 17 and 8, and the team won 40 games. Garnett has improved his game in some capacity in each of his seven years in the league to become the most versatile player in basketball. He has grown several inches, and lists himself at 6–11, but he's actually a bit over 7 feet tall. His long arms allow him to play bigger than his size; plus, he has great vertical lift. Consequently, he jumps over everybody on offense and matches up well with big forwards and centers on defense. His quick feet and long strides propel him past close-up defenders at the perimeter and enable him to defend quick points, 2-guards, or small forwards.

Routinely, KG scores 20-plus points, pulls double-digit rebounds, dishes about five assists, picks a couple of steals, and blocks a couple of shots. He does all that while defending the opponent's best player. Nobody plays with more intensity and emotion than Garnett. He's involved in every play at both ends of the floor. He handles the ball, sets screens, makes pinpoint passes, knocks down perimeter shots or makes crushing dunks, and rebounds misses. Then he's the first player back on defense, playing tough D on his man, helping out teammates, blocking shots, and rebounding the ball. He does it all with a sense of urgency—communicated by fierce facial expressions, chest thumping, and triumphant howls—like a timberwolf.

Garnett is the ultimate team player. Everything he does is focused on making the team win. He practices hard, is attentive to the coaches' instructions about the game plan, and gives encouragement to his teammates. When practice ends, he's in the weight room, pumping iron to add strength to his wiry frame. He sets a perfect example for others.

He has also become the team leader. He started off deferring to veteran players like Porter and Sam Mitchell, but now feels the responsibility is on his shoulders. "I'm the veteran now. It's up to me to set an example and become more vocal with my teammates," he says. Garnett finds team leadership is easy. "I show everybody that I work hard. Then I expect them to do that too. I talk when I have to, but I let my actions and attitude show what needs to be done. I love basketball, so it's easy for me to come to practice or games for a couple of hours and put all my efforts into what has to be done. My teammates pick up on that."

Former teammate (2000–2001) LaPhonso Ellis, then with Miami, told Steve Aschburner, staff writer for the Minneapolis *Star Tribune* during the 2002–2003 season, "The thing that left an impression on my mind is that he [Garnett] came to work every single day, to get something out of practice every single day."

He is also thinking about his future. Kevin is involved in several business and charitable activities. He's a spokesman for American Express, the Upper Deck Company, JOMO Energy Company, and AND 1 athletic apparel, and now has his own clothing line—OBF (Official Block Family). And at the 2002 All-Star Game, he announced the start of 4XL (For Excellence & Leadership Foundation), a group that conducts job searches for teenagers. KG also works with the Ronald McDonald House and Make-A-Wish to help promote their efforts with terminally ill children. Approximately six times a year, he brings a group of needy kids to a T'Wolves game.

He can cite, chapter and verse, the lessons he's learning as a basketball player that carry over to his personal and business life. "The same things apply: You've got to work hard, know where you're going, show people you care, and communicate—you've really got to communicate. It's harder in real life, because it never stops. In basketball, you spend whatever time is required with the team, then you're done for the day. But the responsibilities with your family, friends, and businesspeople keep going—they're never over." Garnett uses the same formula for success in both endeavors: hard work, a caring attitude about others, and unbridled enthusiasm.

Leader or not, those factors are sure to add up to success in anyone's life.

EPILOGUE

The Triangle Defense

Family, Fun, Friends

I TAKE A GREAT DEAL of satisfaction in all I've accomplished as a basketball coach and as a media commentator, but the personal relationships I formed in my life have brought my greatest rewards.

Family Ties

I believe my greatest achievement is that I am a parent of a strong family. Winning games and championships, with the acclaim that accompanies them, seem highly important at the time, but the love and caring shared within a good family yield the richest of all rewards or honors. For me, the family is really what life is all about.

It is generally acknowledged that the family is the primary unit of society and the backbone of a nation. History shows that when family unity is strong, society flourishes; when it weakens, the strength of the nation dissipates. I was privileged to have had a secure and happy early childhood, but I was also no stranger to the pain caused by the dissolution of one's family.

As described in the Introduction, my childhood home was in Milford, Connecticut. My loving parents, Jack and Anne, took a keen interest in my activities and friendships and those of my three older sisters. Although we grew up in the Depression days of the 1930s, my father did well enough in his mortgage business to enable us to live in comfortable homes, and we always had enough to eat. But money was scarce. My mother gave me 10 cents a day for school lunch, and I got another dime to go to the movies on Saturday afternoon. To supplement my 60-cents-a-week "income," I scavenged for empty soda bottles that were worth a 5-cent deposit when returned to the grocery store. Our faith sustained us as well. I was raised as a Catholic, and the family regularly attended Sunday Mass.

My dad supported my interest in sports; he came to see me play baseball and basketball and did what he could to sharpen my skills in both sports. (He also took me to see amateur boxing bouts.) During baseball season, as soon as dinner was over, my dad and I went to the side yard, where he pitched batting practice for me. The family dog, an Irish setter named Lady, took her position in the outfield and retrieved balls that I hit her way. When we had fielding practice, Lady crouched behind me to pick up any grounders that got past me. It was a nightly ritual that lasted until it got dark or my father's arm got too sore. I was in my early teens then, and home life was good.

When my sisters left home to get married and start their careers, our family unit began to unravel. My father and mother frequently disagreed on many issues, which ultimately led to their separation; and my mother and I moved to Upper Darby, Pennsylvania. The family was never the same after that.

Family became an important part of my life again after I married Jean and we had our five children (in the first 10 years of our marriage). I worked hard to make enough money for us to have more than just the basic necessities, and Jean worked equally hard as wife, mother, and homemaker. Our children were our treasures, and we have remained close to them now that they are adults and have their own families. Including our children's spouses and our 13 grandchildren, our family now numbers

25. Just thinking about that gives me a great sense of satisfaction. I count our children and their spouses as my best friends.

My wife and I both are grateful, and take pleasure in seeing, that all our children and their spouses are leading happy and productive lives. I look on them and their combined 13 children as members of one closely knit, expanded family. It is wonderful to watch each family interact with love and caring, and to observe the joy and interest they take in each other when the families are together. That all have achieved some level of success in their chosen professions is a bonus.

Susan, the oldest, earned her doctorate in English literature from the Catholic University and currently teaches a writing program for prospective attorneys in the Law School at Quinnipiac University, Hamden, Connecticut. Her husband, Vince Dailey, the ultimate sports buff, has his own business in computer equipment sales. The Daileys have two adult children, Geoff, who's in the business world, and Melissa, who teaches at the secondary school level.

Older son, John, received his Ph.D. in Education from the University of Buffalo, and is the Hollis Caswell Professor of Educational Studies at Carleton College, Northfield, Minnesota. His wife, Michele, has a master's degree in education (also from UB), and is a full-time mom to 13-year old twin boys, Nick and Jake, and their 11-year old brother, Luke.

The next in line, Sharon, graduated from St. Joseph's, later received a master's degree in education from the University of Oregon, and worked successfully in several fields including teaching, insurance, and interior design before and during her marriage. She is the wife of Jim O'Brien, coach of the Boston Celtics. I take vicarious pleasure watching Jim establish himself among the top-ranked coaches in the NBA. I help him with preseason training camp and we talk frequently during the season. I can relate to his problems (not much different from those I had) and share his joy in victory, as well as the agony and frustration that goes with defeat. Jim handles "those two imposters" better than I did. The O'Briens have three adult children, two exceptional college graduates, Shannon and Jack, and the sweet, lovable Caitlyn.

Christopher graduated from Rollins College, Winter Park, Florida, where he majored in communications. Chris worked a variety of jobs in television before landing at ESPN, where, after several years as coordinating producer of SportsCenter, he's now a senior editor for ESPN.com. His wife, Cristina, whom he met at Rollins, is an administrative assistant with a computer firm not far from their home in Unionville, Connecticut. But her main job is overseeing the activities of their three beautiful girls, Chloe, 11, Tessa, 13, and Sophia, 15.

Carolyn, the "baby," lives in Los Angeles with her husband, Andy. She's a graduate of the University of Oregon, and a former journalist who now is executive director of Olive Branches, a community-improvement, nonprofit organization. Carolyn always has a few things going on and a few more waiting to happen. Andy, after some years as a television writer, directed Norman Lear and Alan Horn's media environmental awareness program before going into business for himself as a public-interest consultant. The Ramsay-Goodmans have two children, Daniel, an active boy of 14, and Olivia, a precocious girl of 5.

The five siblings had a wonderful role model in their mother. I met Jean when she was a student at the St. Joseph's College Evening Division, doing coursework on a part-time basis to earn a degree in English literature while also working full-time as an executive secretary at a Philadelphia bank. After we married and our children started coming, she put her degree work on hold, later to return to her formal studies at St. Joe's when I took the coaching job there. When I left St. Joseph's to go to the 76ers, Jean transferred to West Chester State (Pennsylvania) University, which was closer to where we lived, and continued to pursue her degree. But she had to relocate her studies again when I left Philadelphia to coach the Buffalo Braves. There Jean enrolled at the University of Buffalo where she acquired enough credits to receive her bachelor's degree, cum laude, from West Chester. Always an excellent student, she kept copious notes from every class and studied intently after completing her daily household responsibilities. She loved to read and seemed always to have a book in her hand. Such diligence and determination didn't go unnoticed by our children and surely influenced them in their later academic pursuits.

That is quite a range and amount of activity for one family, and best of all, everyone seems satisfied with their places in life—which is not to say that some things couldn't be better. But overall, there's a high level of satisfaction and happiness among us.

Our grandchildren show every sign of continuing the tradition. Ranging in age from 5 to 30, they all have endearing qualities and unique personalities that make their parents and grandparents glow with pride.

We hold a family reunion each summer—usually at our home in Ocean City, New Jersey—and it is one of the highlights of the year for all of us. We begin planning for the next year even as we're enjoying the present event. The grandkids love being together and have developed close bonds that will last their lifetimes.

All Work and No Play . . .

The best work in life is that which gives pleasure and satisfaction. Under those conditions, work doesn't seem like work at all. I am fortunate indeed to have had—and continue to have—that kind of opportunity. My various jobs have all been involved with a game—basketball. There have been some gut-wrenching moments, to be sure, but I've had many wonderful times, too. Here are a few anecdotes that still bring a smile to my face.

Jack Attack

Every fan of basketball knows that Jack Nicholson, the Oscar-winning film actor, is a die-hard fan of the Los Angeles Lakers. In the old Forum, he held a group of season tickets for seats abutting the visitors' bench. As a great admirer of Nicholson's talent I always looked forward to chatting with him when my teams played the Lakers. He and I were both riding a wave of success, I with the soon-to-be championship Blazers, and he with his brilliant performance in *One Flew over the Cuckoo's Nest*.

The Blazers' first meeting with the Lakers in the 1977 Conference Finals began in Los Angeles. They were coming off a grueling, seven-game series that they had won against Golden State and were tired. We were rested, and by half-time had built a commanding lead. As I returned to the bench for the second half, Nicholson intercepted me and said, "Jesus Christ, Jack, take it easy on us." I laughed and told him that we had to do what we could when we could do it.

Game 2 was an entirely different story. The Lakers were sharp and in control of the game through the first three periods. Nicholson was ecstatic, standing and shouting encouragement to the Lakers' players, while making derogatory comments about the Blazers. But in the fourth period, Herm Gilliam, our backup 2-guard caught fire and single-handedly got us back in the game, which we won in the closing seconds. As the game ended, Lloyd Neal, who as a reserve player had watched Nicholson's antics during the game, shouted into his face, "How you like that, Cuckoo Man?" A dejected Nicholson had no response, and Neal's comment became a kind of rallying cry for our team: "How you like that, Cuckoo Man?" seemed to fit any occasion and evoked gales of laughter.

The rivalry between the two teams heated up the next season. Norm Nixon was in the Lakers backcourt then, and in an early season game in Los Angeles, another encounter with Nicholson took place. A Lakers player was shooting a free throw in front of our bench, and I took the dead-ball occasion to call out an offensive play to my point guard, Dave Twardzik, for our ensuing possession. I wasn't paying attention to Nixon who was standing nearby. But according to my assistant, Jack McKinney, Norm had asked Nicholson what I had said and Nicholson told him.

The incident took place just before halftime, and after I had talked to the team and they had returned to the court, McKinney told me about the Nixon-Nicholson exchange. We decided to have some fun with Mr. Jack.

When I returned to my bench position, Nicholson was seated at his usual spot near our bench. I walked over to him, angrily grabbed him by his lapels, and raised him halfway out of his chair. "If you ever give one of my plays to a Lakers' player again, I'll tear your head off," I said in my most threatening manner.

Nicholson, usually Mr. Cool in his screen appearances, was clearly flustered. "Jack . . . I . . . I . . . wouldn't do that," he sputtered. "What do I know about basketball? What could I tell them?"

With that, I released my hold of him and broke out laughing, and he showed me his best demonic grin. It was great fun.

The Schonz

Bill Schonley was the radio broadcaster of Blazer games. Schonz, as he was affectionately called, loved the Blazers and enjoyed being around the players and coaches. He also became the butt of many pranks—especially when the team traveled. Ron Culp, the team trainer and traveling secretary, took delight in creating incidents that would bedevil Schonz. Culp waited until Schonley was on air for his pregame program from a court-side location adjacent to the Blazers' bench, then would casually drift up to his spot, and under the guise of picking up a towel, bend over, carefully raise Schonz's pants legs, and spray his ankle with ethyl chloride, a freezing-cold substance used to stanch the flow of blood. Schonz would gasp and try not to allow the shock of the cold spray disrupt the flow of his broadcast voice, while Culp would convulse at side-court.

Another standing prank involved one of Schonley's prized possessions, a houndstooth hat that he wore at a jaunty angle on every trip. Once the team convened at the airport, and as soon as Schonz had placed the hat down in the gate area, or after he had nodded off to sleep when the plane was airborne, Culp or a player would spirit the hat away and keep it out of sight, sometimes for the entire trip. The hat always miraculously reappeared as the plane touched down at the home terminal. Schonz fumed and fussed, but he loved the attention. And there seemed no end to the ways the team found to lavish that attention on him.

On one trip, Culp arranged for the bellman at our hotel to transfer all of Schonz's belongings to another nearby room after we had left for dinner. When we returned, Schonley entered his room to find his clothes, toilet articles, broadcast gear—everything—gone! He immediately called Culp, who suggested that Schonz must have a key to the wrong room. Schonley insisted that this was the room he had checked into. Culp suggested that they take up the matter with the hotel manager. After Culp and Schonz left the room to go to the lobby, the bellman returned all the stuff, so that when he, Culp, and the manager arrived back at the room, everything was just as he had left it when he checked in. The manager, who was in on the ploy, berated Schonz for bringing him to the room without cause. Schonz, of course, realized he had been duped again.

Bite of the Apple

All NBA teams like to visit New York City. I'm no exception. The cosmopolitan atmosphere, the bustling crowds, the museums, theaters, and restaurants make it a highlight of any road trip.

On one Blazers trip to the Big Apple, Culp, McKinney, Schonley, and I had gone to dinner and were leisurely walking along Broadway on our way back to our hotel. There's always something of interest happening on the streets of New York. On this night, Culp tired of the scene before the rest of us and went back to his room. As McKinney, Schonley, and I neared our hotel, a middle-aged woman, dressed in a long, wraparound shawl-like robe, approached us and asked in a heavily accented voice if we'd like some female companionship. We smiled and told her no thanks.

But as we walked away, McKinney hatched a plan to have the woman visit Culp—the straightest of all the straight livers I've ever known—in his hotel room. McKinney went back to the woman, told her the plan, and paid her an agreed-on $20. She accompanied us to the hotel, where we all took the elevator to Culp's floor. Schonley, McKinney, and I positioned ourselves out of sight, but close enough to see the woman knock on Culp's door and hear their conversation.

When Culp opened the door and saw the woman, he started to close the door immediately. But she was not to be put off that easily. Sticking her leg in the doorway, she said, "What's a matter? You no like nice Greek lady?"

From our secluded vantage point, McKinney, Schonley, and I stifled our laughter.

Culp, determined to usher her from his room, put his hands on her shoulders and gently pushed her out the door. "Hey," the woman shouted, "don't put your hands on me."

As soon as she was out of the room, we could hear Culp lock and bolt his door and refuse to respond to the woman's repeated knocks. We motioned to the woman to rejoin us; McKinney gave her an additional $10 for her trouble, and we escorted her back to the street.

None of us mentioned the incident for a long time, and neither did Culp. Then on another trip, when we were having dinner together, McKinney asked of no one in particular, "Hey, you no like nice Greek lady?"

Culp, as if waiting for that moment, said with a laugh, "I knew it was you, McKinney—and that someday you'd have to bring it up. Don't ever do anything like that again."

It was something you could only do once.

Suit of a Different Color

Joe Wesner, one of my teammates at St. Joseph's, didn't get much playing time, but he always suited up for games. One evening at dinner in the boardinghouse where several of the players lived, Joe said in jest that there really was no need for him to put on his game uniform; he could just wear his jock strap and sweatsuit for the game. Someone said that he'd put up $5 to see Joe do that. At first, Wesner balked at the idea, but when others kicked in more money and the amount reached $20, he agreed to go out sans uniform for the next game at Convention Hall.

The game was against Idaho, and was regarded as a tough battle. But the Hawks were flying high that night and we built up a big lead, so Coach Ferguson began substituting more freely than usual. Finally, with about two minutes left in the game, Ferg looked down the bench and called for Joe. Wesner never turned his head, pretending he hadn't heard, and kept looking out at the court. Ferg tried again. No response. On the third summons, Wesner—still sitting—turned to Ferg with a questioning look. Ferg said, "Come on, get in there."

Wesner knew he had to do something, because despite his stalling tactics, there was still about a minute left. So he went over to Ferg, knelt on one knee, and asked for instructions. The rest of the players on the bench were doing their best to keep from rolling off their seats. Ferg laughed and said that he just wanted him to get in the game. Wesner rose and went slowly to the scorer's table—still in his sweats. There was a dead ball with about 30 seconds left in the game, when substitutions can be made, but the officials, seeing Wesner still in warm-ups, resumed play. The clock finally ran out before there was another occasion for subbing players, and Wesner breathed a huge sigh of relief and trotted to the locker room ahead of the team. Later he collected his $20.

Playing the Big House

The Sunbury Mercuries played on weekends in the Eastern League. We usually played Saturday night at home and Sunday in another city. Each year, when the schedule gave us an open Sunday, we played an afternoon game at the Lewisburg Federal Penitentiary against a team of inmates. The games at the penitentiary were always fun. There was high interest in the game. A point spread was established and large quantities of cigarettes were bet on the outcome. During one pregame, a prisoner approached us as we prepared to go on the floor to warm up. "Don't let up! Don't let up! I've got lots of sticks [cigarettes] on you guys." The Mercuries were big fan favorites, and the "home" team got more derision than support. The prison team trained all year for that game, and of course, we saw the same players year after year—they never lost their eligibility. We never lost to them—but we didn't run up the score either.

The warden always offered us accommodations at the prison after our game on Saturday night, and one year, my teammate Dick Koecher and I, looking to save on hotel room costs, took him up on his invitation.

The rest of the players thought it was too risky. They predicted all kinds of dire consequences: "They might take us hostage," or "Some psycho could come after us in our sleep." Dick and I remained unperturbed, and after the game, we drove out to the prison gate, were ushered inside, and sat down to a nice postgame meal. We visited for a while with the warden and his wife, and then he led us to our "accommodations," a cell in a separate section of the facility where there were no other prisoners. The cell door was left unlocked and open. It contained two double-deck cots; the restroom was located down the hall.

Koecher suddenly became ill at ease, but I assured him that we were safe. The warden wouldn't take any risks regarding our safety, I reasoned. I got into bed and went to sleep.

When I awoke in the morning, I looked across at Koecher, who had the blankets pulled up over his nose. He was staring at me wide-eyed, and motioned with them in the direction of the cell door. Rising up on one elbow, I saw an inmate standing in the doorway with a broom.

When he saw I was awake, he came toward my bunk, unbuttoned his fatigue jacket and pulled it open to show me something. I wasn't sure what I was going to see, but I have to admit the warnings of our teammates flashed through my mind. Instead, I quickly realized I was face to face with an avid Sunbury fan. Pinned to the inside of his jacket was a series of Mercuries game write-ups. He told us that he listened to all of our games on radio and clipped the articles about the team from the local paper. He just wanted to tell us how honored he was to have us stay in his section of the prison. I chatted with him for a short while, and when I looked over at Koecher, he just rolled his eyes and got out of bed.

Money Flies, Coaches Don't

Nothing engenders wild excitement for teams and fans like a great win, and people do crazy things in an effort to express their joy, myself among them. Once during my tenure as coach at St. Joseph's, we won a big game at Wake Forest on a last-second jump shot. I became so elated that, as I ran off the court, I took off my sport coat, swung it above my head several times, and let it fly. The coat flattened out and sailed over the first several rows of seats, landing amid the Wake Forest fans. I didn't care. "They can keep it," I thought, as I joined my team exulting in the locker room.

It was not until the excitement had subsided that I remembered I kept the team travel money—about $500 dollars in cash—in an envelope in my inside jacket pocket. I quickly sent a manager out to see if he could recover the coat. Minutes later he returned with the jacket—with the money still inside. An amused Wake Forest student had been waiting outside the locker room for me to reclaim the airborne coat.

On another occasion, again after a last-second St. Joseph's win, I ran ahead of the players and, as I got to the locker room, jumped in the air and hit the door with both feet, expecting it to swing open. The only problem was that the door was locked, and I bounced backward off it onto my backside. The players enjoyed that scene immensely.

Buffaloed

Buffalo, New York, is dead center of the snowbelt; it gets heavy accumulations of the white stuff from November to April, meaning that travel there during those months is always an iffy proposition. Coming back from a road trip, we never knew what conditions would greet us.

I had cautioned those of my players who drove to the airport always to note where they parked their cars because snow might have blanketed the area by the time we got back. But on one memorable occasion I neglected to take my own advice when we left on a five-day trip. Sure enough, the night before we returned, a major storm passed through Buffalo. On arrival the next day, and after I had picked up my bags and walked out of the terminal, I was greeted with about two feet of snow on the roofs of all the cars, making identification impossible.

I began trudging around, sweeping the snow off various cars, hoping to find mine. In the midst of my search, Bob McAdoo came tooling by in his car. He slowed down, lowered the window, and asked with a smile, "Having trouble finding your car, Coach?" I didn't want to admit that I couldn't find my car and told him I'd be okay, that I knew where the car was (it took me another half hour to find it). But Bob Mac knew the truth and told the players all about my plight before I arrived at practice the next day. They took great pleasure in mimicking my warning about paying attention to where they parked their cars, a well-deserved ribbing I had to take in silence.

Friends Indeed

When I think about the richness in my life, in addition to my family and the fun I've had over the years, I count my wealth in the many enduring friendships that have sustained me. These events, among many, stand testimony to the durability of these bonds.

In my last season coaching St. Joseph's (1966), we played Fairfield University at New Haven Arena. It had been some 25 years since I had left nearby Milford to move to Philadelphia with my family, and I had maintained only occasional contacts with my old friends from there. As the teams warmed up for the game, I saw a group of men emerge from the stands and approach me at courtside. As they drew closer, I realized they were some of my teammates from Milford High School. Though it was unnecessary—for I recognized them all—each shook hands with me and told me his name. As if no time had passed, standing before me were Tom Long, Roy Lund, Teddy Paul, Ko Phillips, Biff Johnson, and Powerhouse Jensen. Later I learned that they had followed my basketball career and had even gone to Madison Square Garden, along with Father Cullinan, the Catholic priest at St. Mary's Church where I had been an altar boy, to see me play as a collegian.

Several years later, in 1992, when I was inducted into the Naismith Basketball Hall of Fame, it was Long and Lund who arranged a reception at Milford with that same group, along with many others I hadn't seen in 50 years. Many had married their high school sweethearts and still lived in the community. It was a warm, nostalgic evening.

Then, shortly after my 70th birthday in 1995, Paul Westhead, one of my former players at St. Joseph's, called to say that a number of former Hawks wanted to get together to celebrate the occasion. I'm not much for recognizing my birthdays, but he assured me that it would be a casual reunion, and I looked forward to seeing those players again.

The event was held in a banquet room on the St. Joseph's campus, and almost every man who had played on my teams from 1955 to 1966 was there. It was a magical night. I was especially moved when one representative from each graduating group gave a brief account of their experiences, and each player gave me a letter describing how playing on my Hawks' team had influenced his life.

As for my future, I don't know how long I will continue to work actively in the wonderful world of basketball. I truly love it, but there comes a time when everyone must step back and consider his obligations.

My family comes first for me, and I've reached a point where I need to be more available for my wife, Jean. If I can do that and still find a way to make a contribution to this great game, I'll stay on. If not, I'll step away with no regrets.

Bearing the mantle of leadership is not for the faint of heart. But if you yearn for the challenges it offers and then can stand strong to meet those challenges successfully, you will be able to look back with pride on a life fully lived.

Index